WORLD CLUB
FOOTBALL DIRECTORY
——1985-86——

WORLD CLUB
FOOTBALL DIRECTORY
——1985-86——

Keir Radnedge

Macdonald
Queen Anne Press

A Queen Anne Press BOOK

© Keir Radnedge 1985

First published in Great Britain in 1985 by
Queen Anne Press, Macdonald & Co (Publishers) Ltd,
Maxwell House, 74 Worship Street,
London EC2A 2EN

A BPCC plc company

British Library Cataloguing in Publication Data
    World club football directory.—1985–86–
    1. Soccer clubs – Directories
    796.334′025   GV942
    ISBN 0–356–10971–2

Cover photograph of Michel Platini in match-winning form
for Juventus, courtesy of Colorsport

Typeset by J&L Composition Ltd, Filey, North Yorkshire

Reproduced, printed and bound in Great Britain by
Hazell, Watson & Viney Limited,
Member of the BPCC Group,
Aylesbury, Bucks

CONTENTS

INTRODUCTION

Football is an international game, and thus its triumphs and its tragedies are international. The exploits of the great players are recognised as widely as the grief was felt after the appalling events at Bradford and Brussels – as well as Mexico City – scarred the game's image and reputation in 1985. That football can survive such disasters is due to the tradition and continuity established over the years, largely thanks to the great clubs – from Real Madrid to River Plate. It is because of their continuing achievements that the *World Club Football Directory* has been extensively revised and updated.

TEXT KEY

Details for all clubs are listed in the same way: name, year of foundation (not always straightforward, because of mergers), stadium (and capacity), club address and honours list. Club colours are described in a basic shirts/shorts formula, although this is another awkward area. A surprisingly large number of clubs play in colour combinations which vary from the strip registered with their domestic federations. As for addresses, many clubs beyond Europe, North America and the major South American countries use their federation as a 'post office'. In such cases the federation address is given. As regards honours, the term 'league' describes the home-and-away match system most commonly used to decide a nation's top club. The term 'championship' is used, particularly with reference to South America but increasingly in Scandinavia as well, where a play-off or bonus-points system tops up the league formula. Note that in South America, Scandinavia, the Soviet Union and parts of Africa, the season runs from spring to autumn and is thus contained in a calendar year.

ALBANIA

One event, not directly connected with football but which occurred during the season, could have major repercussions on the sport in this secretive country: the death of Communist dictator Enver Hoxha. For more than forty years Hoxha had kept Albania at arm's length from the rest of Europe, and that included football. Albanian clubs have on political grounds refused to play Soviet teams, and foreign clubs have always found enormous difficulties obtaining the required visas. With the death of Hoxha, all may gradually change; only time will tell. In the meantime, domestic football continues to revolve around the Tirana clubs, and the capital regained the league title with the success of 17 Nëntori.

It was the sixth time they had won the championship, and they led for most of the season after going clear at the top in November thanks to a 1–0 win over neighbours Dinamo Tirana. A week later top striker Arben Minga scored a rare league hat-trick in a 5–2 win over Lokomotiva to emphasise Nëntori's confidence. By the start of January they were four points clear of Luftëtari at the top, and refused to be upset by a cup semi-final defeat at the hands of Partizani (0–0, 0–2) in February. By early March, Nëntori's league lead had been stretched by six points – which was the margin by which they finished ahead of Dinamo after completion of the twenty-six round league programme.

Nëntori were sure of the title with three weeks of the season remaining. Key players were the captain, Baçi, the midfield general Mema and the attacking trio of Minga, Muça and Kola. Between them these three scored the vast majority of the club's forty-five goals – the best attacking record in an unadventurous league. The man behind the club's sixth success in twenty years was senior coach Enver Shehu. He was assistant manager for the league triumphs in 1965, 1966, 1968 and 1970, and has been number one for the successes in 1982 and this past season.

Runners-up were a revived Dinamo, who had struggled to stay clear of the relegation zone, and finished eleventh the previous season. Their best players were the record international and centre-back Targaj and the talented young midfielder, Demollari. Dinamo were more effective than Nëntori in the second half of the championship, collecting nineteen points compared with Nëntori's seventeen. But Nëntori, of course, had made a much stronger start to the season.

Vllaznia finished third, thanks to the goals of Fakja, and Partizani finished fourth, and were surprisingly beaten by Flamurtari in the cup final. Partizani have a number of promising young players, but still lean heavily on the experience of international goalkeeper Perlat Musta, runner-up in the Albanian Sportsman of the Year poll, and powerful winger Kushta. He was their top scorer with nine goals.

Behind them in the table, in fifth place, came Flamurtari. Their victory in the cup final was their first-ever major trophy, though they did have some luck along the way. In the first round they beat Besa of Kavaja 1–0, 3–1, and then defeated prospective second division champions Apolonia only on the away goals rule after drawing 1–1, 0–0 in the two-leg tie.

It took the away goals rule again for Flamurtari to overcome Vllaznia in the semi-finals and earn a showdown with Partizani. The final was played in the

Labinoti stadium in Elbasan and Flamurtari began as clear outsiders. Partizani had tradition on their side, having won the cup eleven times since the game was reorganised in Albania after the war. Flamurtari went ahead through Ruçi in the thirty-second minute only for Hametaj to equalise three minutes before the interval. Partizani failed to press home their advantage after the break, however, and in the forty-ninth minute Bubeqi broke away for what proved Flamurtari's winner.

The biggest disappointment of the season was the collapse of 1984 champions Labinoti. They struggled deep in the relegation zone for most of the season, and ensured survival in the first division only by scraping a 2–2 draw against bottom club Skënderbeu on the last day of the campaign thanks to an eighty-eighth minute goal. An even later saving goal was scored by Naftëtari. They achieved a 2–2 draw away to a newly-crowned champions Nëntori in their last game with a ninetieth-minute equaliser. Thus Besa went down to the second division along with Skënderbeu.

In the World Cup qualifiers the national team, under Shyqryi Rreli, achieved one of their most famous results when they defeated Belgium 2–0 in Tirana thanks to goals from Mirel Josa and Minga. Temporarily at least, the Albanians stood joint top of their group along with the Belgians and Poland.

1984–85 League Table

	P	W	D	L	F	A	Pts
17 Nëntori	26	15	9	2	45	22	39
Dinamo	26	13	7	6	42	22	33
Vllaznia	26	13	3	10	33	23	29
Partizani	26	12	5	9	26	19	29
Flamurtari	26	8	11	7	22	20	27
Tomori	26	9	9	8	20	23	27
Luftëtari	26	8	10	8	24	24	26
Traktori	26	7	10	9	15	28	24
Beselidhja	26	8	8	10	18	32	24
Lokomotiva	26	7	9	10	25	26	23
Labinoti	26	7	9	10	28	32	23
Naftëtari	26	6	11	9	23	29	23
Besa	26	7	8	11	28	32	22
Skënderbeu	26	3	9	14	15	32	15

Cup final: Flamurtari 2, Partizani 1.
Top scorers: Arben Minga (17 Nëntori) and F. Fakja (Vllaznia) 13 goals each.

BESA KAVAJE
Founded: 1925 (as Adriatiku).
Colours: White/black.
Stadium: Besa (12,000).
Club address: Klubi Sportiv Besa, c/o Albanian football federation, Rruga Kongresi Permetit 41, Tirana.
League: – .
Cup: – .

DINAMO TIRANA
Founded: 1950.
Colours: All white.

Stadium: Dinamo (12,000). Big matches in the national stadium, Qemal Stafa (19,293).
Club address: Klubi Sportiv Dinamo, c/o Albanian football federation, Rruga Kongresi Permetit 41, Tirana.
League: 1950, 1951, 1952, 1953, 1955, 1956, 1960, 1967, 1973, 1975, 1976, 1977, 1980 (13 – joint record with Partizani).
Cup: 1950, 1951, 1952, 1953, 1954, 1960, 1971, 1974, 1978, 1982 (10).

FLAMURTARI (Vlöre)
Founded: 1923 (as Jeronim de Rada).
Colours: White/black.
Stadium: Flamurtari (10,000).
Club address: Klubi Sportiv Flamurtari, c/o Albanian football federation, Rruga Kongresi Permetit 41, Tirana.
League: – .
Cup: 1985.

LABINOTI (Elbasan)
Founded: 1923 (as Afërdita e Dërparimi).
Colours: Red/black.
Stadium: Labinoti (12,000).
Club address: Klubi Sportiv Labinoti Elbasan, c/o Albanian football federation, Rruga Kongresi Permetit 41, Tirana.
League: 1984.
Cup: 1975.

17 NËNTORI TIRANA
Founded: 1920 (as AGIMI, later Sport Club).
Colours: Blue and white stripes/white.
Stadium: Qemal Stafa (19,293).
Club address: Klubi Sportiv 17 Nëntori, c/o Albanian football federation, Rruga Kongresi Permetit 41, Tirana.
League: 1965, 1966, 1968, 1970, 1982, 1985 (6).
Cup: 1963, 1976, 1977, 1983, 1984 (5).

PARTIZANI TIRANA
Founded: 1946 (as Vshtria Kombëtare).
Colours: All blue.
Stadium: Qemal Stafa (19,293).
Club address: Klubi Sportiv Partizani, c/o Albanian football federation, Rruga Kongresi Permetit 41, Tirana.
League: 1947, 1948, 1949, 1954, 1957, 1958, 1959, 1961, 1963, 1964, 1971, 1979, 1981 (13 – joint record with Dinamo).
Cup: 1948, 1949, 1957, 1958, 1961, 1964, 1966, 1968, 1970, 1973, 1980 (11 – record).

VLLAZNIA SHKODER
Founded: 1919.
Colours: White/black.
Stadium: Vllaznia (10,000).

Club address: Klubi Sportiv Vllaznia, c/o Albanian football federation, Rruga Kongresi Permetit 41, Tirana.
League: 1945, 1946, 1972, 1974, 1978, 1983 (6).
Cup: 1965, 1972, 1979, 1981 (4).

ALGERIA

The Algerian season reached a dramatic climax on the very last day of competition. JET of Tizi Ouzou had been assured of the league title for a couple of weeks. But because of a suspension they were not qualified for the following season's African Champions' Cup, so the place would go to the league runners-up, whose identity remained uncertain until the last round of matches. MP Oran, Collo and MAHD were all in the running. Both Collo and MAHD won their last home matches by 1–0 – against Annaba and Belcourt respectively – but were finally pipped when MP Oran snatched victory over Bel Abbès in their decisive game thanks to an eighty-eighth minute penalty converted by Sebba.

Both Collo and MAHD had a better goal difference overall than MP Oran. But MP finished ahead of both because of a better record in the first half of the season. The same unusual rule had to be called into play to decide the relegation issue. Tiaret and Kouba knew they were going down before the last round of matches. But Bel Abbès, MP Algiers, Guelma and three other teams above them were all in danger of filling the third and last relegation spot. In the end, just as the Bel Abbès' match was decisive at the top of the table, so it provided the solution at the bottom. Bel Abbès' late, late defeat against MP Oran meant they went down to the regional league.

As for the champions, JET, they finished their season in style with a 5–0 thrashing of Mascara – who finished in fourteenth place after being badly affected by the loss through injury of their star player, Lakhdar Belloumi. The story of what happened to Belloumi illustrates that for all black Africa's demands for a greater say in world football's administration, they still have plenty of problems to sort out in the organisation of the game on their own continent.

Belloumi, voted both Footballer of the Year and Sportsman of the Year in Africa in 1982, was the star of the Algeria team who did so well in the finals of the 1982 World Cup in Spain. His admirers compared him with a mixture of Platini and Maradona. But such praise also made him the obvious target for unscrupulous opponents. Sad proof came in an early round of the 1985 African Champions' Cup between Mascara – who had won the domestic title for the first time a year earlier – and Ittihad of Tripoli, the Libyan champions. Mascara won 4–0 at home, but the Libyans went – literally – over the top in the return. A series of rugged tackles ended with Belloumi being badly fouled by Ittihad defender Bani Abou Bakr, and carried off suffering from a broken leg.

As the match went on there were arguments between the reserves and coaches and Mascara were lucky, in the end, to lose only 3–0 and squeeze through 4–3 on aggregate. That was too much for the Libyan fans. Several hundred stormed onto the pitch at the final whistle, the police were over-whelmed, and several Mascara players and officials were injured and bruised on their way to the dressing rooms. The Mascara president suffered a broken arm and the club's general manager complained later he was assaulted even on arrival at hospital for attention to suspected broken ribs.

1984–85 League Table

	P	W	D	L	F	A	Pts
JET Tizi Ouzou	38	19	11	8	58	18	87
MP Oran	38	17	10	11	38	35	82
Collo	38	17	10	11	43	35	82
MAHD	38	17	10	11	43	35	82
Tlemcen	38	16	9	13	41	34	79
EP Sétif	38	12	13	10	39	39	78
ASC Oran	38	12	15	11	33	27	77
Boufarik	38	12	15	10	39	35	77
USMH	38	11	16	10	38	31	76
Belcourt	38	10	18	10	37	38	76
Bordi Menaiel	38	12	13	13	36	40	75
Chief	38	11	15	12	36	40	75
Annaba	38	10	16	12	46	49	74
Mascara	38	13	10	15	50	56	74
Aim'Lila	38	11	14	13	26	33	74
Guelma	38	12	11	15	32	37	73
MP Algiers	38	9	17	12	40	39	73
Bel Abbès	38	12	11	15	46	49	73
RS Kouba	38	8	13	17	32	44	67
Tiaret	38	7	13	18	24	60	65

Note: 3 points for a win, 2 points for a draw, one point for a defeat in which game was completed.
Cup final: MP Oran 2, CRE Constantine 0.

JET
Founded: 1946 (as Jamia Sarih Kawkabi. Reorganised 1962).
Colours: Green/white.
Stadium: Stade Omnisport (Tizi-Ouzou; 30,000).
Club address: Jeunesse Électronique de Tizi-Ouzou (JET), c/o Fédération Algérienne de Football, 4 rue Emir Abdelkrim El Khattabi, Algiers.
League: 1973, 1974, 1977, 1980, 1982, 1983, 1985 (7).
Cup: 1977.
Afr. Champions' Cup: 1981.
Afr. Cup-winners' Cup: – .

MOULOUDIA CHALIA
Founded: 1921.
Colours: Green/red.
Stadium: Important matches in the Stade Olympique (Algiers; 80,000).
Club address: Mouloudia Chalia, c/o Fédération Algérienne de Football, 4 rue Emir Ebdelkrim El Khattabi, Algiers.
League: 1972, 1975, 1976, 1978, 1979 (5).
Cup: 1971, 1973, 1976, 1983 (4).
Afr. Champions' Cup: 1976.
Afr. Cup-winners' Cup: – .

ARGENTINA

It may be significant, or it may be merely ironic, that the two nations who went to war just a few years ago over the Falkland Islands should also be the two nations whose football is suffering the most from terrace violence. The governments of both Britain and Argentina have been seeking ever more deperately this past year – in the wake of death and tragedy – to control and then cure the sport of crowd trouble.

Incidents at matches in the 1985 national championship led the Argentine government to suspend competition for two weeks, and rush through parliament laws providing tougher sanctions against those convicted of violence at matches. Among the sentences are jail terms for up to six years for fans carrying knives, guns or other dangerous weapons. Provision was also made to ban from football grounds – by use of a police station report system – any hooligans who used whistles to confuse players, incite stampedes on the terraces, or assault other fans.

The final straw which galvanised politicians into action was the death of a fourteen-year-old boy, attending his first football match, who was shot and killed at the game between world club champions Independiente and Boca Juniors in the Independiente stadium at Avellaneda, an industrial suburb to the south of Buenos Aires. Boca president Antonio Alegre resigned in protest. He said: 'There is no doubt that the fans of Boca Juniors were responsible for what is a tragedy not only for the family and the club but for Argentine football in general.' The victim, Adrian Silvio Scassera, was just the latest in a list of fans who had died in nearly thirty years of sporadic terrace violence in Argentina. The first was Mario Linker, a supporter killed during rioting at a game between Velez Sarsfield and River Plate in 1958. Between his death and that of Scassera, a dozen other fans had been killed at top-level games.

Of course Latin American crowds have always had a reputation as volatile and easily excited. But since Argentina's return to democratic rule, the violent tension repressed under the military dictatorships of Videla, Galtieri and company appears to have burst into the open, and football happened to provide the convenient battleground. Argentine newspapers and magazines have picked out and pictured some of the ringleaders of terrace violence. But the police have never been able to get to them for fear of provoking even greater trouble and possible loss of life.

Such enormous, socially-based problems have afflicted the Argentine game at a particularly vulnerable moment. Crowds are down, and a string of clubs, including even the great Boca Juniors, former world and South American Club Champions, teeter on the brink of bankruptcy. These financial problems, allied to Argentina's inflationary spiral, meant that it was almost commonplace for playing staffs to stage strikes until they were paid at least some of the monies owed to them, often from two or three months back.

One club which doesn't need to worry quite as seriously about its cashflow is 1984 first division champions Argentinos Juniors. When they sold Diego Maradona first to Boca four years ago, they took advantage of their share in the windfall of his successive £3 million transfer to Barcelona. There was no reckless spending, just sensible dealing in the transfer market to come up with players such as Hector Commisso from River Plate and striker Pedro Pasculli who was Argentinos' top scorer in their triumphant march to the title.

Argentinos were pursued relentlessly all the way to the last match by Ferro Carril Oeste and Estudiantes de la Plata. But at least they didn't have to worry about Independiente. The latter were so concerned to win first the South American Club Cup, then the World Club Cup (1–0 against Liverpool in Tokyo) that they fielded their reserves in league matches and finished not far above the relegation zone.

Estudiantes built up a big lead at the top of the table early in the season. But they too found the pressures of domestic and South American Cup competition too intense. Estudiantes started dropping silly points at home. As coach Eduardo Manera said: 'We have played 175 games in the last two years without the players being able to take a proper holiday. If they go on like this, under this sort of pressure, the only concern next year will be avoiding relegation. They won't have any legs left.'

As for FC Oeste, their problem was a lack of power in attack, apart from national team winger Marcico. They rarely scored more than one goal per game and in the end that absence of firepower told against them.

Argentinos, Estudiantes and FC Oeste all came to the last game of the season with a chance of the title. Estudiantes were home to none other than FC Oeste, while Argentinos had a home game against mid-table Temperley. FC Oeste worked hard against all the odds, wasted a string of chances, but forced Estudiantes to concede a 1–1 draw. Argentinos, meanwhile, gained a 1–0 victory thanks to a penalty from 1978 World Cup-winning defender Jorge Olguin, which left goalkeeper Casse on his back and Argentinos on top of the table. Celebrating fans forced a premature end to the match in the eighty-sixth minute, but the result was allowed to stand.

By winning that last match Argentinos escaped what was promising to be a political row fuelled by Independiente's decision to field reserves in an earlier game against Estudiantes. Independiente lost 2–1, but of course Argentinos did not need to put into effect a protest against the result when they finished three points clear of Estudiantes at the end of the season.

Relegation was no simple matter either. The rules vary from season to season. This time the teams going down were decided on a total of points gained over the last three seasons. That meant Rosario Central and Atlanta. Their relegation was not a surprise. Atlanta tried four different coaches throughout the season while Rosario – who had used seven coaches over two years – failed to replace half a dozen key players who had had to be sold to raise cash over the same period.

Boca Juniors finished fourth from bottom, making more news with their financial crises than their football. Several times the famous old Bombonera stadium nearly went under the auctioneer's hammer, but each time somebody came up with enough cash to pay off immediate debts. Not that Boca could use their stadium – it had long since been declared unsafe for use, and not until this year was it reopened. Boca were reduced in the end to asking the government for a £3 million loan, and an official receiver was appointed to try to sort out the club's finances. One controversial move was to sell star forward Ricardo Gareca to deadly rivals and neighbours River Plate. Boca officials refused to release him and provoked a general strike by all Argentina's professional players. Eventually the transfer went through – though River themselves had the finance available only thanks to their earlier transfer of 1978 World Cup-winning goalkeeper Ubaldo Fillol to the Brazilian club, Flamengo.

On the international scene, Argentina impressed with a European tour in the autumn of 1984, which included victories over Belgium, Switzerland and West Germany. But they then needed the reinforcement of their overseas-based players when it came around to their World Cup qualifying commitments against Colombia, Peru and Venezuela. That meant the recall from Italy of Diego Maradona (Napoli) and Daniel Passarella (Fiorentina), and from Spain of Jorge Valdano (Real Madrid). Maradona remains the most popular Argentine player, but the South American Footballer of the Year for 1984 was in fact an Argentine-based Uruguayan, Enzo Francescoli of River Plate. He was the Argentine first division's top scorer, and also played a key role in seeing Uruguay back to the World Cup finals in Mexico in 1986 for the first time in twelve years.

1984 First Division Table

	P	W	D	L	F	A	Pts
Argentinos Juniors	36	20	11	5	69	36	51
FC Oeste	36	19	12	5	46	18	50
Estudiantes de la Plata	36	21	6	9	49	27	48
River Plate	36	15	13	8	51	38	43
Racing Córdoba	36	16	11	9	42	31	43
Velez Sarsfield	36	14	14	8	43	32	42
Newell's Old Boys	36	17	4	15	36	39	38
San Lorenzo	36	11	15	10	47	46	37
Talleres Córdoba	36	11	12	13	56	55	34
Chacarita Juniors	36	11	12	13	30	37	34
Instituto Cordoba	36	13	7	16	46	47	33
Platense	36	10	13	13	34	45	33
Temperley	36	9	13	14	23	28	31
Independiente	36	10	11	15	45	59	31
Unión Santa Fe	36	11	8	17	43	46	30
Boca Juniors	36	10	10	16	34	49	30
Huracán	36	9	9	18	36	55	27
Rosario Central	36	7	11	18	28	41	25
Atlanta	36	8	8	20	32	61	24

Top scorer: Enzo Francescoli (River Plate) 24 goals.

ARGENTINOS JUNIORS
Founded: 1904.
Colours: All red.
Stadium: Share use of Ferro Carril Oeste's Estadio Martin de Gainza (30,000).
Club address: Argentinos Juniors, c/o AFA, Viamonte 1366/76, 1053 Buenos Aires.
First division/metropolitan champ: 1984.
National championship: – .

BOCA JUNIORS
Founded: 1905.
Colours: All blue with a broad yellow hoop round the shirt.
Stadium: La Bombonera ("Chocolate Box" – 58,850).

Club address: Club Atlético Boca Juniors, Brandsen 805, 1161 Buenos Aires.
First Division/metropolitan champ.: 1919, 1920, 1923, 1924, 1926, 1930, 1931, 1934, 1935, 1940, 1943, 1944, 1954, 1962, 1964, 1965, 1976, 1981 (18).
National champ.: 1969, 1970, 1976 (3).
World Club Cup: 1977.
S. American Club Cup: 1977, 1978. Runners-up in 1963 and 1979.
Interamerican Cup: Runners-up in 1978.

ESTUDIANTES DE LA PLATA
Founded: 1905.
Colours: Red and white stripes/black shorts.
Stadium: La Plata (25,000).
Club address: Club Estudiantes de la Plata, Calle 53, 620, 1900 La Plata, Provincia de Buenos Aires.
First division/metropolitan champ.: 1913, 1967, 1982 (3).
National champ.: 1983.
World Club Cup: 1968. Runners-up in 1969, 1970.
S. American Club Cup: 1968, 1969, 1970. Runners-up in 1971.
Interamerican Cup: 1969.

FERRO CARRIL OESTE
Founded: 1904.
Colours: Green/white.
Stadium: Martín de Gainza (30,000).
Club address: Club Ferro Carril Oeste, Cucha Cucha 350, 1405 Buenos Aires.
First division/metropolitan champ.: – .
National champ.: 1982, 1984.

HURACÁN
Founded: 1908.
Colours: All white.
Stadium: Estadio Tomás Adolfo Ducó (48,500).
Club address: Club Atlético Huracán, Avenida Caseros 3121/59, 1263 Buenos Aires.
First division/metropolitan champ.: 1921, 1922, 1925, 1928, 1973 (5).
National champ.: – .

INDEPENDIENTE
Founded: 1904.
Colours: Red/blue.
Stadium: Cordero (55,000).
Club address: Club Atlético Independiente, Mitre 470, 1870 Avellaneda, Provinica de Buenos Aires.
First division/metropolitan champ.: 1922, 1926, 1938, 1939, 1948, 1960, 1963, 1970, 1971, 1983 (10).
National champ: 1967, 1977, 1978 (3).
Interamerican Cup: 1973, 1974, 1976.
World Club Cup: 1973, 1984. Runners-up in 1964, 1965, 1972 and 1974.
S. American Club Cup: 1964, 1965, 1972, 1973, 1974, 1975, 1984 (7 – record).

NEWELL'S OLD BOYS
Founded: 1903.
Colours: Red and black stripes/black.
Stadium: Parque Independencia (35,000).
Club address: Club Atlético Newell's Old Boys, Parque Independencia, 2000 Rosario, Provincia de Santa Fe.
First division/metropolitan champ.: 1974.
National champ.: – .

QUILMES ATHLETIC CLUB
Founded: 1897.
Colours: All white.
Stadium: Quilmes (25,000).
Club address: 'Quilmes', c/o Asociacion del Futbol Argentino, Viamonte 1366/76, 1053 Buenos Aires.
First division/metropolitan champ.: 1912, 1978.
National champ.: – .

RACING CLUB
Founded: 1903.
Colours: Sky blue and white stripes/black.
Stadium: Mözart y Cuyo (70,100). Formerly Estadio Presidente Perón.
Club address: Racing Club, Mitre 934, 1970 Avellaneda, Provincia de Buenos Aires.
First division/metropolitan champ.: 1913, 1914, 1915, 1916, 1917, 1918, 1919, 1921, 1925, 1949, 1950, 1951, 1958, 1961, 1966 (15).
National champ.: – .
World Club Cup: 1967.
S. American Club Cup: 1967.

RIVER PLATE
Founded: 1901.
Colours: white with a red sash/black.
Stadium: Antonio Liberti 'Monumental' (76,000).
Club address: Club Atlético River Plate, Avenida Figueroa, Alcorta 7597, 1428 Buenos Aires.
First division/metropolitan champ.: 1920, 1932, 1936, 1937, 1941 1942, 1945, 1947, 1952, 1953, 1955, 1956, 1957, 1975, 1977, 1979, 1980 (17).
National champ.: 1975, 1979, 1981 (3).
S. American Club Cup: Runners-up in 1966 and 1976.

ROSARIO CENTRAL
Founded: 1889.
Colours: Blue and yellow stripes/blue.
Stadium: Cordiviola (40,567).
Club address: Club Atlético Rosario Central, Avenida Genova y Bvd Avellaneda, 2000 Rosario.
First division/metropolitan champ.: – .
National champ.: 1971, 1973, 1980 (3).

SAN LORENZO DE ALMAGRO
Founded: 1908.
Colours: Blue and red stripes/black.
Stadium: Share Estadio Amalfitani of Velez (49,300).
Club address: Club Atlético San Lorenzo de Almagro, Avenida La Plata, 1250 Buenos Aires.
First division/metropolitan champ.: 1923, 1924, 1927, 1933, 1946, 1959, 1968, 1972 (8).
National champ.: 1972, 1974.

VELEZ SARSFIELD
Founded: 1910.
Colours: White with blue 'V'/blue.
Stadium: Jose Amalfitani (49,300).
Club address: Club Atlético Velez Sarsfield, Avenida Juan B. Justo 9200, 1408 Buenos Aires.
First division/metropolitan champ.: – .
National champ.: 1968.

AUSTRALIA

South Melbourne Hellas and Newcastle Rosebud collected the glory at the end of a 1984 season in which much of the football was overshadowed by continued wrangling over sponsorship and organisation.

The problems arise fundamentally out of concern over the credibility of a full national championship. High travel costs make sponsorship cash a necessity in a country where soccer is far from being the national sport, and where modest attendances still lean heavily on immigrant identification with clubs.

The championship was launched in 1977, but for 1984 it was decided to split into a National Conference (based in Melbourne, Brisbane and Adelaide) and an Australian Conference (Sydney, Newcastle, Canberra), with a play-off series to sort out the overall champions.

South Melbourne Hellas lost six of their thirty matches in the National Conference, but still ended up five points clear of Heidelberg Alexander and Melbourne Croatia. Yet it was their neighbours, Croatia, who came the closest to wrecking Hellas' title ambitions.

In their National Conference semi-final, Hellas were lucky to be only 1-0 down to Croatia when John Yzendoorn powered forward from the centre of defence to equalise. That took the tie into extra time, where Doug Brown scored twice to destroy Croatia and earn a place in the National Conference final against Heidelberg.

Once again, Hellas took their time. They were 1-0 down, equalised, then went 2-1 behind; Heidelberg appeared in command. But then referee Doug Rennie sent off Heidelberg strongman Charlie Yankos for a foul on the Hellas midfield star, Oscar Crino. Not only were Heidelberg now down to ten men, they had lost the one player able to keep any sort of grip on Crino, who proceeded to take them apart.

On the hour it was Crino who equalised at 2-2, and after Yzendoorn scored another of his 'specials', Crino turned up in the penalty box in the eighty-fourth minute to assure Hellas a 4-2 victory. Their prize was a place in the overall final against Sydney Olympic.

Olympic had, in fact, finished runners-up in the Australian Conference to the championship's all-time top team, Sydney City Hakoah. But in the Conference final Olympic came back to beat their neighbours 2-1 in extra time.

Luck turned against them, however, in the final against Hellas, who, like Olympic, include the controversial Scot Tommy Docherty among their past team managers. The first leg of the final was played in Sydney, but Olympic's star striker, Jim Patikas, was injured early on. Two goals from Charlie Egan brought Hellas a 2-1 victory they repeated in front of their own fans for a 4-2 aggregate.

It was Hellas's first championship, and owed much to the power of Yzendoorn, the skill of Crino and the tackling of Alan Davidson, who then flew to England to join Nottingham Forest.

Yet both Hellas and Olympic were eliminated in the first round of the National Cup. Hellas' neighbours, Melbourne Croatia, did reach this final, only to go down 1-0 to Newcastle Rosebud. Derek Todd scored the only goal after half an hour before a 4,000 crowd in Sydney.

National Conference

	P	W	D	L	F	A	Pts
S. Melbourne Hellas	28	18	4	6	48	20	40
Heidelberg Alexander	28	14	7	7	37	27	35
Melbourne Croatia	28	13	7	8	38	31	35
Brisbane Lions	28	12	6	10	38	36	30
Brunswick Juventus	28	13	4	11	36	42	30
Preston-Makedonia	28	11	6	11	42	33	28
Adelaide C. Juventus	28	10	5	13	33	34	25
Footscray JUST	28	10	5	13	29	33	25
Green Gully	28	9	6	13	34	36	24
Brisbane City	28	8	5	15	21	39	21
West-Adelaide Hellas	28	8	5	15	40	52	21
S. George Cross	28	5	6	17	24	57	16

Australian Conference

	P	W	D	L	F	A	Pts
Sydney City Hakoah	28	17	8	3	67	21	41
Sydney Olympic	28	16	8	4	61	27	40
Marconi	28	12	8	8	58	39	32
APIA Leichhardt	28	12	8	8	43	35	32
Blacktown City	28	12	6	13	43	48	30
Sydney Croatia	28	8	11	9	32	38	27
Penrith	28	8	10	10	29	40	26
Newcastle-Rosebud	28	11	4	13	35	52	26
Canberra Arrows	28	12	1	15	46	39	25
St George Budapest	28	8	9	11	38	41	25
Melita Eagles	28	8	8	12	23	38	24
Woollongong	28	5	5	18	22	59	15

Play-offs: National Conference: Brisbane Lions 4, B.U. Juventus 2 – Melbourne Croatia 2, Heidelberg-Alexander 1 – Heidelberg 0, Brisbane Lions 0 (3-2 pens). **Semi-finals:** SM Hellas 3, Melbourne Croatia 2 aet – Heidelberg 3, Melbourne Croatia 1. **Final:** SM Hellas 4, Heidelberg 2.
Australian Conference: Sydney Olympic 2, Marconi 1 – APIA 3, Blacktown 1 – APIA 3, Marconi 3 (4-3 pens). **Semi-finals:** Sydney City Hakoah 1, Sydney Olympic 1 (4-2 pens) – Sydney Olympic 3, APIA 0. **Final:** Sydney Olympic 2, Sydney City Hakoah 1.
Championship final: SM Hellas bt Sydney Olympic 2-1, 2-1.
National Cup: Newcastle-Rosebud 1, Melbourne Croatia 0.
Top scorer: D. Brown (SM Hellas) 22 goals.

MARCONI-FAIRFIELD
Founded: 1965.
Colours: Green/white.
Stadium: Marconi (12,000).
Club address: Marconi-Fairfield, Marconi Road, Bossley Park, New South Wales 2176.
National League: 1979.
National Cup: 1980.

NEWCASTLE-ROSEBUD
Founded: 1983.
Colours: Green/brown.
Stadium: Adamstown Oval (7,000).
Club address: Newcastle-Rosebud United, Adamstown Oval, Bryant Street, Adamstown, New South Wales.
National championship: –.
National Cup: 1984.

SOUTH MELBOURNE HELLAS
Founded: 1950.
Colours: All blue.
Stadium: Middle Park (15,000).
Club address: South Melbourne Hellas, Middle Park Stadium, Aughtie Drive, Middle Park, Melbourne, Victoria.
National championship: 1984.
National Cup: –.

ST GEORGE BUDAPEST
Founded: 1957.
Colours: Red/white.
Stadium: St George (15,000).
Club address: St George Budapest, 84 Victoria Avenue, Mortdale, New South Wales 2223.
National league: 1983.
National Cup:–.

SYDNEY CITY HAKOAH
Founded: 1939 (as Hakoah).
Colours: Sky blue/white.
Stadium: Sydney Athletic Field (10,000).

Club address: Sydney City/Hakoah, 61 Hall Street, Bondi, New South Wales 2026.
National League: 1977, 1980, 1981, 1982 (4).
National Cup: – .

SYDNEY OLYMPIC
Founded: 1950 (as Panhellenic; name change 1977).
Colours: All blue.
Stadium: Pratten Park (10,000).
Club address: Sydney Olympic, Pratten Park Stadium, Ashfield, Sydney.
National championship: –.
National Cup: –.

WEST ADELAIDE HELLAS
Founded: 1946.
Colours: Blue/white.
Stadium: Hindmarsh Stadium (14,600).
Club address: West Adelaide Hellas, 98 North Terrace, Adelaide, South Australia 5000.
National League: 1978.
National Cup: Runners-up in 1981.

AUSTRIA

Rapid Vienna stole most of the biggest headlines with their remarkable run to the Cup-winners' Cup final. But on the domestic scene it was traditional rivals FK Austria who led the way. Rapid made the bigger transfer market splash before the season in signing striker Peter Pacult in exchange for Christian Keglevits, but while he was settling in it was the other 'P' – FK Austria's Toni Polster – who was making progress up the scoring charts. Polster scored a hat-trick in a 5-1 league win over Spittal, and then another treble in a 5-0 thrashing of Wiener SC in the Cup.

Already the tone for the campaign had been set. FK Austria even allowed themselves the privilege of parting with veteran right-back Robert Sara. He joined little Favoritner AC. They needed his experience to steady their defence, but must have wondered about their newcomer when he was booked and conceded a penalty on his debut in a 2-0 defeat by Admira.

Rapid were also quickly into disciplinary problems. Veteran Czechoslovak midfield star Antonin Panenka scored a hat-trick with two free kicks and a penalty in a Cup-winners' Cup tie against Besiktas of Turkey. But in the league he was sent off for the first time in his distinguished career in a 1-1 draw against Eisenstadt after coming on as a substitute.

Rapid had a chance to make up ground on FK Austria when the teams met in the big Viennese derby at the start of November. But with midfield general Herbert Prohaska in sure-footed form in midfield, the match ended in a 2-2 draw. Prohaska, happily settled back in Vienna after his years in Italy with Internazionale and Roma, was playing his best football for several years and gained due reward in the annual Footballer of the Year poll. Here again FK Austria outstripped Rapid for honours. Rapid's sweeper Heribert Weber was runner-up, but third place went to another FK Austria star, Hungarian Tibor Nyilasi. But then, Austrian football had seen rather a lot of his achievements since he had just inspired Hungary to eliminate the Austrian national team from the World Cup!

It must be said that while FK Austria ran ahead in the league and Rapid won through to the final of the Cup-winners' Cup – thanks to their controversial, replayed second-round victory over Celtic – the national team was struggling. Erich Hof quit as national manager in November, to be succeeded by the Yugoslav Branko Elsener. He wanted Rapid's skipper and centre-forward Hans Krankl to make an international comeback. But Krankl was hard to convince, and felt he had a more suitable role to play in encouraging some of the new youngsters at Rapid. One such was goalkeeper Michael Konsel. He stepped in after the winter break following injury in an indoor tournament to Herbert Feurer, the veteran whose chequered season had included becoming the victim of an irate fan in the middle of the replayed European tie with Celtic at Old Trafford. Konsel stepped in so impressively that Feurer had to sit out the rest of the season on the substitutes' bench.

Rapid were undergoing a period of change. Panenka announced his intention to retire into the world of hotel management back in his native Czechoslovakia at the season's end, and Yugoslav coach Otto Baric accepted an offer to move during the summer to Stuttgart in West Germany. That was, for Baric, some consolation for what he felt had been an unjustified three-match touchline ban imposed by UEFA after the stormy night at Celtic Park when Rapid had threatened a walk-off after midfielder Rudi Weinhofer was struck by a mystery missile.

FK Austria's European adventures were ended by Liverpool in the quarter-finals of the Champions' Cup, but they refused to let that defeat upset their domestic form, virtually assuring themselves of the championship with a 1-0

1984–85 League Table

	P	W	D	L	F	A	Pts
F K Austria	30	25	4	1	85	17	54
Rapid Vienna	30	18	9	3	85	30	45
Linzer ASK	30	17	4	9	49	37	38
SSW Innsbrück	30	12	8	10	51	44	32
Admira Wacker	30	11	10	9	49	42	32
Sturm Graz	30	13	6	11	51	52	32
Klagenfurt	30	10	11	9	39	38	31
Eisenstadt	30	9	10	11	39	31	28
VÖEST Linz	30	10	8	12	39	43	28
Grazer AK	30	8	12	10	31	35	28
Donawitz	30	11	5	14	38	47	27
Wiener SK	30	10	5	15	40	55	25
Spittal	30	9	6	15	28	55	24
Favoritner AC	30	7	7	16	26	62	21
Salzburg	30	7	4	19	35	69	18
Vienna	30	4	9	17	33	51	17

Cup final: Rapid bt FK Austria 6-5 on pens after 3-3 draw.
Top scorer: Polster (FK Austria) 24 goals.

win over Rapid – still in second place – in mid-May. Nyilasi scored the only goal in the only memorable moment of the 162nd championship derby between the clubs, and a game which was also marked down as having been one of the worst.

There were other events on the club scene – though, as usual, they had to take second place to the FK Austria/Rapid duel. Favoritner coach Peter Blusch, former Eintracht Frankfurt defender, was 'sent off' in one game for coaching from the touchline. Also on the management front, Sturm Graz brought Hermann Stessl home from Portugal – he later returned to FK Austria – while Admira re-engaged their old boss Felix Latzke.

ADMIRA WACKER
Founded: 1905.
Colours: White/black.
Stadium: Bundesstadion Südstadt (15,600).
Club address: F C Admira Wacker, 2344 Maria Enzersdorf, Johann Steinböckstrasse, Vienna.
League: 1927, 1928, 1932, 1934, 1936, 1937, 1939, 1947, 1966 (9).
Cup: 1928, 1932, 1934, 1964, 1966 (5).

CASINO SALZBURG
Founded: 1933.
Colours: Claret/blue.
Stadium: Salzburger stadion (22,000).
Club address: S V Casino Salzburg, 5020 Salzburg, Schumacherstrasse 14.
League: – .
Cup: Runners-up in 1974, 1980 and 1981.

F K AUSTRIA
Founded: 1911.
Colours: All mauve.
Stadium: Horr (20,000). But important matches in the Prater (69,996).
Club address: F K Austria Memphis, 1010 Vienna, Schellinggasse 6.
League: 1924, 1926, 1949, 1950, 1953, 1961, 1962, 1963, 1969, 1970, 1976, 1978, 1979, 1980, 1981, 1984, 1985 (17).
Cup (Vienna Cup until 1950): 1921, 1924, 1925, 1926, 1933, 1935, 1936, 1948, 1949, 1950, 1960, 1962, 1963, 1967, 1971, 1974, 1977, 1980, 1982 (19 – record).
Cup-winners' Cup: Runners-up in 1978.

GRAZER A K
Founded: 1902.
Colours: All white, with red trimmings.
Stadium: Bundesstadion Liebenau (19,000).
Club address: Grazer A K Ring Schuh, Wickenburggasse 40, 8010 Graz.
League: – .
Cup: 1981.

LINZER A S K
Founded: 1908.
Colours: Black and white stripes/white.

Stadium: Linzer stadion (22,000).
Club address: LASK (Linz), 4020 Linz, Köglstrasse 14.
League: 1965.
Cup: 1965.

RAPID
Founded: 1899.
Colours: White with green trimmings/white.
Stadium: Hanappi stadion (20,000).
Club address: S K Rapid Wien, 1140 Vienna, Keisslergasse 6.
League: 1912, 1913, 1916, 1917, 1919, 1920, 1921, 1923, 1929, 1930, 1935, 1938, 1940, 1941, 1946, 1948, 1951, 1952, 1954, 1956, 1957, 1960, 1964, 1967, 1968, 1982, 1983 (27 – record).
Cup: 1919, 1920, 1927, 1946, 1961, 1968, 1969, 1972, 1976, 1983, 1984, 1985 (12).
Cup-winner's Cup: Runners-up 1985.

S S W INNSBRUCK
Founded: 1914.
Colours: Green/black.
Stadium: Tivoli stadion (14,400).
Club address: S S W Innsbruck, 6020 Innsbruck, Höttinger Au 73 b.
League: 1971, 1972, 1973, 1975, 1977 (5).
Cup: 1970, 1973, 1975, 1978, 1979 (5).

STURM GRAZ
Founded: 1909.
Colours: White/black.
Stadium: Bundesstadion Liebenau (19,000).
Club address: S K Sturm Graz, 8010 Graz, Maiffredygasse 14.
League: – .
Cup: Runners-up in 1948 and 1975.

VÖEST LINZ
Founded: 1946.
Colours: White/black.
Stadium: Linzer stadion (22,000).
Club address: S K VÖEST Linz, 4020 Linz, Muldenstrasse 5.
League: 1974.
Cup: – .

WIENER SPORT-CLUB
Founded: 1883.
Colours: White/black.
Stadium: Elterleinplatz (12,000).
Club address: Wiener Sport-Club, 1170 Vienna, Elterleinplatz 7.
League: 1922, 1958, 1959 (3).
Cup: 1923.

BELGIUM

The Heysel Stadium disaster, in which thirty-eight fans – mainly Italian – died at the European Cup final cast an horrific pall over the close of the Belgian season. While the Belgian authorities were quick to identify English hooligans as the culprits, they were not without blame themselves – for insufficient security arrangements, a fiasco over ticket sales and segregation, and a failure to ensure that the Heysel met the safety standards necessary for a volatile, capacity crowd.

Among the achievements virtually forgotten in this major crisis for the Belgian government – never mind Belgian football – was the runaway success of the Brussels club Anderlecht in the league championship. They had signalled their intentions right from the start, when they began the campaign with victories by 9-2 over promoted neighbours Racing Jet and 7-1 against Lokeren. Five of those sixteen goals fell to the personal count of Alex Czerniatynski.

The unknown quantity was the source of any real challenge to the Anderlechtois. Standard Liège, their traditional rivals, had been brought to their knees by the scandals which had forced the suspensions and resignations of president Roger Petit and coach Raymond Goethals, and bans on a string of international players. It seemed initially as if the so-called 'third' Liège club, Seraing, with their three stars from Zaire, might step into those championship-challenging shoes. But their dreams were quickly cut short in October when they lost 4-2 at home to Anderlecht, with Czerniatynski collecting two more goals.

Such was the competition for places at Anderlecht that goalkeeper Jacques Munaron rejected club instructions to undergo a minor operation to correct a knee injury for fear that he might lose his place in the team! Nothing and nobody, it appeared, could stop them. Anderlecht thrashed Gent 5-1 at home, scored a 3-1 away win over Waterschei – with two goals from the young Dane, Per Frimann – and then massacred Waregem 8-2 in the Parc Astrid. Czerniatynski scored a hat-trick and the newly-fit Erwin Vandenbergh collected two goals in a victory made even more remarkable for the fact that Waregem were then second in the table!

That success crowned a wonderful four days, since only the previous Wednesday Anderlecht had scored a 3-0 victory over Real Madrid in the first leg of their UEFA Cup third round tie – a victory club skipper Frankie Vercauteren had dedicated to his father, who had died three days before the game.

Anderlecht travelled to Madrid for the return in cheerful mood. They had won the UEFA Cup in 1983, finished runners-up in 1984 and now fancied their chances of regaining the trophy. But all those runaway victories in the league had blunted their sense of competitive reality. In the Estadio Bernabeu they strolled out expecting Madrid to concede. Instead, they were overturned 6-1, and kicked out of the UEFA Cup on a 6-4 aggregate. It was a ferocious blow to their pride – and one for which the election of brilliant young schemer Enzo Scifo as Footballer of the Year did little to console them. Scifo, the son of Italian parents, who had decided too hastily, he now felt, to adopt Belgian citizenship the previous year to play in the European championship finals, was undoubtedly the star of the Anderlecht show. He scored two fine goals in a 6-0 thrashing of Seraing in February as the league leaders recovered their domestic equilibrium, and was inspirational in midfield on the run-in to the title.

Anderlecht eventually made sure of the championship with four games to go, and reached one hundred goals in league competition for the first time in their last match – a 4-3 win over Lokeren. Fittingly, it was Czerniatynski who scored the hundredth goal. But that wasn't enough to bring him the league's top scorer award. The penalty for being dropped for a few weeks in midseason was that Czerniatynski finished with twenty-one goals, one fewer than Gent's Ronny Martens. If that was one minor disappointment, another was Anderlecht's narrow failure to complete the league season unbeaten. With two games to go they lost their first game 3-1 away to Kortrijk.

Standard struggled throughout the season with never a hope of catching Anderlecht. West German veteran striker, Horst Hrubesch, was out injured for three months, and a string of poor results led to Louis Pilot, the former Luxembourg boss, being fired at the end of March. Runners-up spot went, in the end, to the reviving Club Brugge, while neighbours Cercle beat Beveren on penalties after a 1-1 draw in the cup final. But that was a success which made little impact, coming, as it did, just three days after the Heysel disaster.

1984–85 League Table

	P	W	D	L	F	A	Pts
Anderlecht	34	26	7	1	100	25	59
Club Brugge	34	19	10	5	80	46	48
FC Liège	34	17	12	5	64	36	46
Waregem	34	19	7	8	64	39	45
Beveren	34	17	7	10	67	32	41
Gent	34	14	12	8	62	36	40
Antwerp	34	13	13	8	44	46	39
Standard Liège	34	10	13	11	42	43	33
Waterschei	34	9	14	11	29	37	32
Lokeren	34	10	10	14	55	59	30
KV Mechelen	34	9	10	15	37	54	28
Cercle Brugge	34	10	9	15	33	51	28
Kortrijk	34	8	11	15	41	64	26
Seraing	34	9	8	17	42	64	26
Lierse	34	7	11	16	26	58	25
Beerschot	34	7	10	17	38	60	24
St Niklaas	34	6	9	19	42	78	21
Racing Jet	34	5	9	20	38	76	19

Cup final: Cercle Brugge bt Beveren 5-4 on penalties after a 1-1 draw.
Top scorer: Ronny Martens (Gent) 22 goals.

ANDERLECHT
Founded: 1908.
Colours: Mauve/white.
Stadium: Stadion Constant Vanden Stock (40,300).
Club address: Anderlecht RSC, Stadion Vanden Stock, Theo Verbeecklaan 2, 1070 Brussels.
League: 1947, 1949, 1950, 1951, 1954, 1955, 1956, 1959, 1962, 1964, 1965, 1966, 1967, 1968, 1972, 1974, 1981, 1985 (18 – record).
Cup: 1965, 1972, 1973, 1975, 1976 (5).

Cup-winners' Cup: 1976, 1978. Runners-up in 1977 and 1984 (UEFA Cup).
UEFA Cup: 1983. Runners-up (in the Fairs' Cup) in 1970, 1984.
European SuperCup: 1976, 1978.

ANTWERP
Founded: 1880 (Belgium's oldest club).
Colours: White/red.
Stadium: Bosuil stadion (60,000).
Club address: Antwerp F C, Bosuil stadion, Oude Bosuilbaan 54a, 2100 Deurne.
League: 1929, 1931, 1944, 1957 (4).
Cup: 1955.

BEERSCHOT
Founded: 1899.
Colours: Mauve/white.
Stadium: Olympisch stadion (25,000).
Club address: K Beerschot VAV, De Geyterstraat 133, 2020 Antwerp.
League: 1922, 1924, 1925, 1926, 1928, 1938, 1939 (7).
Cup: 1971, 1979.

BEVEREN
Founded: 1934.
Colours: Yellow/blue
Stadium: Freethiel (21,000).
Club address: S K Beveren-Waas, Freethiel stadion, Klapperstraat 151, 2750 Beveren.
League: 1979, 1984.
Cup: 1978, 1983.

CERCLE
Founded: 1899.
Colours: Green/black.
Stadium: Olympiastadion (32,000).
Club address: KSV Cercle Brugge, Magdalenastraat 9, 8200 St-Andries-Brugge 2.
League: 1911, 1927, 1930.
Cup: 1927, 1985.

CLUB BRUGGE
Founded: 1891.
Colours: All sky blue.
Stadium: Olympisch Stadion (32,000).
Club address: Club Brugge KV, Olympisch Stadion, Olympialaan 74, 8200 Brugge 2.
League: 1920, 1973, 1976, 1977, 1978, 1980 (6).
Cup: 1968, 1970, 1977 (3).
Champions' Cup: Runners-up in 1978.
UEFA Cup: Runners-up in 1976.

GENT
Founded: 1898.
Colours: All blue.
Stadium: Ottenstadion (25,000).
Club address: A A Gent, Ottenstadion, Tennis-straat 9, 9219 Gent-brugge/Gent.
League: – .
Cup: 1964, 1984.

LIÉGEOIS
Founded: 1892.
Colours: All blue.
Stadium: Stade de Rocourt (34,000).
Club address: R F C Liégeois, Stade de Rocourt, Chaussée de Tongres, 4420 Liège.
League: 1896, 1898, 1899, 1952, 1953 (5).
Cup: – .

LIERSE
Founded: 1906.
Colours: Yellow/black.
Stadium: Het Lisp (20,000).
Club address: K Lierse SV, Het Lisp stadion, Voetbalstraat 4, 2500 Lier.
League: 1932, 1942, 1960 (3).
Cup: 1969.

LOKEREN
Founded: 1970.
Colours: White/black.
Stadium: Daknam-stadion (18,000).
Club address: K S C Lokeren, Daknam-stadion, Daknamstraat 91, 9100 Lokeren.
League: – .
Cup: – .

R W D MOLENBEEK
Founded: 1973 (out of the succession of mergers between Brussels/Molenbeek clubs Racing, White Star and Daring).
Colours: White and red halves/black.
Stadium: Edmond Machtens-stadion (31,750).
Club address: R W D Molenbeek, Machtens-stadion, rue Charles Malis 61, 1080 Brussels.
League: 1975.
Cup: – .

SERAING
Founded: 1900.
Colours: Red/black
Stadium: Stade du Pairay (18,000).
Club address: R F C Seraing, Stade du Pairay, Rue de la Bouverie 253, 4100 Seraing/Liège.

League: – .
Cup: – .

STANDARD LIÈGE
Founded: 1898.
Colours: All white (red trimmings).
Stadium: Stade de Sclessin (43,000).
Club address: R Standard Liège C L, Stade de Sclessin, Rue de la Centrale 2, 4200 Sclessin/Ougrée/Liège.
League: 1958, 1961, 1963, 1969, 1970, 1971, 1982, 1983 (8).
Cup: 1954, 1966, 1967, 1981 (4).
Cup-winners' Cup: Runners-up in 1982.

WAREGEM
Founded: 1946.
Colours: White/red.
Stadium: Regenboogstadion (20,000).
Club address: K S V Waregem, Regenboogstadion, 8190 Waregem.
League: – .
Cup: 1974.

WATERSCHEI
Founded: 1925,
Colours: Yellow/black.
Stadium: André Dumont-stadion (22,200).
Club address: K Waterschei T H O R Genk, André Dumont-stadion, Stadion-plain 4, 3600 Genk-Waterschei.
League: – .
Cup: 1980, 1982.

BOLIVIA

The industrial town of Santa Cruz de la Sierra, in the east of Bolivia, has suddenly become that country's football capital. Not only did Oriente Petrolero from Santa Cruz win the first stage of the 1984 championship, but neighbours and rivals Blooming then collected the overall title for the first time in their thirty-eight year history. Both teams thus competed in the South American club championship this year, one of the few occasions on which the capital, La Paz, has been without a presence in the continent's prestige club competition.

Oriente, three times champions in the 1970s, began the League first round as if eager to make up for their disappointment the previous year, when they lost the title in a play-off against Bolivar from La Paz.

Indeed, Bolivar were Oriente's closest challengers for the first round leadership, and looked the better team for much of the time. Chilean coach Andres Prieto had already agreed to go home at the season's end to take over Chile's Cobreloa. But he wanted to go out on top, and Bolivar's record of seventy-one goals in twenty-eight games, and twenty-two conceded, was by far the best.

Those twenty-eight games included one unusual away match against San Jose, a mid-table team, in Oruro, south of La Paz. When the twenty-two players walked out for the match they found that stadium workers had stolen the cross-bars as part of their protest against the rejection of demands for a pay rise. Cross-bars were hastily borrowed from a nearby training pitch, and the match got under way half an hour late!

Another team to suffer from the problems which seem to be part and parcel of football in Bolivia, were the Petrolero club from Cochabamba. The players missed their flight to La Paz for a match against The Strongest, who were duly awarded a walkover and the points. The Strongest have been champions of Bolivia eighteen times, a record. But their last championship triumph was back in 1977, and they rarely threatened to regain their crown – finishing the first round seven points behind Oriente.

For the second stage of the championship the top eight from the first round were split into two groups of four, then two groups of two, with the winners emerging for the title play-off – Bolivar against Blooming.

Bolivar put their faith in the left-sided midfielder, Erwin Romero, a schemer who is the best-paid player in Bolivia at around 600 dollars a month. Romero has averaged twenty-five goals a season ever since returning in 1980 from an unhappy spell in Argentina with Quilmes of Buenos Aires. But even his sharp-shooting skills were not enough to provide Bolivar with a third successive title. Blooming coach Paul Pino was delighted with his men's 4-3 win in the first leg in Santa Cruz.

But he knew the return would be tough up in La Paz, 10,000 feet above sea-level. Blooming flew there on the day of the game to try to minimise the effects of altitude. But they were run off their feet and beaten 6-3, yet this was not a total disaster. In the play-offs, if the two teams are level on points, goal difference is immaterial – so they played a third time. Bolivar were favourites, but this time Blooming goalkeeper Terrazas was in inspired form, and the hero of a 1-0 win.

1984 Professional Championship
First Round Final Table

	P	W	D	L	F	A	Pts
Oriente	25	17	5	3	58	25	39
Bolivar	26	17	5	4	71	22	39
Blooming	26	17	4	5	62	29	38
Jorge Wilsterman	26	15	4	7	54	31	34
The Strongest	26	13	6	7	57	35	32
Petrolero	26	11	7	8	33	34	29
Chaco	25	10	4	11	41	43	24
San Jose	26	6	11	9	43	43	23
Aurora	26	6	9	11	35	42	21
Real	25	8	4	13	29	39	20
Gaubira	26	8	4	14	35	58	20
Magisterio	26	5	5	16	35	77	15
Municipal	25	6	2	17	23	54	14
Primero de Mayo	26	3	6	17	22	66	12

Top eight qualified for final round

Second Round

Section A	P	W	D	L	Pts
The Strongest	6	3	2	1	8
Oriente	6	3	2	1	8
Jorge Wilsterman	6	3	1	2	7
San Jose	6	0	1	5	1

Section B	P	W	D	L	Pts
Bolivar	6	5	0	1	10
Blooming	6	4	0	2	8
Petrolero	6	2	1	3	5
Chaco	6	0	1	5	1

Semi-finals – Section A	P	W	D	L	F	A	Pts
Bolivar	2	1	0	1	5	2	2
Oriente	2	1	0	1	2	5	2

Section B	P	W	D	L	F	A	Pts
Blooming	2	1	1	0	4	2	3
The Strongest	2	0	1	1	2	4	1

Championship final: Blooming bt Bolivar 4-3, 3-6, 1-0.

AURORA
Founded: 1935.
Colours: Sky blue/white.
Stadium: Félix Capriles (35,000).
Club address: Aurora, Jordán 3797, Cochabamba.
Championship: – .

BLOOMING
Founded: 1946.
Colours: Sky blue/white.
Stadium: Ramon 'Tauhichi' Aguilera (40,000).
Club address: Blooming, 24 de Setiembre, Santa Cruz de la Sierra.
Championship: 1984.

BOLIVAR
Founded: 1925.
Colours: All blue.
Stadium: Important matches in the Estadio Nacional Olímpico (55,000).
Club address: Bolivar Independiente Unificada, Ed. Litoral, Calle Colón, La Paz.
Championship: 1939, 1940, 1941, 1942, 1950, 1953, 1954, 1956, 1968, 1976, 1978, 1982, 1983, 1984 (14).

DEPORTIVO CHACO
Founded: 1944.
Colours: Green and white stripes/white.
Stadium: Nacional Olímpico (55,000).
Club address: Deportivo Chaco Petrolero, YPFB, La Paz.
Championship: – .

GUABIRÁ
Founded: 1962.
Colours: Red/blue.
Stadium: Ramon 'Tauhichi' Aguilera (40,000).
Club address: Guabirá, Ingenio Azucarero, Guabirá, Santa Cruz de la Sierra.
Championship: 1975.

JORGE WILSTERMAN
Founded: 1949.
Colours: Red/blue.
Stadium: Estadio Félix Capriles (35,000).
Club address: Club Jorge Wilsterman, San Martín S–0348, Cochabamba.
Championship: 1958, 1959, 1966, 1967, 1972, 1973, 1980, 1981 (8).

MUNICIPAL
Founded: 1944.
Colours: Crimson/white.
Stadium: Luis Lastra (10,000).
Club address: Deportivo Municipal, Honorable Municipalidad de la Paz.
Championship: 1955, 1960, 1961, 1965 (4).

ORIENTE PETROLERO
Founded: 1955.
Colours: Green/white.
Stadium: Ramon 'Tauhichi' Aguilera (40,000).
Club address: Oriente Petrolero, YPFB, Santa Cruz de la Sierra.
Championship: 1971, 1974, 1979 (3).

PETROLERO
Founded: 1950.
Colours: Green and white stripes/white.
Stadium: Félix Capriles (35,000).
Club address: Petrolero, YPFB, Cochabamba.
Championship: 1962, 1970.

THE STRONGEST
Founded: 1908.
Colours: Black and yellow stripes/black.
Stadium: Achumani (40,000).
Club address: The Strongest, Comercio esq. Colón 512, La Paz.
Championship: 1914, 1916, 1917, 1920, 1924, 1929, 1930, 1932, 1935, 1937, 1938, 1943, 1945, 1952, 1963, 1964, 1975, 1977 (18 – record).

BRAZIL

After six years of financial crises, a rapid turnover in coaches and players, Santos FC at last regained a little of their old respect by winning the São Paulo (Paulista) state championship for the first time since 1978. Santos led almost from start to finish. Palmeiras were their only consistent pursuers, although

Corinthians came through strongly and might have snatched the crown right at the end of the term. Instead, in front of a 100,000 crowd in the Morumbi stadium, it was Santos who won a climactic fixture against Corinthians by 1–0 thanks to a goal from their revitalised centre-forward Serginho. He had been pilloried by fans at home after the 1982 World Cup finals, but a transfer to Santos worked wonders, and he was joint Paulista league top scorer with sixteen goals.

Yet it says much for the collapse of Santos since Pele retired from their ranks in the mid-1970s, that at the end of the season the directors collected almost as much praise for their nimble footwork in a financial disaster zone as the players for their work on the pitch. Brazil's rampant inflation had long since wiped out all the savings built up over the 1960s and early 1970s when Santos travelled the world like a touring circus – showing off Pele, Zito, Gilmar, Coutinho, Pepe, Mengalvio, Dorval and company to all and sundry for lucrative fees. In fact, just the week before Santos' vital last league game against Corinthians, they very nearly had all water to stadium and training grounds cut off because payment of the water rates was three months overdue! Further, it illustrates the financial state of Brazilian football that Santos should have been praised because they were rarely more than ten days (!) in arrears in paying the players' wages.

Santos began the state season with problems among the playing staff, principally concerning Serginho. He was accused publicly of faking injury to avoid the two awkward South American Cup-ties in Colombia early in the season. It was only after the dismissal of former Santos and Brazil centre-back Chico Formiga as coach that president Milton Teixeira succeeded in cooling a number of squabbles within the playing staff and bringing Serginho back into the fold.

Carlos Castilho, Brazil's 1954 World Cup goalkeeper, took over as coach, and Santos sealed their victory in the controversial absence of Pele. He had been specifically asked by the club to stay away from their last match against Corinthians so as not to distract the fans or put extra pressure on his successors. Pele would hardly have impressed by them. It's a sad comment on the state of Brazilian game when it comes to attackers, that Santos won the Paulista title with only fifty-four goals in thirty-eight games. The 'secret' of their success rested thus not with the forwards but with the talent of Uruguayan goalkeeper Rodolfo Rodriguez. His finest save, like Serginho's most vital goal, was reserved for the Corinthians clash, when somehow he kept out an apparently goal-bound header from Lima which could have turned the match and the league table around.

Another foreign goalkeeper emerged as a key figure in the Carioca (Rio de Janeiro) championship, Ubaldo Fillol, the Argentine World Cup-winning goalkeeper of 1978, who had joined Flamengo from River Plate. Fillol saw Flamengo get off to an excellent start when they won the first stage of the league, the Guanabara Cup. In the decisive match Flamengo beat Fluminense – still suffering from the hangover of their 1984 national championship success – by 1–0. But Fluminense also had an in-form goalkeeper of their own in Brazilian international Paulo Vitor. And, as the season went on, he came into his own.

Defeat in the Guanabara Cup cost coach Luis Henrique his job, and Carlos Albertos Torres – Brazil's 1970 World Cup-winning skipper – took over. He found a team unbalanced by a contract dispute which kept midfielder Delei on the sidelines and a knee operation which had similarly ruled out defender Ricardo. But he benefited from the return home, after a controversial stay in Spain with Sevilla, of the unpredictable outside-right Carlos Alberti Pintinho, and the emergence of a useful new defender in Vica to fill the gap left by

1984 São Paulo League Table

	P	W	D	L	F	A	Pts
Santos	38	22	13	3	54	19	57
Corinthians	38	22	10	6	56	28	54
São Paulo	38	20	13	5	51	23	53
Palmeiras	38	20	10	8	52	26	50
Ponte Preta	38	17	11	10	51	37	45
Guarani	38	15	13	10	49	36	43
América	38	13	16	9	34	31	42
Marilia	38	14	12	12	41	29	40
Santo André	38	11	18	9	38	38	40
Botafogo de RP	38	13	13	12	42	37	39
Inter Limeira	38	13	12	13	31	35	38
XV Di Jau	38	9	17	12	34	44	35
Juventus	38	9	13	15	36	44	32
Portuguesa	38	11	8	19	30	41	30
Comercial	38	9	12	17	28	51	30
XV Di Piracicaba	38	7	16	15	32	51	29
Ferroviaria	38	8	12	18	35	54	28
São Bento	38	8	12	18	28	50	28
Taquaritinga	38	6	12	20	28	51	26
Taubate	38	5	10	23	23	48	20

Top scorers: Chiquinho (Botafogo de RP) and Serginho (Santos) 16 goals each.

Rio de Janeiro
Two-round points totals: 1. Flamengo and Fluminense each 33; 3. Vasco da Gama and Bangu each 29; 5. Botafogo 28; 6. América 21; 7. Américano 18; 8. Goytacaz 17; 9. Volta Redonda 16; 10. Olaria 15; 11. Campo Grande 12; 12. Friburguense 11.
Play-off tournament: Fluminense 2, Vasco da Gama 0 – Flamengo 1, Vasco da Gama 0 – Fluminense 1, Flamengo 0.
Final points totals: Fluminense 37; Flamengo 35; Vasco da Gama 29.
Top scorers: Claudio Adão (Bangu) and Baltazar (Botafogo) 12 goals each.

Minas Gerais
Championship play-off: Cruzeiro bt Atletico Mineiro 4–0, 0–1 (4–1 on agg).
Top scorer: Carlos Alberto Seixas (Cruzeiro) 14 goals.

Rio Grande do Sul
Final round points totals: 1, Internacional 15; 2, Gremio and Brasil each 12; 4, N. Hamburgo 11; 5, Juventude 8; 6, Pelotas 7.
Top scorer: Ademir (Pelotas) 21 goals.

Other State Championships
Baiano: Bahia. Parana: Pinheiros. Pernambuco: Nautico. Cearense: Ceara. Para: Paysandu. Santa Catarina: Joinville. Goias: Vila Nova.

National championship: Curitiba bt Bangu 6-5 on pens after 1-1 draw.

Ricardo. Above all, Carlos Alberto Torres put new life back into the midfield pairing of Jandir and the Paraguayan Romerito – who was to end up as reverted for the 1984 season to a straight league championship with the top Fluminense's top scorer with eleven of the club's forty goals (in twenty-four games).

Brazilian football is a complex organisation. Whereas São Paulo had club at the end taking the prize, the Carioca set-up had a play-off system grafted onto it. Flamengo made certain of qualifying for those play-offs with their Guanabara Cup success, and Vasco da Gama, thanks to a 2–1 victory over Fluminense, carried off the second qualifying place by winning the second half of the programme for the Taça Rio de Janeiro. Fluminense's only chance of retaining their Rio title was if they grabbed the third place in the play-offs by virtue of finishing with the highest total of points over the two halves of the season.

Flamengo could have barred the way had they won their last-but-one game against Campo Grande, but they drew only 1–1, and star forward Tita missed a penalty. Fluminense duly beat Volta Redonda and then faced Flamengo in the last match of the league programme. Assis and Washington put Fluminense 2–0 ahead, and not even the expulsion of Washington late in the game could prevent a 2–1 victory which secured Flu's place in the play-offs.

Romerito inspired them to a 2–0 victory over Vasco in the first match and that meant Fluminense against Flamengo – the oldest rivals in Rio – with the Carioca championship at stake. A crowd of 153,000 turned out at the Maracana stadium. On the bench were two former World Cup colleagues, Carlos Alberto for Fluminense against Flamengo boss Mario Zagalo, who had been Brazil's manager when Carlos Alberto was their triumphant captain in Mexico. Flamengo had the better of the opening exchanges, but Fluminense had the first chance when Rene crossed, only for Washington's header to be well stopped by Fillol in front of a crowd which included Mick Jagger. It was still 0-0 at half-time, and again Flamengo made the brighter start on the resumption. Páula Vitor had to be at his best to save from Tita, Andrade and Adalberto. Flamengo were now pushing further into attack, and it was with Adalberto out of position that Fluminense took decisive advantage on a counter-attack. Rene sent Aldo clear down the wing and Assis headed his cross beyond Fillol. Fluminense had completed the double of state and national championships, and had successfully retained their Carioca title.

ATLETICO MINEIRO
Founded: 1914.
Colours: Black and white stripes/black.
Stadium: Important matches in the Magalhaes Pinto stadium (110,000).
Club address: Clube Atletico Mineiro, Avenida Olegario Maciel 1516, Lourdes, Belo Horizonte.
Minas Gerais champ.: 1914, 1925, 1926, 1931, 1932, 1936, 1938, 1939, 1941, 1942, 1946, 1947, 1949, 1950, 1952, 1953, 1954, 1955, 1956, 1958, 1962, 1963, 1970, 1976, 1978, 1979, 1980, 1981, 1982, 1983 (30).
National champ.: 1977.

BAHIA
Founded: 1931.
Colours: White/sky blue.

Stadium: Important matches in the Otavio Mangabeira stadium, Salvador (84,300).
Club address: Esporte Clube Bahia, Rua Carlos Gomes 85, 2nd andar, Centro, Salvador.
Baiano champ.: 1931, 1933, 1934, 1936, 1938, 1940, 1944, 1945, 1947, 1948, 1949, 1950, 1952, 1954, 1956, 1958, 1959, 1960, 1961, 1962, 1967, 1970, 1971, 1973, 1974, 1975, 1976, 1977, 1978, 1979, 1981, 1982, 1983, 1984 (34).
National champ.: – .

BOTAFOGO
Founded: 1904.
Colours: Black and white stripes/black.
Stadium: Estadio General Severiano ('Sugar Loaf'; 23,000). Important matches in Maracana stadium (200,000).
Club address: Botafogo de Futebol e Regatas, Rua Xavier Curado 1705, Rio de Janeiro 21610.
Rio champ.: 1907, 1910, 1930, 1932, 1933, 1934, 1935, 1948, 1957, 1961, 1962, 1967, 1968 (13).
Rio/São Paulo champ.: 1962, 1964 (shared with Santos), 1966 (shared).
National champ.: – .

CORINTHIANS
Founded: 1910.
Colours: White/black.
Stadium: Important matches in the Morumbi stadium (150,000).
Club address: Sport Club Corinthians Paulista, Rua São Jorge 777, Tatuapé, São Paulo 03087.
São Paulo champ.: 1914, 1916, 1922, 1923, 1924, 1928, 1929, 1930, 1937, 1938, 1939, 1941, 1951, 1952, 1954, 1977, 1979, 1982, 1983 (19).
Rio/São Paulo champ.: 1950, 1953, 1954, 1966 (shared).
National champ.: – .

CRUZEIRO
Founded: 1921.
Colours: Blue/white.
Stadium: Magalhaes Pinto (110,000).
Club address: Cruzeiro Esporte Clube, Rua Guajaras 1722, Barro Preto, Belo Horizonte.
Minas Gerais champ.: 1928, 1929, 1930, 1940, 1943, 1944, 1945, 1959, 1960, 1961, 1965, 1966, 1967, 1968, 1969, 1972, 1973, 1974, 1975, 1977, 1984 (21).
National champ.: – .
World Club Cup: Runners-up in 1976.
South American Club Cup: 1976. Runners-up in 1977.

FLAMENGO
Founded: 1895 as a sailing club, 1911 as a football club.
Colours: Black and red hoops/white.
Stadium: Estadio da Gavea (20,000) but important matches in the Maracana stadium (200,000).

Club address: Clube de Regatas do Flamengo, Praça Nossa Senhora Auxiliadora, Gavea, Rio de Janeiro.
Rio de Janeiro champ.: 1914, 1915, 1920, 1921, 1925, 1927, 1939, 1942, 1943, 1944, 1953, 1954, 1955, 1963, 1965, 1972, 1974, 1978, 1979, 1981 (20).
Rio/São Paulo champ.: 1961.
National champ.: 1980, 1982, 1983 (3).
World Club Cup: 1981.
South American Club Cup: 1981.

FLUMINENSE
Founded: 1902.
Colours: Red and green stripes/white.
Stadium: Estadio Laranjeiras (20,000) but important matches in the Maracana (200,000).
Club address: Fluminense Futebol Clube, Rua Alvaro Chaves 41, Rio de Janeiro 22231.
Rio de Janeiro champ.: 1906, 1907 (shared, sometimes cons. unofficial), 1908, 1909, 1911, 1917, 1918, 1919, 1924, 1936, 1937, 1938, 1940, 1941, 1946, 1951, 1959, 1964, 1969, 1971, 1973, 1975, 1976, 1980, 1983, 1984 (26).
Rio/São Paulo champ.: 1957, 1960.
National champ.: 1970, 1984.

GREMIO
Founded: 1903.
Colours: Blue and black stripes/black.
Stadium: Estadio Olimpico (100,000).
Club address: Gremio Foot-Ball Porto-Alegrense, Largo dos Campeóes, Azenha, Porto Alegre.
Rio Grande do Sul champ.: 1911, 1912, 1913 (shared), 1914 (shared) 1915 (shared), 1919, 1920 (shared), 1921, 1923, 1925, 1926, 1930, 1931, 1932, 1933, 1935, 1937, 1938, 1939, 1946, 1949, 1956, 1957, 1958, 1959, 1960, 1962, 1963, 1964, 1965, 1966, 1967, 1968, 1977, 1979, 1980 (36).
National champ.: 1981.
World Club Cup: 1983.
S. American Club Cup: 1983. Runners-up 1984.

GUARANI
Founded: 1930.
Colours: Green/white.
Stadium: Brino de Ouro (30,000).
Club address: Guarani FC, Estadio Brinco de Ouro, Campinas.
São Paulo champ.: – .
National champ.: 1978.

INTERNACIONAL
Founded: 1910.
Colours: Red/white.
Stadium: Estadio Beira Río (100,000).
Club address: Sport Club Internacional, Avenida Padre Cacique, Menino de Deus, Porto Alegre.

Rio Grande do Sul champ.: 1913 (shared), 1914 (shared), 1915 (shared), 1916, 1917, 1920 (shared), 1922, 1927, 1934, 1936, 1940, 1941, 1942, 1943, 1944, 1945, 1947, 1948, 1950, 1951, 1952, 1953, 1955, 1961, 1969, 1970, 1971, 1972, 1973, 1974, 1975, 1976, 1978, 1981, 1982, 1983, 1984 (37).
National champ.: 1975, 1976, 1979 (3).
S. American Club Cup: Runners-up in 1980.

PALMEIRAS
Founded: 1914.
Colours: Green/white.
Stadium: Parque Antártica (35,000).
Club address: Sociedade Esportiva Palmeiras, Rua Turiacu 1840, Agua Branca/São Paulo.
São Paulo champ.: 1920, 1926, 1927, 1932, 1933, 1934, 1936, 1940, 1942, 1944, 1947, 1950, 1959, 1963, 1966, 1972, 1974, 1976 (18).
Rio/São Paulo champ.: 1951, 1965.
National champ.: 1967, 1969, 1972, 1973 (4).
S. American Club Cup: Runners-up in 1961 and 1968.

SANTOS
Founded: 1912.
Colours: All white.
Stadium: Vila Belmiro (20,000) but important matches in the early 1960s were played in Maracana (200,000) and lately in the Morumbi (150,000).
Club address: Santos Futebol Clube, Rua Princesa Isabel, Vila Belmiro, Santos/São Paulo.
São Paulo champ.: 1935, 1955, 1956, 1958, 1960, 1961, 1962, 1964, 1965, 1967, 1968, 1969, 1973 (shared), 1978, 1984 (15).
Rio/São Paulo champ.: 1959, 1963, 1964 (shared), 1966 (shared) (4).
National champ.: 1968.
World Club Cup: 1962, 1963.
S. American Club Cup: 1962, 1963.

SÃO PAULO
Founded: 1930.
Colours: All white, with one red and one black hoop.
Stadium: Morumbi (150,000).
Club address: São Paulo Futebol Clube, Praça Gomes Pedrosa, Jardim Leonor, São Paulo.
São Paulo champ.: 1931, 1943, 1945, 1946, 1948, 1949, 1953, 1957, 1970, 1971, 1975, 1980, 1981 (13).
Rio/São Paulo champ.: – .
National champ.: 1977.
S. American Club Cup: Runners-up in 1974.

VASCO DA GAMA
Founded: 1898 as a sailing club, 1915 for football.
Colours: All white with a black sash.
Stadium: Estadio de São Januario (50,000) but important matches in Maracana (200,000).

Club address: Clube de Regatas Vasco da Gama, Rua General Américo de Moura 131, Rio de Janeiro.
Rio de Janeiro champ.: 1923, 1924, 1929, 1934, 1936, 1945, 1947, 1949, 1950, 1952, 1956, 1958, 1970, 1977, 1982 (15).
Rio/São Paulo champ.: 1958, 1966 (shared).
National champ.: 1974.

BULGARIA

Official unease has existed over the state of football in Bulgaria for several years and everything came to a head after the cup final between top clubs CSKA Sofia and Levsky Spartak. Levsky had won the league title ahead of CSKA, and a long rivalry existed between the two dominant clubs of the capital. But both went out of control when CSKA won the cup final 2–1 in a brawl of a game which saw five players booked and three (Nikolov and Spassov of Levsky and Yanchev of CSKA) sent off.

The central committee of the Communist Party went into emergency session the next day, and came up with swingeing punishments on clubs, players and officials. They decided that CSKA (the army team) and Levsky (team of the transport and interior ministries) should be disbanded; officials should be suspended *sine die* from sports administration including team coaches Vasil Metodiev (Levsky), a national team aide, and Manolo Manolev (CSKA); international players Borislav Mikhailov, goalkeeper, and Plamen Nikolov, right-back and Footballer of the Year, from Levsky should be banned for life, along with Emil Velev and Emil Spassov (both Levsky) and Christo Stoikhov (CSKA). One year's suspension was inflicted on several other players including Levsky's goalscorer in the final, Nasko Sirakov, a senior member of Bulgaria's World Cup squad.

The committee also recommended that the cup should be withheld, and that both clubs' records should be erased from the 1984–85 league championship. It considered the cup final brawl a 'scandalous, disgraceful event . . . a shame without precedent in Bulgarian football.' It further suggested that the centralised system of having four major Sofia clubs backed by various government ministries should be replaced by a suburbs/geographical arrangement. All these changes were put through at high speed in time for the start of the 1985–86 league, with CSKA renamed Sredec, and Levsky Vitosha.

CSKA had been founded in 1948 as the army team, then known as CDNA, and had since taken over at least eight other sports clubs – their merger with Red Banner in 1964 leading to the change of name to CSKA Septemvrijsko Zname. The idea of an army team collaring all the best players was a popular one in Eastern Europe in the 1950s, with Honved in Hungary, Dukla Prague in Czechoslovakia and Vorwärts in East Germany. That the system contained flaws and could not be rigidly maintained they found out rather sooner than the Bulgarians, though CSKA had proved durable and awkward European competitors, claiming the record of eliminating Ajax Amsterdam, then Nottingham Forest as well as Liverpool when all those clubs were defending their Champions' Cup crowns.

As for Levsky, they had been the country's most popular club, having been founded in 1914 and with a record of consistent success ever since their first league title in 1933. In 1984 they won both the league and cup, so it was in just failing successfully to retain both those prizes that they lost their nerve and their temper against CSKA in the cup final. It must be said that the cup final was not the first time Levsky had been in trouble during the season. In April they were banned from playing matches in their own stadium for three rounds of the championship – in which they were clear leaders – after their supporters attacked a bus carrying fans from the Pirin club, who had just inflicted, by 1–0, Levsky's first home defeat of the campaign.

They managed to hang on at the top, even so, to pip CSKA to the league title. But the army team's failure to land what would have been a record twenty-fourth championship was owed to their appalling start to the season. They lost all their first three games and were, for the first time in their history, bottom of the table. It wasn't until early October that they signalled their readiness to move up the table, when they thrashed Minior 8–1 with a hat-trick from Marjov and two goals from Slavkov.

Lokomotiv of Sofia had been the early league leaders. But their dreams of glory ended at the start of November when they were thrashed 5–0 at home by Levsky, who thus leap-frogged into a lead they quickly extended thanks to a 7–2 victory over Beroe. National team striker Rusi Gochev scored a hat-trick, and Levsky had more to celebrate when right-back Nikolov – later one of the cup final culprits – was voted Footballer of the Year.

By the end of the first half of the season and the winter break, CSKA had pulled up to third place. The determination to overhaul Levsky led to a roughhouse, with three players seriously injured, in CSKA's home match against Slavia. But try as they could, with both fair means and foul, it just wasn't enough.

Provisional 1984–85 League Table

	P	W	D	L	F	A	Pts
Levsky Spartak*	30	18	6	6	66	37	40
CSKA Sofia*	30	15	7	8	66	36	36
Trakia Plovdiv	30	15	5	10	68	32	33
Lokomotiv	30	13	8	9	48	44	33
Pirin	30	12	7	11	42	43	31
Botev	30	13	3	14	48	42	29
Slavia Sofia	30	14	2	14	49	48	29
Etar Tirnovo	30	14	1	15	49	50	28
Spartak Pleven	30	11	8	12	47	52	27
Cherno More	30	11	7	12	41	45	26
Sliven	30	11	5	14	41	45	26
Beroe S. Z.	30	11	5	14	41	51	26
Dunav	30	10	7	13	39	51	26
Spartak Varna	30	10	7	13	35	49	26
Minior	30	11	5	14	32	65	25
Chernomoretz	30	8	5	17	35	57	21

*Because of the disbanding of Levsky and CSKA the championship was awarded to Trakia.
Note: No points awarded for goal-less draws.

Cup final: CSKA Sofia 2, Levsky Spartak Sofia 1. (Cup withheld).
Top scorer: Getov (Slavia) 26 goals.

AKADEMIK SOFIA
Founded: 1947.
Colours: All blue.
Stadium: Akademik Sports Complex (15,000).
Club address: Akademik Sofia, c/o Bulgarian football federation, Stadium Vassil Levsky, Sofia.
League: – .
Cup: – .

BEROE STARA ZAGORA
Founded: 1920.
Colours: White-green-red.
Stadium: Stadium Stara Zagora (15,000).
Club address: F C Beroe, I. Aleksiev 10, 6000 Stara Zagora.
League: – .
Cup: – .

BOTEV VRAZA
Founded: 1921.
Colours: Red/black.
Stadium: Hristo Botev (24,000).
Club address: F C Botev, Jordan Lütibrodsski 23, 3000 Vraza.
League: – .
Cup: – .

DUNAV ROUSSE
Founded: 1949.
Colours: All white.
Stadium: Rousse (20,000).
Club address: Dunav Rousse, A. Zlatarov 31, Rousse.
League: – .
Cup: – .

ETAR TIRNOVO
Founded: 1924.
Colours: Violet/black.
Stadium: Spartak (10,000).
Club address: Etar Tirnovo, A. Stamboliyski, Veliko Tirnovo.
League: – .
Cup: – .

LOKOMOTIV PLOVDIV
Founded: 1936.
Colours: White/black.
Stadium: Deveti Septemvri (50,000).
Club address: Lokomotiv Plovdiv, Otez Paisiy 31, Plovdiv.
League: – .
Cup: – .
League Cup: 1983.

LOKOMOTIV SOFIA
Founded: 1929.
Colours: Red and black stripes/black.
Stadium: Lokomotiv (30,000).
Club address: F C Lokomotiv, Georgi Dimitrov 106, 1233 Sofia.
League: 1940, 1945, 1964, 1978 (4).
Cup: 1948, 1953, 1982 (3).

SLAVIA SOFIA
Founded: 1913.
Colours: All white.
Stadium: Slavia (35,000).
Club address: F C Slavia, 9 Septemvri 128, 1618 Sofia.
League: 1928, 1930, 1936, 1939, 1941, 1943 (6).
Cup: 1952, 1963, 1964, 1966, 1975, 1980 (6).

SPARTAK VARNA
Founded: 1914.
Colours: White/blue.
Stadium: Spartak (25,000).
Club address: FC JSK-Spartak, Varnensska Komuna 1, 9000 Varna.
League: 1932.
Cup: – .

SREDEC
Founded: 1948 as CDNA. Reorganised June 1985.
Colours: All red.
Stadium: Nardonia Armia (35,000) but important matches in the National Vassil Levsky stadium (70,000).
League: 1948, 1951, 1952, 1954, 1955, 1956, 1957, 1958, 1959, 1960, 1961, 1962, 1966, 1969, 1971, 1972, 1973, 1975, 1976, 1980, 1981, 1982, 1983 (23 – record).
Cup: 1951, 1954, 1955, 1960, 1961, 1965, 1969, 1972, 1973, 1974 (10).

TRAKIA
Founded: 1912.
Colours: Yellow/black.
Stadium: Hristo Botev (40,000).
Club address: F C Trakia, D. Blagoer 10, 4000 Plovdiv.
League: 1929, 1967.
Cup: 1981.

VITOSHA
Founded: 1914 as Levsky; merged with Spartak Sofia in 1969. Reorganised June 1985.
Colours: All blue.
Stadium: Levsky-Gerena (45,000). Important matches in the Vassil Levsky (70,000).
League: 1933, 1937, 1942, 1946, 1947, 1949, 1950, 1965, 1968, 1970, 1974, 1977, 1984 (13).
Cup: 1942, 1946, 1947, 1949 (Levsky won the third replay with CDNA 1-0 after extra time), 1950, 1956, 1957, 1959, 1967, 1968 (for Spartak), 1970, 1971, 1976, 1977, 1979, 1984 (16 for Levsky – record).

CAMEROON

Cameroon football, riding high on the performance of the national team in the 1982 World Cup finals, came down to earth with a bump in 1984. On the domestic front little changed. Tonnerre of Yaoundé won the championship for the third consecutive season – though after surprisingly losing their last game 3–1 to Dynamo Douala. It was only on goal difference that they finished ahead of Canon. This was a vast change from the previous year, when Tonnerre finished twelve points clear of runners-up Etoile Filante. Early in the campaign newly-promoted Rail FC of Douala had led the way thanks to their transfer market captures of François N'Doumbé Lea and Rene Ndjea from Union. In the end, however, the inexperience of the rest of the squad proved their undoing and they finished in third place.

On the international club scene it was Canon who carried Cameroon hopes furthest, in the African Cup-winners' Cup. In the Champions' Cup Tonnerre had fallen surprisingly to Shooting Stars of Nigeria in the second round. Tonnerre crashed 4–0 away, and a 1–0 victory back in Yaoundé was mere consolation.

As for Canon, all went reasonably smoothly considering that the players they lost have over the past few years looked like a 'Who's Who' of African football. Goalkeeper Thomas Nkono, defender Aoudou and midfielders Mbida and Theophile Abega had all been tempted by professional offers in Europe. Their departures had been reflected in the size of Canon's 5–0 defeat at the hands of Al Ahly of Egypt in the 1983 Champions' Cup. In less than a year, however, they had rebuilt around Mbarga in defence, Kunde in midfield and Nguea and Dagobert Dong in attack. Canon beat Avia Sport 3–1, 1–1 and Dynamo Filma 5–0, 0–3 to earn a Cup-winners' quarter-final against Enugu, of Nigeria.

In brilliant style Canon avenged Tonnerre's defeat in Nigeria in the other competition. Canon won 5–0 in Yaoundé, and could afford the luxury of a 3–0 defeat – Nigerian goals from Okonkwo, Igwilo and Nosike all in the second half – in the return. That earned a semi-final against Al Ahly of Libya. Kunde gave Canon a narrow lead in the home, first leg. But the Libyans reversed the score in Tripoli and won the tie on penalties, and yet Canon still reached the final. This was because the Libyans' opponents in the final were to have been the similarly-named Al Ahly of Egypt. The two countries are engaged in a 'cold war', so the Libyans refused to turn up for the first leg of the final. The African confederation, controversially, then ordered Canon to take their place – which they were, of course, happy to do.

A crowd of 80,000 filled the Cairo International Stadium for the first leg of the 'new' final and saw Canon leave well satisfied after losing just 1–0 to a thirty-fifth minute goal by Magdi Abdel Ghani for Al Ahly. When Dong equalised the aggregate nine minutes into the second half of the return in Yaoundé, the Cameroon team appeared on their way to regaining the Cup they first won in 1979. Al Ahly held out after that, however, and – to the massive disappointment of the 40,000 Cameroon fans – won the crown 4–2 on a penalty shoot-out.

1984 Championship

Final leading placings: 1, Tonnerre Yaoundé; 2, Canon Yaoundé; 3, FC Rail Douala.
Relegated: Foudre and Kohi.

CANON
Founded: 1930.
Colours: All red.
Stadium: Ahmadou Ahidjo (50,000).
Club address: Canon Yaoundé, c/o Fédération Camérounaise de Football, BP 1116 Yaoundé.
League: 1970, 1974, 1977, 1979, 1980, 1982 (6).
Cup: 1967, 1973, 1975, 1976, 1977, 1978, 1983 (7).
Afr. Champions' Cup: 1971, 1978, 1980 (3 – record).
Afr. Cup-winners' Cup: 1979. Runners-up in 1977, 1984.

TONNERRE
Founded: 1935.
Colours: Green/red.
Stadium: Ahmadou Ahidjo (50,000).
Club address: Tonnerre Kalara Club, c/o Fédération Camérounaise de Football, BP 1116, Yaoundé.
League: 1982, 1983, 1984 (3).
Cup: 1974.
Afr. Champions' Cup: – .
Afr. Cup-winners' Cup: 1975. Runners-up in 1976.

UNION DOUALA
Founded: 1958.
Colours: All white.
Stadium: Réunification (Douala; 40,000).
Club address: Union Douala, c/o Fédération Camérounaise de Football, BP 1116, Yaoundé.
League: 1969, 1976, 1978 (3).
Cup:1961, 1969, 1980 (3).
Afr. Champions' Cup: 1979.
Afr. Cup-winners' Cup: 1981.

CANADA

It was a huge irony that Toronto Blizzard should have been beaten in the North American Soccer League's 1984 Superbowl by a team, Chicago Sting, who were about to abandon ship. The NASL has, of course, suspended operations this year after its collapse in just a few years from twenty-four teams to a mere three. This section is not the correct place to review the contributory factors. Soccer is strong in Canada, with its big-city ethnic leagues and there is sympathy with those Canadian officials who felt the NASL collapsed because of blunders on the American side of the border.

Clubs who couldn't make soccer work either folded or switched to the indoor soccer leagues. Of the three Canadian teams left in the NASL in 1983, Montreal Manic folded soon after that tournament ended, and Vancouver Whitecaps stepped out once they had been beaten by Chicago in the 1984 semi-finals.

This left Toronto high and dry – their sensible development under former

Fleet Street journalist Clive Toye an object lesson to the rest. Hardly surprisingly, Toye was chosen to take over as the NASL's interim commissioner after the death of Howard Samuels during the winter.

Toronto finished second behind Chicago in the Eastern Conference of the 1984 NASL, then beat San Diego in the semi-final to qualify to meet the Sting in the best-of-three Superbowl. The fact that the championship play-off had been reorganised in this way pointed up concern over the future. Previous Superbowls had drawn disappointing attendances if New York Cosmos hadn't been playing, and it was thought that a best-of-three series, with home-and-away matches to capitalise (literally) on home-town support, would prove a better economic proposition. In fact, there were only 8,352 fans in Chicago for the first leg.

No love was lost between the teams. Officials on both sides had criticised the other's style and tactics. Toronto were also angry at Chicago's impending defection, and all this bitterness was reflected in the game.

Referee David Socha had to show the yellow caution card to no fewer than twelve players in the first match, seven of Chicago and five of Toronto. The Blizzard even took the lead after barely fifteen minutes when skipper Bruce Wilson – who played for Chicago in 1978 and 1979 – saw his powerfully-hit through ball slip through both hands and legs of Sting goalkeeper Victor Nogueira.

Chicago were still a goal down at half-time. But within five minutes of the restart they equalised through Pato Margetic, and then collected a fortunate winner from Chilean forward Manuel Rojas just before the end.

Toronto remained favourites, even so. The crowd was better at the Varsity Stadium in Toronto, albeit just 16,842. But their chants for Toronto were silenced by an early goal from Chicago defender Mark Simanton. The Blizzard refused to panic. After all, a simple victory even by only 2-1 would be enough to take the Superbowl to the third game. The equaliser appeared to be only a matter of time, particularly when David Byrne shot against a post just before half-time, and then veteran Italian international Roberto Bettega smashed the rebound against the other upright.

But for all their pressure, Toronto couldn't get the ball past one-time Crystal Palace goalkeeper Paul Hammond. And, as so often happens, Chicago broke away to score a second through Margetic in the sixty-eighth minute. It seemed all over. But Toronto brought on John Paskin as substitute for Pasquale DeLuca and with his first touch of the ball he scored. Two minutes later Bettega, one-time hero of Juventus, equalised. Despite Toronto's frenzy, the last word was to be reserved for the Argentine, Margetic, who scored Chicago's last-ever goal in the NASL eight minutes from the end. This time Toronto were too drained to produce another comeback.

In spite of this failure, Toronto had done Canadian football proud, and would not have been disgraced in class company. In the summer of 1984 they beat Benfica 2-0 in a friendly – and the Portuguese were lucky to escape so lightly – and then lost only 2-1 to the touring Italians of Juventus, Bettega's old team-mates. Bettega's regret from that game was that he had failed to score an equaliser which would, he thought, have helped underline the progress being made by football in Canada.

Not that anyone need worry too much, as the Canadian national team proved by reaching the quarter-finals of the Olympic Games football tournament in

Los Angeles. In the first round Canada drew 1-1 with Iraq, lost 1-0 to Yugoslavia and then beat Cameroon 3-1 to qualify for a quarter-final against Brazil. Canada even went ahead in the fifty-eighth minute through Dale Mitchell, and were unlucky to have a further 'goal' disallowed for a controversial offside decision. Brazil equalised to send the game into extra time, where Canada's hero Mitchell hit the bar before they were beaten in a penalty shoot-out.

1984 NASL League Table

Eastern Conference	P	W	D*	L	F	Bns APts	Pts
Chicago Sting	24	13		11	50	49 44	120
Toronto Blizzard	24	14		10	46	33 35	117
New York Cosmos	24	13		11	43	41 39	115
Tampa Bay Rowdies	24	9		15	43	61 35	87

Western Conference	P	W	D*	L	F	Bns APts	Pts
San Diego Sockers	24	14		10	51	42 40	118
Vancouver Whitecaps	24	13		11	51	48 43	117
Minnesota Strikers	24	14		10	40	44 35	115
Tulsa Roughnecks	24	10		14	42	46 38	98
Golden Bay Earthquakes	24	8		16	60	62 49	95

Note: Six points for a victory (including overtime wins), four points for a shoot-out victory, one bonus point for every goal scored per game to a maximum of three.
* No draws in the NASL.

Championship semi-finals: Chicago Sting bt *Vancouver Whitecaps* 0-1, 3-1, 4-3 – *Toronto Blizzard* bt San Diego Sockers 2-1, 1-0.
Superbowl: Chicago Sting bt *Toronto Blizzard* 2-1, 3-2.
Top scorer: Steve Zungul (Golden Bay) 20 goals.
(N.B.: Canadian teams are italicized.)

TORONTO BLIZZARD
Founded: 1971. Abandoned competition 1985.
Colours: Red and white/blue.
Stadium: Varsity (21,700).
Club address: Toronto Blizzard, 720 Spadina Avenue, Suite 409, Toronto, Ontario M5S 2T9.
NASL championship: 1976 (as Toronto Metros-Croatia). Runners-up in 1983.

VANCOUVER WHITECAPS
Founded: 1974 (Abandoned competition 1984).
Colours: Blue/white.
Stadium: B. C. Place (60,000).
Club address: Vancouver Whitecaps, c/o Canadian Soccer Association, 333 River Road, Ottawa, Ontario KIL 8B9.
NASL championship: 1979.

CHILE

Chilean football is steeped in so much trouble it's hard to know where to begin to review a season which ended with the twenty-six first division clubs sharing debts of £12 million. The final ignominy came in the spring of 1985 when sequestrators walked into the offices of the Chilean federation and confiscated chairs, desks and other office equipment. A secretary was typing out fixture lists when the typewriter was snatched away. The confiscation was made under a court order after a claim by a former Brazilian player of Universidad de Chile, Liminho, that he was owed £15,000 in back pay. The club claimed that their debts were guaranteed by the federation, and so the court officials went in.

It was yet another blow to the credibility of an organisation which thought it had found a bright new broom in newly-elected President Antonio Martinez (from the Everton club of Vina del Mar) a year earlier, only to see him arrested on bank fraud charges and resign in November. The problem by then was that Martinez had totally reorganised the league, splitting the original first division into two, with a play-off system to decide the champions. Yet this was just an interim measure intended as a stepping-stone towards a major streamlining of Chilean football; an attempt to bring competition back into line with the other South American seasons, finishing in December, rather than dragging on until February or March as had been the case.

The club who benefited from the new deal were Universidad Catolica. They hadn't won anything for nearly twenty years when Martinez took office. But by the end of 1984 they had won the pre-season Pollagol tournament (run for the pools punters), and then the championship. The star was left-sided midfield player Jorge Aravena, nicknamed The Mortar because of the power of his shooting. He hit sixteen goals to finish as the league's second-highest scorer behind poor Victor Cabrera who topped the chart with eighteen, yet saw his club, Atacama, relegated. Catolica's other heroes were skipper and fellow midfielder Miguel Angel Neira, goalkeeper Marcos Cornez and centreforward Osvaldo Hurtado, who was later voted Footballer of the Year. Team manager was Ignacio Prieto, who played in midfield for the Catolica team who had last won the championship in 1966. Now Catolica had helped him complete a remarkable double, because brother Andres had coached Bolivar to the Bolivian title a year earlier.

The surprise of the four-team mini-league was the poor showing of Cobreloa, from the Andean mining town of Calama. Cobreloa had been runners-up in the South American Club Cup in 1981 and 1982 and had won their first round league by a clear three points from Cobresal. In the play-offs they lost their first match to Catolica and virtually gave up. It was a sad send-off for Argentine coach Vicente Cantatore, who had built the team but was now moving on.

More disappointing still, perhaps, was the form of Colo Colo. They have won the Chilean title on a record fourteen occasions, but could finish only third in their first round group. Much of the time appeared to be spent trying to sort out rows between the veteran striker Carlos Caszely and the Brazilian midfielder, Vasconcelos. After a slow start to the season Colo Colo did put together a fifteen-game unbeaten run. But this was ended by defeat at the hands of Cobreloa, and then, the bubble having burst, the team threatened to go on strike in a pay row. Colo Colo is a Chilean nickname for a wildcat – apparently a most appropriate title.

Their fans claimed that Universidad Catolica were lucky to have been placed in the weaker Group B of the championship. But Catolica were given a good run for their money by a revived Union Española. Union were outstanding in the mid-1970s when they once reached the final of the South American Club Cup. Their problem now was up front, for they scored just thirty-four goals in twenty-six league games and their top marksman, Luis Gonzalez, found the net on only nine occasions.

As for Universidad de Chile – popularly known merely as 'U' – it was an unhappy season. Not only were they up to their ears in debt, but they also had the bitter experience of watching Catolica, a club founded as an offshoot of the 'U', take the title. At the season's end they appointed former national manager Luis Ibarra as team manager in the hope of better things to come.

Finally, a word about one of the Group B strugglers, Audax Italiano. They finished ninth in the thirteen team division, but laid claim to a world record through veteran central defender Hernan Castro. He claims to have been sent off no fewer than twenty-nine times in top-flight competition! No wonder the average first division attendance in Chile is down to around 5,000.

Championship First Round

Group A	P	W	D	L	F	A	Pts
Cobreloa	26	18	5	3	47	14	41
Cobresal	26	16	6	4	44	20	38
Colo Colo	26	14	8	4	52	21	36
Arica	26	11	8	7	36	33	30
Magallanes	26	10	9	7	43	39	29
Iquique	26	7	12	7	23	28	26
Palestino	26	10	5	11	44	37	25
San Felipe	26	7	10	9	23	29	24
San Luis	26	9	6	11	28	49	24
Wanderers	26	6	10	10	21	28	22
Antofagasta	26	6	5	15	24	47	17
La Serena	26	2	9	15	26	48	13
Atacama	26	3	7	16	26	55	13

Group B	P	W	D	L	F	A	Pts
Univ. Catolica	26	15	7	4	46	18	37
Union Española	26	13	9	4	34	16	35
Naval	26	12	7	7	32	18	31
O'Higgins	26	11	7	8	31	30	29
Un. de Chile	26	10	8	8	29	23	28
Rangers	26	8	9	9	34	35	25
Huachipato	26	10	5	11	34	36	25
Everton	26	8	9	9	22	28	25
Trasandino	26	9	6	11	38	37	24
Audax Italiano	26	8	8	10	37	40	24
F. Vial	26	8	6	12	25	36	22
Green Cross	26	6	7	13	18	36	19
Coquimbo	26	4	6	16	17	41	14

Final Round

	P	W	D	L	F	A	Pts
Univ. Catolica	3	2	1	0	4	0	5
Cobresal	3	1	1	1	1	1	3
Union Española	3	1	1	1	1	2	3
Cobreloa	3	0	1	2	1	4	1

Top scorer: Victor Cabrera (Atacama) 18 goals.

COBRELOA
Founded: 1976.
Colours: All orange.
Stadium: Estadio Cobreloa (20,000).
Club address: Club de Deportes Cobreloa, Atacama 1482, Casilla 156, Calama.
League: 1980, 1983.
South American Club Cup: Runners-up in 1981 and 1982.

COLO COLO
Founded: 1925.
Colours: White/black.
Stadium: Estadio Colo Colo (10,000). Important matches in the Estadio Nacional (74,159).
Club address: Colo Colo, Cienfuegos 41, Santiago.
League: 1937, 1939, 1941, 1944, 1947, 1953, 1956, 1960, 1963, 1970, 1972, 1979, 1982, 1984 (14 – record).
South American Club Cup: Runners-up in 1973.

EVERTON
Founded: 1909.
Colours: Blue and yellow stripes/blue.
Stadium: Estadio Sausalito (25,000).
Club address: Everton, Viana 161, Viña del Mar.
League: 1950, 1952, 1976.

HUACHIPATO
Founded: 1947.
Colours: Blue and yellow stripes/blue.
Stadium: Estadio Las Higueras (10,000).
Club address: Deportes Huachipato, Parque Araucaria, Talcahuano.
League: 1974.

O'HIGGINS
Founded: 1916.
Colours: All sky blue.
Stadium: Estadio El Teniente (20,000).
Club address: Deportes O'Higgins, Avenida Brazil 1079, Rancagua.
League: – .

PALESTINO
Founded: 1920.
Colours: Green, red and white stripes/black.
Stadium: Estadio Santa Laura (35,000).
Club address: Palestino, Avenida Pte Kennedy 9351, Santiago.
League: 1955, 1978.

UNION ESPAÑOLA
Founded: 1897 as Iberico. Renamed 1924.
Colours: Red/black.

Stadium: Estadio Santa Laura (35,000).
Club address: Union Española, Carmen 102/110, Santiago.
League: 1943, 1951, 1973, 1975, 1977 (5).
S. American Club Cup: Runners-up in 1975.

UNION SAN FELIPE
Founded: 1956.
Colours: All white.
Stadium: Estadio Municipal (12,000).
Club address: Union San Felipe, Prat 320, San Felipe.
League: 1971.

UNIVERSIDAD CATOLICA
Founded: 1937.
Colours: White with a blue hoop/blue.
Stadium: Estadio Nacional (74,159).
Club address: Club de Deportes Universidad Catolica, Avenida Andrés Bellol 2782, Santiago.
League: 1949, 1954, 1961, 1966, 1984 (5).

UNIVERSIDAD DE CHILE
Founded: 1911.
Colours: All blue.
Stadium: Estadio Nacional (74,159).
Club address: Universidad de Chile, Marín 0525, Santiago.
League: 1940, 1959, 1962, 1964, 1965, 1967, 1969 (7).

WANDERERS
Founded: 1892.
Colours: Green/white.
Stadium: Estadio Playa Ancha (18,000).
Club address: Wanderers, Lira 575, Valparaíso.
League: 1958, 1968.

COLOMBIA

Colombia is another of those South American countries where the championship is organised in several stages to make it last for nine or ten months of the year but with several 'high spots' to maintain interest. First, the fourteen first division clubs play in two separate groups. Then there are play-offs to determine the first round champions. Next comes a second round in which everybody plays everybody else both home and away. Finally, the top eight teams, in terms of total points over the two previous stages, face each other home and away to decide the 'real' champions – which, in 1984, turned out to be América of Cali.

The Colombian championship could not be complete without a row. Last year this centred on the rent being charged by the local authority in Medellin to top clubs Nacional and Independiente. The local authority blamed tax increases, and the clubs threatened to boycott the championship. It took a month to bring about a peace settlement, and then Nacional and Independiente took their places in the competition, and life went on again as if nothing had happened.

Colombian clubs have always had a reputation for free-spending on foreign players. That tradition began at the turn of the 1950s when the pirate clubs, led by Millionarios of Bogota, benefited from their status outside FIFA to sign some of the world's top players without paying a peso in transfer fees. Argentina's Jose Pedernera, Alfredo Di Stefano and Nestor Rossi were among the players lured to Colombia, as well as England centre-half Neil Franklin.

Nowadays the imports are 'legal' signings, but they are still important to the Colombian game. América of Cali, champions three years in a row, relied heavily on Argentine goalkeeper Falcioni, Uruguayan forward Ruben Paz – who cost a record £200,000 from Internacional of Brazil – and Peruvian World Cup stars Cesar Cueto and Guillermo La Rosa.

Yet América are one of the few Colombian clubs to employ a Colombian team manager. While Atlético Junior of Baranquilla contracted the former Argentine defender Josa Varacka, while Independiente of Santa Fe took on the controversial Argentine Juan Carlos Lorenzo, América were happy to retain for a seventh year Dr Gabriel Ochoa Uribe.

In the 1950s he was a goalkeeper with Millionarios in the pirate years, later qualified in medicine, and introduced a string of innovations after being first appointed by América in 1978. He was the first coach in Colombia to install video cameras to assist coaching, and he was the first to use a small tape recorder for making notes during a game.

That attention to detail put América out in front of their rivals throughout the 1984 season. They won their first round group, won the play-off against Atlético Junior, won the second round league, and then finished two points clear of Millionarios in the final round.

The irony was that a few months earlier América had signed Millionarios' star player, Willington Ortiz. Millionarios thought he was over the hill. But Ortiz played some superb football for América until an old back injury caught up with him. Millionarios, despite the name, also ran into cash problems and, midway through the season, had to sell Uruguayan centre-forward Wilmar Cabrera to Valencia of Spain. All things considered, to finish as overall runners-up was a remarkable performance.

Not so impressive were two of Colombia's most famous clubs, Deportivo Cali and Independiente Santa Fe, who both failed to make the 'cut' and missed out on the money-spinning final round of the championship. Cali, who remain the only Colombian team ever to have reached the final of the South American Club Cup (in 1978), were still paying the price for the financial extravagance which that success had encouraged. To stay afloat they had to sell a string of key players and, as a result, finished third from bottom in the second round of the championship.

As for Santa Fe, they were delighted with Argentine striker Hugo Gottardi, who was the first round's top scorer with twelve goals. But midway through the second round, when results didn't measure up, they axed coach Lorenzo. He then insisted on turning up at training every day until Santa Fe paid up his contract. The consequent turmoil ruined any chance of the team forcing their way up among the top eight final round qualifiers.

1984 Championship – First Round

Group A	P	W	D	L	F	A	Pts
Atlético Junior	14	11	0	3	27	9	22
Nacional Medellin	14	8	2	4	19	8	20
Quindio	14	5	4	5	12	21	14
Indep. Santa Fe	14	5	2	7	17	24	12
Deportivo Cali	14	5	1	8	13	16	11
Dep. Pereira	14	4	2	8	15	19	10
Cucuta	14	1	3	10	14	32	5

Group B	P	W	D	L	F	A	Pts
América Cali	14	9	2	3	27	14	20
Deportes Tolima	14	6	6	2	16	11	18
Millionarios	14	5	6	3	23	15	16
Bucaramanga	14	5	3	6	25	26	13
Union Magdalena	14	5	3	6	14	16	13
Indep. Medellin	14	4	4	6	9	12	12
Caldas	14	3	4	7	11	20	10

First round play-offs: América bt Atlético Junior for first place, Nacional Medellin beat Tolima for third place.

Second Round

	P	W	D	L	F	A	Pts
América Cali	26	13	10	3	41	20	36
Nacional Medellin	26	13	9	4	39	21	35
Millionarios Bogotá	26	11	9	6	39	20	31
Indep. Medellin	26	10	11	5	32	18	31
At. Junior Barranquilla	26	13	5	8	34	31	31
Bucaramanga	26	13	3	10	33	33	29
Union Magdalena	26	11	5	10	28	29	27
Indep. Sante Fe	26	9	8	9	36	31	26
Deportes Tolima	26	7	10	9	25	27	24
Pereira	26	8	7	11	30	44	23
Caldas	26	8	6	12	28	40	22
Deportivo Cali	26	6	9	11	29	38	21
Quindio	26	5	6	15	25	42	16
Cucuta	26	1	10	15	25	51	12

Final Round

Teams qualified were the eight with most points in aggregate from the first and second rounds (América 56, Nacional 55, At. Junior 53, Millionarios 47, Medellin 43, Bucaramanga 42, Tolima 41, Union Magdalena 40).

	P	W	D	L	F	A	Pts
América Cali	14	6	6	2	15	9	20
Millionarios Bogotá	14	6	6	2	16	8	18
Medellin Independiente	14	4	7	3	13	10	15
Deportes Tolima	14	5	4	5	12	13	14
Junior Barranquilla	14	4	5	5	11	15	14
Bucaramanga	14	5	3	6	13	15	13
Nacional Medellin	14	3	4	7	11	16	11
Union Magdalena	14	3	5	6	7	12	11

AMÉRICA
Founded: 1927.
Colours: All red.
Stadium: Important matches in the Estadio Pascual Guerrero (61,000).
Club address: Club Deportivo América, Calle 24N 5B-22, apartado 1383, Cali.
Championship: 1979, 1982, 1983, 1984 (4).

ATLÉTICO JUNIOR
Founded: 1936.
Colours: Red and white stripes/black.
Stadium: Metropolitano (70,000) or Romelio Martíniz (20,000).
Club address: Club Atlético Junior, Barranquilla, depto Atlántico.
Championship: 1977, 1980.

DEPORTIVO CALI
Founded: 1936.
Colours: Green with white trimming/white.
Stadium: Estadio Pascual Guerrero (61,000).
Club address: Club Deportivo Cali, Calle 34N 2bis-75, apartado 4593, Cali.
Championship: 1965, 1967, 1969, 1970, 1974 (5).
South American Club Cup: Runners-up in 1978.

INDEPENDIENTE SANTA FE
Founded: 1936.
Colours: Red with white trimming/black.
Stadium: El Campin (Estadio Distrital Nemesio Camacho – 57,000).
Club address: Club Independiente Santa Fe, Avenida 39 15–22, Apartado 4988, Bogotá.
Championship: 1948, 1958, 1960, 1966, 1971, 1975 (6).

MILLIONARIOS
Founded: 1938.
Colours: Blue/white.
Stadium: El Campin (Estadio Distrital Nemesio Camacho – 57,000).
Club address: Club Deportivo Los Millionarios, Calle 39A – No 14–32, Bogotá.
Championship: 1949, 1951, 1952, 1953, 1959, 1961, 1962, 1963, 1964, 1972, 1978 (11 – record).

NACIONAL
Founded: 1936.
Colours: Green and white stripes/white.
Stadium: Estadio Atanasio Girardot (47,000).
Club address: Club Atletico Nacional, Carrera 76 48A-11, Medellín.
Championship: 1954, 1973, 1976, 1981 (4).

TOLIMA
Founded: 1936.
Colours: Yellow/black.

47

Stadium: Murillo Toro (25,000).
Club address: Deportes Tolima, Ibagüé, Depto de Tolima.
Championship: – .

CYPRUS

Omonia of Nicosia raced unbeaten to the league title for the fifth successive season to take their record total of championships to fourteen. Their success had never been in doubt, and they had the trophy sewn up long before the end of a season which they closed with a nine-point advantage over Apoel. In similar manner Omonia striker Saavidis finished as top league scorer on twenty-four goals with an advantage of nine over runner-up Ioannu from Apoel. There were occasional moments when Apoel managed to steal the limelight from Omonia – one of those being the Footballer of the Year poll when the winner was Nikos Pantzarias, the Apoel defender. He is Cyprus' record international, with more than fifty appearances for his country against his name, and this was the second successive year in which he had been voted the nation's top player.

The season began on a note of celebration. The year 1984 marked the fiftieth anniversary of the Cyprus federation. Special events began with a youth tournament and string of coaching camps in the summer soon after the national team had achieved the notable feat of defeating a weakened Glasgow Celtic 2–1 in a Limassol friendly in May. This was the first of a string of international matches through to the end of the year which included a 2–0 home defeat by Greece in September, and then Cyprus' first international victory for years by 1–0 over Luxembourg in Nicosia. Celebrations reached their climax late in October when Cyprus drew 0–0 with Canada in a match staged in the presence of a string of visiting dignitaries, including FIFA president Joao Havelange, and the President of the European federation, UEFA, Jacques Georges.

On the domestic front, Omonia had already established their lead in a season they finished unbeaten. In Saavidis they have apparently discovered a striker with the nose for goal and ability – at least in domestic competition – in the penalty box to shake off all attentions. Those were the hallmarks of Sotiris Kaiafas, one-time Golden Boot winner as Europe's top league scorer, who starred for Omonia in the 1970s after joining them as a sweeper!

The win over Luxembourg apart – Tsikos scored the all-important goal in the fifty-second minute – the 1984–85 season was a disappointment for Cyprus at international level. They had not expected to turn Europe upside down in the World Cup qualifiers. But at least they had thought they should have been able to hold Austria or Hungary or Holland, their group rivals, to one drawn match on home ground. But, beaten 2–1 in Nicosia by Austria in May 1984, they lost 2–1 in front of 8,000 of their own fans against Hungary in November and then 1–0 against Holland in December. The last defeat was the most galling because the Dutch won only with a late, late goal from Feyenoord striker Peter Houtman. Officials and players held out little hope for the away games – and were proved right. Cyprus crashed 7–1 away to Holland – after surprising even themselves by taking a brief, seventh-minute lead through Marangos – then lost 2–0 in Hungary and 4–0 in Austria. Saavidis played in all three games but found international defences a very different proposition from domestic opposition!

	P	W	D	L	F	A	Pts
Omonia	26	17	9	0	70	22	43
Apoel	26	13	8	5	43	26	34
Anorthosis	26	12	9	5	38	22	33
AEL	26	8	12	6	33	29	28
Apollon	26	9	10	7	35	30	28
Pezoporikos	26	8	9	9	32	27	25
EPA	26	7	11	8	26	29	25
Alki	26	8	9	9	23	27	25
Paralimni	26	7	10	9	44	40	24
Salamina	26	6	12	8	25	29	24
Olympiakos	26	8	8	10	35	40	24
Aris	26	6	12	8	35	39	24
Aradippu	26	7	6	13	22	38	20
Evagoras	26	1	5	20	14	67	7

Cup final: AEL 1, EPA 0.
Top scorer: Saavidis (Omonia) 24 goals.

A E L
Founded: 1933.
Colours: Blue/yellow.
Stadium: Tsirion (20,000).
Club address: Athletiki Enosis Limassol, PO Box 210, Limassol.
League: 1941, 1953, 1955, 1956, 1968 (5).
Cup: 1939, 1940, 1948, 1985 (4).

ALKI F C
Founded: 1948.
Colours: Red/blue.
Stadium: G S Z Stadium, Larnaca (10,000).
Club address: Alki F C, Louki Akrita 23, Larnaca.
League: – .
Cup: – .

ANORTHOSIS (Famagusta).
Founded: 1911.
Colours: Blue/white.
Stadium: G S E Stadium (10,000).
Club address: Anorthosis FC, Athenon Ave, No 77, P O Box 756, Larnaca.
League: 1950, 1957, 1958, 1960, 1962, 1963 (6).
Cup 1949, 1971.

APOEL
Founded: 1926.
Colours: Blue/yellow.
Stadium: Makarion Athletic Centre (20,000).
Club address: Apoel FC, P O Box 1133, Nicosia.

League: 1936, 1937, 1938, 1939, 1940, 1947, 1948, 1949, 1952, 1965, 1973, 1980 (12).
Cup: 1937, 1941, 1947, 1950, 1963, 1968, 1969, 1976, 1978, 1979, 1984 (11).

APOLLON
Founded: 1954.
Colours: Blue/white.
Stadium: Tsirion (20,000).
Club address: Apollon FC, P O Box 1912, Limassol.
League: – .
Cup: 1966, 1967.

E P A
Founded: 1932.
Colours: Yellow/black.
Stadium: G S Z Stadium (10,000).
Club address: E P A FC, 3 Gregory Afxentiou Street, P O Box 316, Larnaca.
League: 1945, 1946, 1970 (3).
Cup: 1945, 1946, 1950, 1953, 1955 (5).

OLYMPIAKOS
Founded: 1931.
Colours: Green/black.
Stadium: Important matches at the Makarion Athletic Centre (20,000).
Club address: Olympiakos FC, Athenas Avenue, P O Box 2339, Nicosia.
League: 1967, 1969, 1971 (3).
Cup: 1977

OMONIA
Founded: 1948.
Colours: Green/white.
Stadium: Important matches at the Makarion Athletic Centre (20,000).
Club address: Omonia FC, Papanikolis 5, Nicosia.
League: 1961, 1966, 1972, 1974, 1975, 1976, 1977, 1978, 1979, 1981, 1982, 1983, 1984, 1985 (14 – record).
Cup: 1965, 1972, 1974, 1980, 1981, 1982, 1983 (7).

PARALIMNI
Founded: 1936.
Colours: Red/white.
Stadium: G S E Stadium (10,000).
Club address: Athletic Union of Paralimni, P O Box 12, Paralimni.
League: – .
Cup: – .

PEZOPORIKOS
Founded: 1927.
Colours: Green/white.
Stadium: G S Z Stadium (10,000).
Club address: Pezoporikos FC, P O Box 60, Larnaca.

League: 1954.
Cup: 1970.

CZECHOSLOVAKIA

Sparta, one of the oldest and certainly still the most popular of Czech clubs, squeezed through at the end to win the league title on goal difference from long-time leaders Bohemians. But there were a string of heart-stopping moments as Bohemians – their mascot appropriately a kangaroo – threw away a three-point lead over the last month of the season.

Bohemians' troubles began in mid-May when they lost surprisingly at home by 2–0 against Lokomotiva Kosice, a very ordinary middle-of-the-table side. That allowed Banik Ostrava to move within two points of Bohemians, and they narrowed the gap still further, to one point, when Bohemians were held 1–1 away by Inter Bratislava. At that stage Banik and Slavia, one point further back, appeared the most threatening rivals to Bohemians' title bid. Sparta were in fourth place, still three points off the pace with five games to go.

Bohemians seemed apparently to put themselves back on course the next week with a 3–1 home win over Dukla, while Banik lost 2–0 away to Vitkovice, so Bohemians led Slavia by two points, and Sparta and Banik by three. Then, with three games remaining, Sparta stepped up the pressure by moving within one point of Bohemians. Banik and Slavia slipped back, and were now virtually out of it, though Banik still had a decisive role to play in the Bohemians/Sparta battle.

In the twenty-eighth round of matches, two from the end of the season, Bohemians thrashed Olomouc and Sparta sneaked a win over bottom club Slovan Bratislava. But in the penultimate games, while Sparta were crushing Tatran Presov 7–0, Bohemians travelled to Ostrava to face a Banik team whose philosophy appeared to be, 'we may not be able to win the league but we are not making it easy for you'. The result was a 2–2 draw. That meant Bohemians and Sparta were level on forty-three points from twenty-nine games. But Sparta – thanks to those seven goals against Presov – now held a clear lead in goal difference and went to the top of the table.

Their last match should have made sewing up the title a mere formality: they were away to mid-table Dukla Banska Bystrica, while Bohemians went to Spartak Trnava. Bohemians, believing it was all over, looked spiritless and weary and lost 1–0, but came off the pitch to learn that Sparta, too, had lost 1–0 – a defeat which, thanks to Bohemians' own pessimism and lack of self-belief, had not mattered.

Sparta may have won the title, but the club and their fans were far from happy. Problem number one was the hooliganism which erupted on the way to Banska Bystrica. Some thirty fans were arrested for causing £30,000 worth of damage to a train. Windows were smashed, seats were slashed and bottles and other missiles thrown out of the windows – some at another train – in scenes reminiscent of train vandalism by football hooligans in Britain and to a lesser extent West Germany and Holland in recent years. It has not been unknown, even in communist Czechoslovakia, for marching fans to damage telephone boxes and parked cars both before and after some of the big Prague derbies. But this was the worst outbreak of hooliganism so far. Sparta's committee met on the Friday, two days after the match, and announced strict curbs. All banners and flags have been banned from home matches, as has the sale of alcohol. Sparta also appealed for other first division clubs to step into line with them in the fight against increasing violence in football.

The other problem for the champions was coach Vladimir Taborsky. The former Czechoslovak international left-back had taken over at the start of the season and had proved hugely popular with the players, but not with the directors. They criticised him for allowing the squad too much freedom from the discipline necessary for top-level sportsmen. The fact that this approach had brought Sparta to the league title was not enough in terms of mitigation, and so Taborsky – two days after landing on top of the Czech football world – was dismissed. The decision was hardly a sudden one. At the same time as Sparta announced Taborsky's departure, they said that Jan Zachar, coach of second division Zbrojovka Brno, would be taking over for the 1985–86 season and the Champions' Cup campaign.

Dukla, who finished fifth in the league, won the cup with a 3-2 defeat of Kosice, which was hardly a surprise. But what did shock the establishment was the relegation of Sloven Bratislava, the only Czechoslovak club to have won a European trophy, the Cup-winners' Cup, in 1969. Slovan and Petrzalka went down when for months it had appeared that Slovan's neighbours, Inter, were the relegation certainties.

1984–85 League Table

	P	W	D	L	F	A	Pts
Sparta Praha	30	19	5	6	64	23	43
Bohemians	30	17	9	4	58	24	43
Slavia Praha	30	16	7	7	59	33	39
Banik Ostrava	30	14	11	5	40	23	39
Dukla Praha	30	13	6	11	51	40	32
Olomouc	30	10	11	9	50	47	31
Dukla B. Bystrica	30	15	1	14	38	44	31
RH Cheb	30	12	6	12	44	38	30
Spartak Trnava	30	10	9	11	33	39	29
Lok. Košice	30	9	9	12	34	44	27
Vitkovice	30	8	10	12	30	41	26
Tatran Prešov	30	9	6	15	28	46	24
Internacional	30	7	9	14	25	33	23
Zilina	30	8	7	15	26	49	23
Petrzalka	30	6	9	15	29	47	21
Slovan Bratislava	30	6	7	17	24	59	19

Cup final: Dukļa Praha 3, Lokomotiv Kosice 2.
Top scorer: Ivo Knoflicek (Slavia) 21 goals.

BANIK OSTRAVA
Founded: 1922.
Colours: Blue/white.
Stadium: Bazaly (35,000).
Club address: TJ Banik Ostrava OKD, Bazaly, 71000 Ostrava 10.
League: 1976, 1980, 1981 (3).
Cup: 1973, 1978.

BOHEMIANS
Founded: 1903.
Colours: Green and white hoops/white.
Stadium: Vrsovice (18,000).
Club address: Bohemians CKD Praha, SNB 31, 10 000 Prague 10.
League: 1983.
Cup: – .

DUKLA
Founded: 1948.
Colours: All yellow with red trimmings.
Stadium: Juliska (28,000).
Club address: VTJ Dukla Praha, Postfach 59, 16 044 Prague 6.
League: 1953, 1956, 1958, 1961, 1962, 1963, 1964, 1966, 1977, 1979, 1982 (11).
Cup: 1961, 1965, 1966, 1969, 1981, 1983, 1985 (7).

INTERNACIONÁL
Founded: 1940.
Colours: Yellow and black stripes/black.
Stadium: Internacionál (40,000).
Club address: T J Internacionál, Vajnorská, 80 100 Bratislava.
League: 1959.
Cup: – .

LOKOMOTIVA KOŠICE
Founded: 1946.
Colours: Blue/white.
Stadium: Čermeli (35,000).
Club address: T J Lokomotiva Košice, Čermelská 3, 04 225 Košice.
League: – .
Cup: 1977, 1979.

SLAVIA
Founded: 1892.
Colours: Red and white halves/white.
Stadium: Dr Vacka (46,200).
Club address: S K Slavia IPS, Stadion Dr V. Vacka, 10 005 Prague 10.
League (includes original Bohemia championship): 1913, 1924, 1929, 1930, 1931, 1933, 1934, 1935, 1937, 1947 (10).
Cup: – .

SLOVAN
Founded: 1919.
Colours: All sky blue.
Stadium: Tehelné Pole (63,000).
Club address: Slovan Bratislava, Tehelné Pole stadion, 80 000 Bratislava.
League: 1949, 1950, 1951, 1955, 1970, 1974, 1975 (7).
Cup: 1962, 1963, 1968, 1974, 1982 (5).
Cup-winners' Cup: 1969.

SPARTA
Founded: 1893.
Colours: Red/white.
Stadium: Letná (38,000).
Club address: Sparta ČKD Praha, Obránců míru 98, 17 082 Prague 7.
League (including original Bohemia championship): 1912, 1919, 1920, 1921, 1922, 1923, 1925, 1926, 1927, 1932, 1936, 1938, 1939, 1946, 1948, 1952, 1954, 1965, 1967, 1985 (20 – record).
Cup: 1964, 1972, 1976, 1980, 1984 (5).

SPARTAK TRNAVA
Founded: 1925.
Colours: Red/black.
Stadium: Spartak-TAZ-stadion (28,000).
Club address: Spartak T A Z Trnava, Spartak T A Z-stadion, 91 760 Trnava.
League: 1968, 1969, 1971, 1972, 1973 (5).
Cup: 1967, 1971, 1975 (3).

TATRAN PREŠOV
Founded: 1931.
Colours: Green/white.
Stadium: Comunale (23,000).
Club address: Tatran Prešov, ul. kpt. Nálepku 6, 08 092 Presov.
League: – .
Cup: – .

UNION TEPLICE
Founded: 1945.
Colours: Yellow/blue.
Stadium: Union-stadion (17,800).
League: – .
Cup: – .

ZBROJOVKA BRNO
Founded: 1913.
Colours: Red/white.
Stadium: Zbrojovka (70,000).
Club address: Zbrojovka Brno, Drobného 45, 65 631 Brno.
League: 1978.
Cup: – .

DENMARK

The exploits of Preben Elkjaer, Michael Laudrup, Morten Olsen and Frank Arnesen thrilled millions who watched, live or on television, the finals of the European championship in the summer of 1984. But they represented a very one-sided view of the Danish game, since all four earn their livings in professional football exile in Italy and Belgium.

Ironically, the very success of the Danish national team under West German manager Sepp Piontek in qualifying for the European finals and then reaching the semi-finals, sent attendances tumbling back home. The reason was the fans' increasing dissatisfaction with the quality of domestic football compared with the televised version being provided by Danish players they had very little chance of ever watching – except for the occasional home international.

Thus domestic attendances were down by an average 500 a match, a certain contribution to the revelation at the season's end that after just seven years of professional football half of the first division clubs are now in debt, despite the continuing sponsorship support of Carlsberg.

The first prize of the 1984 season went to Lyngby who, for six months, could claim to be double-winners. They followed up their championship victory in 1983 by winning the cup the following May thanks to a 2-1 win over KB Copenhagen. A crowd of 25,800 turned out to see a lively match in which Lyngby went ahead two minutes before half-time. Left-back Peter Pakners shipped a free kick over the defensive wall for Michael Lyng to shoot past national team goalkeeper Ole Qvist.

KB came out for the second half throwing caution to the wind and equalised just five minutes after the restart, when Michael Pedersen easily shot past Henrik Christensen in the Lyngby goal. It was another Christensen, however, who had the last word in this final – Fleming Christensen, the twenty-six-year-old winger who had only recently returned to fitness after a broken leg. With quarter of an hour remaining, and KB pressing forward, Christensen saw his chance on the counter-attack to run half the length of the pitch and beat Qvist for the winner.

Qvist, son of a newspaper cartoonist, and a police motorcyclist when not keeping goal for Denmark, had a mixed year. After finishing on the losing side in the cup final he did well in the finals of the European Championship. But in league action KB – the most successful Danish club of all time – struggled. They had only just been promoted back to the top division after being relegated for the first time in their history in 1982. But all of Qvist's heroics in goal weren't enough to prevent them slipping back down again.

KB's last game was against fellow strugglers Herning. They had to win and hope that Esbjerg, just above them, would lose at home to Hvidovre, who were also perched just above the relegation zone. Esbjerg and Hvidovre, perhaps predictably, drew 0-0, which spelled relegation for KB. They also drew, 1-1, and finished one point below both Herning – who were relegated with them – and Esbjerg, who survived.

Matters were equally tight at the top of the table, where leaders Vejle were away to fourth-placed Brøndby, the former club of Michael Laudrup, on the season's last day. Vejle needed a draw to clinch the title ahead of Aarhus and Lyngby, who were level just two points behind, and who had to play each other. Aarhus had the home advantage and romped home 6-0. But they came off the pitch to find their celebrations short-lived. Vejle had held out for a goalless draw against Brøndby. So Aarhus, third in 1983, had to be satisfied with runners-up spot this time.

Like the national team with Piontek, Aarhus had put their faith in a West German coach, Jürgen Wähling, who played a dozen matches in the Bundesliga in the mid-1960s with Tasmania (West) Berlin. Wähling summed up Aarhus' near miss by saying: 'We were outstanding against the top teams, like Vejle, Lyngby and Brøndby. But we dropped too many "silly" points against the strugglers.'

Much of the credit for Vejle's title success was due to one-time Borussia Mönchengladbach team-mates Allan Simonsen and Steen Thyschosen. Simonsen had returned home after his time abroad with Borussia, Barcelona and (briefly) Charlton, fired with ambition to star in the European championship.

Sadly, a badly-timed tackle by Frenchman Yvon Leroux in the opening match of the finals in Paris broke Simonsen's leg. He had intended retiring that summer. But he didn't want to go out like that. Instead, as he battled his way back to fitness, his will to succeed communicated itself to his Vejle team-mates. They promised: 'We will win the league title for Allan.' And they did. Thychosen, the league's top scorer with twenty-four goals, was a key figure. And Simonsen believed he was fit enough to return alongside Thychosen in the last match, away to Brøndby, but Vejle coach Paul Bech wouldn't let him. Simonsen said later: 'I was disappointed at the time. But really he was right.'

1984 League Table

	P	W	D	L	F	A	Pts
Vejle	30	17	7	6	60	36	41
Aarhus GF	30	15	10	5	50	30	40
Lyngby	30	18	2	10	53	34	38
Brøndby	30	14	8	8	49	45	36
Brønshøj	30	11	12	7	40	34	34
Køge	30	12	6	12	39	36	30
Ikast	30	13	3	14	44	45	29
Herfølge	30	10	9	11	37	41	29
OB	30	10	8	12	47	41	28
Naestved	30	9	9	12	46	51	27
Hvidovre	30	7	13	10	28	37	27
Frem	30	10	7	13	44	56	27
Herning	30	9	8	13	30	50	26
Esbjerg	30	11	4	15	45	44	26
KB (Copenhagen)	30	10	5	15	36	46	25
B 1909	30	6	6	18	21	51	18

Cup final (1984): Lyngby 2, KB 1.
Top scorer: Steen Thychosen (Vejle) 24 goals.

A G F
Founded: 1880.
Colours: White/blue.
Stadium: Aarhus (24,000).
Club address: Aarhus Gymnastikforening, Terp Skovvej 1, 8260 Viby J.
League: 1955, 1956, 1957, 1960 (4).
Cup: 1955, 1957, 1960, 1961, 1965 (5).

B1901
Founded: 1901.
Colours: Blue and white stripes/blue.
Stadium: Nykøbing (15,000).
Club address: Nykøbing Falster Boldklub, Ved Kohaven 3, 4800 Nykøbing F.
League: – .
Cup: – .

B1903
Founded: 1903.
Colours: All white.
Stadium: Gentofte (18,000).
Club address: Boldklubben 1903, Lyngbyvej 270, 2900 Hellerup.
League: 1920, 1924, 1926, 1938, 1969, 1970, 1976 (7).
Cup: 1979.

B1909
Founded: 1909.
Colours: Red/white.
Stadium: Odense (20,000).
Club address: Boldklubben 1909, Gillestedvej 12, 5240 Odense.
League: 1959, 1964.
Cup: 1962, 1971.

BRØNDBY
Founded: 1964.
Colours: Yellow/blue.
Stadium: Glostrup (10,000).
Club address: Brøndbyernes Idraetsforening, Klubhuset, Gl.Kirkevej 1, 2600 Glostrup.
League: – .
Cup: – .

ESBJERG
Founded: 1924.
Colours: White/blue.
Stadium: Esbjerg (18,000).
Club address: Esbjerg forenede Boldklubber (EfB), Gl. Vardevej 88, 6700 Esbjerg.
League: 1961, 1962, 1963, 1965, 1979 (5).
Cup: 1964, 1976.

FREM
Founded: 1886.
Colours: Red and blue hoops/white.
Stadium: Important matches in the Idraetspark (48,000).
Club address: Boldklubben Frem, Jul. Andersensvej 3, 2450 Copenhagen SV.
League: 1923, 1931, 1933, 1936, 1941, 1944 (6).
Cup: 1956, 1978.

HVIDOVRE
Founded: 1925.
Colours: Red/blue.
Stadium: Hvidovre (12,000).
Club address: Hvidovre Idraetsforening, Sollentuna Alle 1–3, 2650 Hvidovre.
League: 1966, 1973, 1981 (3).
Cup: 1980.

K B
Founded: 1876.
Colours: Blue and white stripes/blue.
Stadium: Important games in the Idraetspark (48,000).
club address: Kjøbenhavns Boldklub, Peter Bangsvej 147, 2000 Copenhagen F.
League: 1913, 1914, 1917, 1918, 1922, 1925, 1932, 1940, 1948, 1949, 1950, 1953, 1968, 1974, 1980 (15 – record).
Cup: 1969.

LYNGBY
Founded: 1921.
Colours: Blue/white.
Stadium: Lyngby-Taarbaek (14,000).
Club address: Lyngby Boldklub, Lyngby Stadion, Lundtoftvej 53, 2800 Lyngby.
League: 1983.
Cup: 1984.

NAESTVED
Founded: 1939.
Colours: Green/white.
Stadium: Naestved (18,000).
Club address: Naestved IF, Rolighedsvej, 4800 Nykøbing F.
League: –.
Cup: – .

O B
Founded: 1887.
Colours: Blue and white stripes/blue.
Stadium: Odense (20,000).
League: 1977, 1982.
Cup: – .

VEJLE
Founded: 1891.
Colours: Red/white.
Stadium: Vejle (18,000).
Club address: Vejle Boldklub, Vejle Stadion, 7100 Vejle.
League: 1958, 1971, 1972, 1978, 1984 (5).
Cup: 1958, 1959, 1972, 1975, 1977, 1981 (6 – record).

EAST GERMANY

Dynamo Berlin may have made little impact in Europe, but at domestic level they have been virtually unstoppable now for seven years, maintaining their record run by retaining the league title yet again. It is now necessary to look back as far as FC Magdeburg's success in 1978 to find any name other than that of BFC Dynamo on the championship roll of honour. They did concede the cup final, losing 3-2 to Dynamo Dresden, but that was hardly important. Only CDNA (now CSKA) in Bulgaria with nine titles in a row in the 1950s have outstripped Dynamo in consecutive success terms in post-war European football. The only matching string of seven successive titles was put together by Ujpest Dozsa in Hungary in the late 1960s and early 1970s.

Yet Dynamo started the season quietly. The early running was made by Dresden, who began their campaign by thrashing Chemie Leipzig 9-1, after going a goal behind in the fifth minute. It was an appropriate way to celebrate the pre-match presentation of the Footballer of the Year award to veteran sweeper and skipper Hans-Jürgen Dörner. Later in the season Dörner would also become the second East German player to top a hundred international appearances. He reached three figures in the 3-1 World Cup win over Luxembourg, while Magdeburg spearhead Joachim Streich had preceded him to the honour when he made his hundredth appearance for his country in the 1-0 defeat by England at Wembley in September.

For years Streich has been the only consistent forward to play for East Germany at international level. But now Dynamo Berlin appear to have a successor in Rainer Ernst. He scored early-season hat-tricks against Rot-Weiss Erfurt and Karl-Marx-Stadt, and then grabbed two more in the important 2-2 draw away to Dresden. Dresden were then held at home again, this time 1-1 by Vorwärts, and beaten 4-0 away by Carl Zeiss Jena, thus allowing Dynamo to sneak back into the lead at the top of the table when the winter break brought competition to a halt.

Dresden were always trailing after that. Dynamo scored nine against Stahl-Riesa when the season restarted in March – two more goals for Ernst – and though they lost 2-1 at home to Dresden, still held a four-point lead going into the last matches. It was in this game that Ernst's shooting was, for once, awry as he shot a penalty against a post. Not that the old master of the penalty box, Streich, was yet ready to be written off. He celebrated his thirty-fourth birthday in some style in April by scoring all four goals in Magdeburg's 4-2 defeat of Vorwärts, and then ran up four more in the very next home game – a 7-0 victory over Chemie Leipzig. Those goals brought his career league total to 228, easily an East German record.

But while there were plenty of goals at club level, the national team staggered from one failure to another in European championship and World Cup qualifiers. In most countries that would lead to pressure for dismissal of the national manager. But the East German authorities decided that the malaise went deeper than that. Accordingly, once the league season had ended, no fewer than eight of the fourteen first division team managers were dismissed or moved around. Jürgen Bogs remained in charge at Dynamo Berlin, and policeman Klaus Sammer at Dresden. But there was little promise of job security elsewhere. Even third-placed Lok Leipzig dismissed Harro Miller in favour of Hans-Ulrich Thomale, who had steered Wismut Aue to fourth spot.

Competition in the early rounds of the cup was confusing, to say the least, owing to the East German system which allows reserve teams to compete on equal terms with the first-team squads. Thus, in the quarter-finals, Dresden's first-team were drawn against Dynamo Berlin's reserves, who threatened a major surprise when they won the first leg 2-1 in Dresden. Cup-ties in East Germany are also, however, two-leg affairs. Dresden won the return 2-1 in East Berlin, and progressed to the semi-finals by squeezing through 5-3 on penalties. They also lost the home leg in the semi-final, going down 2-0 to

Vorwärts Frankfurt. Once again Dresden turned the score around on their opponents' ground, and won the penalty shoot-out 4-2. Beating the 'real' Dynamo Berlin 3-2 in the final was much more straightforward!

1984–85 League Table

	P	W	D	L	F	A	Pts
BFC Dynamo Berlin	26	20	4	2	90	28	44
Dynamo Dresden	26	15	8	3	69	34	38
Lokomotiv Leipzig	26	17	4	5	55	26	38
Wismut Aue	26	12	8	6	38	33	32
Magdeburg	26	11	9	6	53	35	31
Rot-Weiss Erfurt	26	10	10	6	47	39	30
Carl Zeiss Jena	26	9	7	10	36	27	25
Vorwärts Frankfurt	26	7	8	11	41	38	22
Karl-Marx-Stadt	26	7	7	12	39	48	21
Hansa Rostock	26	6	9	11	37	51	21
Stahl Brandeburg	26	5	10	11	25	39	20
Stahl Riesa	26	6	8	12	29	55	20
Chemie Leipzig	26	4	9	13	26	56	17
Motor Suhl	26	1	3	22	16	92	5

Cup final: Dresden 3, Dynamo Berlin 2.
Top scorer: Rainer Ernst (Dynamo Berlin) 24 goals.

CARL ZEISS JENA
Founded: 1949.
Colours: White and blue hoops/blue.
Stadium: Ernst-Abbe-Sportfeld (20,000).
Club address: F C Carl Zeiss Jena, 6900 Jena, Professor-Ibrahim-Str 33.
League: 1963, 1968, 1970 (3).
Cup: 1960, 1972, 1974, 1980 (4).
Cup-winners' Cup: Runners-up in 1981.

CHEMIE (Halle)
Founded: 1954.
Colours: Red and white hoops/red.
Stadium: Kurt-Wabbel-Stadion (30,000).
Club address: HFC Chemie, 4020 Halle (Salle), Martinstrasse 18.
League: 1949, 1952.
Cup: 1956, 1962.

CHEMIE (Leipzig)
Founded: 1950.
Colours: White/green.
Stadium: Georg-Schwarz-Sportpark (23,000).
Club address: BSG Chemie, 7033 Leipzig, Am Sportpark 2.
League: 1951, 1964.
Cup: 1966.

DYNAMO BERLIN
Founded: 1953.
Colours: Red/white.

Stadium: Sportforum (21,000).
Club address: B F C Dynamo, 1125 Berlin, Steffenstrasse.
League: 1979, 1980, 1981, 1982, 1983, 1984, 1985 (7 – record).
Cup: 1959.

DYNAMO DRESDEN
Founded: 1948.
Colours: Yellow/black.
Stadium: Dynamo-Stadion (38,000).
Club address: Dynamo Dresden, 8010 Dresden, Dr-Richard-Sorge-Strasse 1.
League: 1953, 1971, 1973, 1976, 1977, 1978.
Cup: 1952, 1971, 1977, 1982, 1984, 1985 (6).

HANSA ROSTOCK
Founded: 1950.
Colours: Sky blue/white.
Stadium: Ostseestadion (28,000).
Club address: F C Hansa Rostock, 2500 Rostock, Kopernikusstrasse.
League: – .
Cup: – .

KARL-MARX-STADT
Founded: 1963.
Colours: Blue/white.
Stadium: Kurt-Fischer-Stadion (22,000).
Club address: F C Karl-Marx-Stadt, Sportform Ernst Thälmann, Postfach 216.
League: 1967.
Cup: – .

LOKOMOTIV LEIPZIG
Founded: 1954.
Colours: Yellow/blue.
Stadium: Bruno-Plache-Stadion (22,000). Important matches in the Zentral-stadion (95,000).
Club address: 1. F C Lokomotiv Leipzig, 7039 Leipzig, Connewitzer Strasse 19.
League: – .
Cup: 1957, 1976, 1981 (3).

MAGDEBURG
Founded: 1965.
Colours: All white with blue trimmings.
Stadium: Ernst-Grube-Stadion (35,000).
Club address: 1. F C Magdeburg, 3010 Magdeburg, Gübser Weg, Ernst-Grube-Stadion.
League: 1972, 1974, 1975 (3).
Cup: 1964 (SC Aufbau), 1965 (SC Aufbau), 1969, 1973,1978, 1979, 1983 (7 – record, including S C Aufbau victories).
Cup-winners' Cup: 1974.

VORWÄRTS
Founded: 1948.
Colours: Yellow/red.
Stadium: Stadion der Freundschaft (18,000).
Club address: F C Vorwärts, 1200 Frankfurt/Oder, Oderallee, PSF 69973.
League: 1958, 1960, 1962, 1965, 1966, 1969 (6 – joint record).
Cup: 1964, 1970.

WISMUT AUE
Founded: 1951 (Reorganised 1963).
Colours: Mauve/white.
Stadium: Otto-Grotewohl-Stadion (25,000).
Club address: Wismut Aue, 9400 Aue, Lössnitzer Strasse.
League: 1956, 1957, 1959 (3).
Cup: 1955.

ECUADOR

The Ecuador season, which ended with Nacional winning the championship for the eighth time in all and third in a row, was one long controversy. Liga Deportiva Universitaria of Quito made the running with an early-season cash scandal. It turned out that no one could find any balance sheets for the previous three years. Then the club refused to pay their players in July because too many forged tickets and not enough 'real' ones had been sold for an important league match.

Top club Barcelona then upset their fans by deciding to stop importing foreign stars and rely only on Ecuadorian players – except for Brazilian Paolo Cesar, who had apparently agreed to take out Ecuadorian citizenship. Then coach Washington Munoz further put the cat among the pigeons by dropping popular defender Holger Quiñoñez, because he was 'too rugged'.

Even champions Nacional, despite their success under Brazilian coach Roberto Abrussezzi and their disciplined reputation as befits an army team, had their troubles. One game against Nueve de Octobre was little more than a free-for-all. Top Nacional official Colonel Gerardo Mesias ordered the arrest of the federation's delegate at the game, and instructed his soldiers to seize and smash press cameras.

Then the decisive second round group two league match between Nueve de Octobre (again) and Universidad de Portoviejo had to be rearranged after angry fans smashed down the wire fences meant to keep them off the pitch. Controversy continued as the national team began its World Cup qualifying preparations with a squad which included an Argentine-born goalkeeper in Pedro Latino of Deportivo Quito, but had to make do without the league's Argentine top scorer, Sergio Saucedo, after citizenship moves were abruptly halted by his transfer to Sporting Lisbon.

Nacional supplied six players to the World Cup squad – defenders Hans Maldonaldo and Elias de Negri, midfielders Jose Villafuerte and Carlos Ron, and strikers Ermen Benitez and Fernando Baldeon. Benitez promises to be the country's number one player, and impressed East German national boss Bernd Stange when they played in Ecuador during the winter break. Benitez scored eight goals in four games against East Germany, Finland and the touring Danish champions, Vejle.

The Ecuador championship is played in three stages of home-and-away competition. Nacional were winners all the way. They finished at the top of their seven-team first round group, then three points clear of their deadly rivals Barcelona at the end of the second stage. Eight teams went on to the final round of the championship. Nacional won their last game 1-0 against Deportivo Quito to finish two points clear of Nueve de Octobre.

Unlike certain other South American countries such as Uruguay and Peru, the Ecuadorians do not extend their season even further for more play-offs to sort out their entries for the South American Club Cup. Thus Nacional and Nueve de Octobre qualified, as they had, and in that same order, the previous year.

1984 Championship

First round Group One: Barcelona (Guayaquil) 23 pts; Tecnico Universitario (Ambato) 18; Emelec (Guayaquil) 15; Deportivo Quito 15; Liga Deportiva Universitaria (Quito) 11; Universidad de Portoviejo 11; Aucas (Quito) 7. Group Two: Nacional (Quito) 22 pts; Filanbanco (Guayaquil) 15; Universidad Catolica (Quito) 15; Nueve de Octobre (Guayaquil) 14; America (Quito) 11; Sporting Manta 11; Deportivo Quevedo 9.

Second round Group One: Nacional 21; Barcelona 18; Dep. Quito 15; Un. Catolica 13; Sporting Manta 13; Tecnico Universitario 12; Filanbanco 12. Group Two: Nueve de Octobre 15; LDU 15; Un. Portoviejo 13; Emelec 12; America 12; Dep. Quevedo 12; Aucas 11.

Final Round

	P	W	D	L	F	A	Pts
Nacional	14	8	2	4	20	16	20
Nueve de Octobre	14	7	4	3	29	27	18
LDU Quito	14	7	3	4	18	17	17
Un. Catolica	14	6	3	5	19	15	15
Barcelona	14	6	2	6	26	28	14
Tecnico Univ.	14	5	3	6	19	22	13
Dep. Quito	14	3	5	6	16	20	11
Emelec	14	2	4	8	17	29	8

Top scorer: Sergio Saucedo (Dep. Quito) 25 goals.

AMÉRICA
Founded: 1925.
Colours: Green/white.
Stadium: Olímpico Atahualpa (40,000).
Club address: América, Estadio Olímpico Atahualpa, Quito.
Championship: – .

BARCELONA
Founded: 1925.
Colours: Yellow with red trimming/black.
Stadium: Estadio Modelo (48,772).
Club address: Barcelona, Maldonado 508, Guayaquil.
Championship: 1963, 1966, 1970, 1971, 1981 (5).

DEPORTIVO QUITO
Founded: 1925.
Colours: Blue and red stripes/blue.
Stadium: Olímpico Atahualpa (40,000).
Club address: Sociedad Deportivo Quito, Veintimilla 325, Quito.
Championship: 1964, 1968.

EMELEC
Founded: 1925.
Colours: All blue with white sash.
Stadium: Estadio Modelo (48,772).
Club address: Emelec, Velez 1109, Guayaquil.
Championship: 1957, 1960, 1965, 1972 (4).

EVEREST
Founded: 1925.
Colours: All white.
Stadium: Estadio Modelo (48,772).
Club address: Everest, Estadio Modelo, Guayaquil.
Championship: 1961, 1962.

LIGA DEPORTIVA UNIVERSITARIA (L D U)
Founded: 1925.
Colours: All white.
Stadium: Olímpico Atahualpa (40,000).
Club address: Liga Deportiva Universitaria, Madrid 868, Quito.
Championship: 1969, 1973, 1975 (3).

NACIONAL
Founded: 1964.
Colours: White with blue sash/blue.
Stadium: Olímpico Atahualpa (40,000).
Club address: Club Deportivo El Nacional, Avenida 10 de Agosto, 645, Quito.
Championship: 1967, 1974, 1976, 1977, 1978, 1982, 1983, 1984 (8 – record).

NUEVE DE OCTUBRE
Founded: 1925
Colours: Red/white.
Stadium: Estadio Los Chirijos (10,000).
Club address: 9 de Octubre, Estadio Los Chirijos de Milagro, Guayaquil.
Championship: – .

TECNICO UNIVERSITARIO
Founded: 1925.
Colours: White/red.
Stadium: Estadio Bellavista (20,000).
Club address: Tecnico Universitario, Centro Comercial BL 2, Ambato.
Championship: – .

UNIVERSIDAD CATÓLICA
Founded: 1925.
Colours: Sky blue with black trimming/black.
Stadium: Important matches in Olímpico Atahualpa (40,000).
Club address: Club Deportivo Universidad Católica, Avenida 12 de octubre y Ladrón de Guevara, Quito.
Championship: 1979, 1980.

EGYPT

Zamalek, one of the great names of Egyptian football, won the league championship for the fifth time when their traditional end-of-season meeting with great rivals Al Ahly ended in a 1-1 draw. Thus Zamalek maintained their two-point advantage at the top, but Al Ahly (National) did have the consolation of victory over El Masri of Port Said in the cup final for the second year in a row. Both clubs then went on to greater things in the closing stages of the 1984 African club competitions.

Zamalek's triumph was to win the African Champions' Cup for the first time. They beat Sfax of Tunisia easily in the first round proper, then gained a walk-over against Gor Mahia after their Kenyan opponents lost their heads. In the quarter-finals they thrashed Nkana Red Devils of Zambia, and were then drawn against former African champions JET of Algeria.

The first leg, in Algeria, was something of a disaster. A goal from central defender Ibrahim Youssef helped them hold on at 1-1 for most of the game. But then JET scored twice in the last fifteen minutes. It was the first time an Egyptian club had conceded three goals in an African competition for seven years.

Zamalek were without three senior players because of injury for the return in Cairo. But, roared on by a crowd of 100,000, they pulled one back with Gamal Abdel Hamid's penalty just before half-time. It was Hamid who created the second goal for Nasr Ibrahim to head home after fifty-two minutes, and also the third for Zamalek's Ghanaian international, Emmanuel Quarshie.

Opponents in the final were Shooting Stars of Nigeria. But, like JET before them, they were to be taken apart by Abdel Hamid. He scored two second-half goals to cushion Zamalek for the trip to Lagos, where they profited from an own goal to win the return 1-0 and the cup 3-0 on aggregate.

But if Egyptian football had reason to celebrate, they proved even more dominant in the Cup-winners' Cup, where they had two entries. The first was Arab Contractors, defending the title they had won in 1983; the second was Al Ahly, who qualified by virtue of their 1-0 cup final win over El Masri.

Arab Contractors were founded only in 1976. But, carrying the name of one of the Middle East's major construction companies and backed by owner and millionaire developer Osman Ahmed, it didn't take long to make their mark.

In 1982 they finished runners-up in the league, which, because of the absence of a cup competition that year, qualified Contractors for the 1983 Cup-winners' Cup. They engaged English coach Mike Everitt – one-time Arsenal, Northampton, Plymouth and Brighton half-back – from Zamalek, and won the trophy. In the final Everitt's men beat the Zambian club, Power Dynamos, who were managed by fellow Englishman Billy McGarry.

Contractors also won the domestic league title in 1983, largely thanks to the abilities of their Cameroon goalkeeper Antoine Bell, and Ghanaian midfielder Abdul Razak, a former African Footballer of the Year. They wanted to enter both the 1984 Champions' Cup and defend their title in the Cup-winners' event, but neither the Egyptian FA nor the African Confederation would sanction that. So they settled for defending their title in the Cup-winners' Cup.

Everything went according to plan until Contractors were drawn against Egyptian rivals Al Ahly – managed by former England boss Don Revie – in the semi-finals. Egyptian fans had hoped they would be kept apart by the luck of the draw. But it wasn't to be. Luck was against Contractors on the field as well as off it. In the away leg, they held Al Ahly to a goal-less draw. But a minute before half-time in the return, Al Ahly went ahead through star forward Mahmoud El Khattib. Early in the second half Nasser Mohammed Ali equalised but that was the only time Al Ahly goalkeeper Agmed Shobeir was beaten, and Contractors went out on the away goals rule.

In the final they should have met their namesakes, Al Ahly from Libya. But diplomatic relations between Egypt and Libya being what they were, the Libyans failed to turn up for the first leg in Cairo. Amid controversy, the African confederation set new dates for the final and ordered Al Ahly to play against Canon of Cameroon, who had been beaten in the semi-final by the Libyans. Arab Contractors protested that they ought to be allowed a play-off against Canon to decide the substitute finalists, but to no avail. The Libyans protested that they should share the trophy, claiming, no doubt correctly, that if they had been drawn to stage the first leg of the final in Tripoli, then the Egyptians wouldn't have turned up.

But time was fast running out on the season. The nomination of Canon stood and Al Ahly squeezed to the title, winning 4-2 on penalties in Yaounde, the Cameroon capital, after each side had won their home leg 1-0.

1984 League Table

	P	W	D	L	F	A	Pts
Zamalek	22	15	6	1	26	8	36
Al Ahly	22	14	6	2	30	9	34
Ismaili	22	9	8	5	22	13	26
Masri	22	9	5	8	26	20	23
Arab Contractors	22	6	10	6	15	17	22
Mehalla	22	3	13	6	18	18	19
Menia	22	5	9	8	12	12	19
Tersana	22	6	7	9	14	21	19
Ettihad	22	3	11	8	8	17	18
Olympic	22	5	7	10	15	26	17
Plastic	22	5	7	10	16	28	17
Koroun	22	5	5	12	13	26	15

Cup final: Al Ahly 3, Masri (Port Said) 1.
Top scorer: Ayman Shawki (Koroun) 7 goals.

1984–85 Championship

Final points totals: 1 Ahly 35. 2 Zamalek 32. 3 Ismaili 25. 4 Mehalla 24. 5 El Masry 23. 6 Tarsana 22. 7 Union Recreation 19. 8 Arab Contractors 18. 9 Menia 18. 10 Mansoura 17. 11 Olympic 16. 12 Damiette 15.

ARAB CONTRACTORS
Founded:1976.
Colours: Yellow and black stripes/black.
Stadium: Ismailia (20,000).
Club address: Arab Contractors, c/o Egyptian FA, 5 Shareb Gabalaya, Al Borg Post Office, Cairo.
League: 1983.
Afr. Champions' Cup: – .
Afr. Cup-winners' Cup: 1982, 1983.

AL AHLY (NATIONAL)
Founded: 1907.
Colours: All red.
Stadium: Al Ahly (10,000) but big matches at the Nasser Stadium (100,000).
Club address: Al Ahly, c/o Egyptian FA, 5 Shareh Gabalaya, Al Borg Post Office, Cairo.
League: 1949, 1950, 1951, 1953, 1954, 1956, 1957, 1958, 1959, 1961, 1962, 1975, 1976, 1977, 1979, 1980, 1981, 1982 (18).
Afr. Champions' Cup: 1982. Runners-up in 1983.
Afr. Cup-winners' Cup: 1984.

ZAMALEK
Founded: 1925.
Colours: All white.
Stadium: Zamalek (35,000).
Club address: Zamalek Sporting Club, c/o Egyptian FA, 5 Shareb Gabalaya, Al Borg Post Office, Cairo.
League: 1960, 1964, 1965, 1978, 1984, 1985 (6).
Afr. Champions' Cup: 1984.
Afr. Cup-winners' Cup: – .

ENGLAND

Many reasons could have made the 1984–85 Football League season a memorable one: Everton's revival, which brought them so close to the league-and-cup double; the controversial tackle which meant Manchester United's Kevin Moran becoming the first player to be sent off in an FA Cup final; the contrasting fortunes of Norwich, winning the Milk Cup but being relegated; the rise from the second division of Robert Maxwell's Oxford United; and the slide from first to third division of those great old clubs Notts County and Wolves. But all of this and more paled into insignificance alongside the enormity of the tragedies at Valley Parade, Bradford, on Saturday, 11 May and at the Heysel Stadium, Brussels, just eighteen days later.

At Bradford fifty-five fans died after fire swept through the seventy-six-year-old wooden main stand just forty minutes into the match against Lincoln. The stand, as ill luck would have it, was packed to its capacity of 3,000, because this was the match at which Bradford were celebrating their promotion to the second division.

It seems that a cigarette end caused the blaze, which started amongst rubbish beneath the stand, and engulfed the structure in less than three minutes watched by television cameras and 8,000 other fans around the ground. Some fans, their clothes and hair alight, threw themselves over the terracing and onto the pitch where they were helped to safety and hospital. Others, less fortunate, tried to get out through the exits at the back of the stand, only to find them locked. The government ordered an inquiry, and gradually the story emerged of how vulnerable football grounds were in such tragic circumstances. An extension of the ground safety laws – introduced after the 1971 Ibrox disaster – was ordered – a high-cost operation for the third and fourth division clubs which had previously been exempted from the need to obtain safety designation certificates.

The tragedy of Valley Parade overshadowed events that same afternoon at Birmingham where Leeds fans lived up to their notorious reputation with scenes of hooliganism which went beyond even the excesses of fans of Millwall at Luton a few weeks earlier, and of the hooligans at Chelsea whose antics had prompted the Stamford Bridge club to try to instal an electric fence. The Leeds fans at Birmingham ripped apart a refreshment stand to use lumps of wood as missiles and were prevented from taking over the pitch only by a charge of mounted police. The game was interrupted for nearly thirty minutes after the first half had been completed, and there was more fighting at the end. There was death, too: a fifteen-year-old boy died, crushed between masonry and other falling Leeds fans as a perimeter wall collapsed under pressure from supporters impatient to get out of the ground.

The memories were still fresh when Liverpool travelled to Brussels to play Juventus in the European Champions' Cup final. It could have been a great night for British football: had Liverpool won they would have turned the European Cup into their own property, with what would have been their fifth success in eight years. Instead the match took place in the shadow of death. Blame has been cast in many directions; at the disorganised Belgian police; at the ageing state of the Heysel Stadium; at the lack of proper supporter segregation; and at the irresponsible sale of tickets in Brussels before the match. The fact remains, whatever the attempts to find a disguise elsewhere, that if a couple of hundred hooligans from the Liverpool section had not charged into the mainly Italian crowd in Sector Z there would have been no deaths.

The Italian fans retreated against the side wall and the front of the terracing. Both walls collapsed, and bodies and masonry tumbled to the ground. What happened will remain engraved on the memories of those who were there to see it. The hooligans charged again and the first victims were crushed and trampled by more Italian fans trying to escape onto the pitch. The Belgian police, totally blind to the real tragedy, started trying to get the supporters back, before they realised people were dead and dying. As the rescue work went on at one end, as a field hospital was created in the car park behind Sector Z, so Italian fans at the other end took the opportunity to bait the police and pelt them with missiles. At one end of the stadium, carnage; at the other end, chaos. The Juventus players came out to try to calm their fans, and succeeded only in whipping them to a greater frenzy. Both captains, Liverpool's Phil Neal and Juventus' Gaetano Scirea, appealed for calm. And so, more than an hour after the scheduled kick-off, the match began.

The decision to play the European Cup final drew bitter criticism almost exclusively from people – politicians, sports administrators and ordinary fans – who saw events unfold via television. But in the circumstances it was a tough but practical and correct decision. To have cancelled or postponed then and there would have unleashed a further wave of violence; it would have released thousands of milling fans into the areas around the stadium only to hamper the desperate work of the emergency services; and the decision to play gave the security forces time to draft in riot police from all over Belgium to make sure there could be as little trouble as possible later into the night. Juventus won 1–0, with a disputed penalty converted by European Footballer of the Year Michel Platini, and Liverpool and their shamed supporters went home to one of English football's greatest crises.

With enthusiastic Government approval, the FA announced it would not enter the names of clubs for participation in European competitions in 1985–86; Liverpool withdrew voluntarily; UEFA imposed an indefinite ban, and FIFA temporarily extended that to worldwide proportions.

Many of the clubs bleated, predictably, that it wasn't their fault and that they should not be punished. They wriggled and squirmed too at plans to ban all alcohol at grounds and introduce a computerised membership card system. As a wide spectrum of the media – from the *Sunday Times* to the *Mirror* and taking in specialist publications such as *World Soccer* commented – these clubs appeared to have totally misread the mood of a nation which was becoming sick of football, and the large number of whingers who appeared to be involved in running it.

In truth, punishment was very much a secondary consideration compared with English football's responsibility to protect other countries, their cities, citizens and clubs, from the excesses of the lunatic fringe, however much time that would take. As FA secretary Ted Crocker said sadly: 'The ban will not be a short, sharp shock. It will be a long, sharp shock.'

1984–85 League Tables

	P	W	D	L	F	A	Pts
Everton	42	28	6	8	88	43	90
Liverpool	42	22	11	9	68	35	77
Tottenham	42	23	8	11	78	51	77
Manchester Utd	42	22	10	10	77	47	76
Southampton	42	19	11	12	56	47	68
Chelsea	42	18	12	12	63	48	66
Arsenal	42	19	9	14	61	49	66
Sheffield Wed.	42	17	14	11	58	45	65
Nottingham Forest	42	19	7	16	56	48	64
Watford	42	14	13	15	81	71	55
West Bromwich	42	16	7	19	58	62	55
Luton	42	15	9	18	57	61	54
Newcastle	42	13	13	16	55	70	52
Leicester	42	15	6	21	65	73	51
West Ham Utd	42	13	12	17	51	68	51
Ipswich	42	13	11	18	46	57	50
Coventry	42	15	5	22	47	64	50
Queen's Pk Rangers	42	13	11	18	53	72	50
Norwich	42	13	10	19	46	64	49
Sunderland	42	10	10	22	40	62	40
Stoke	42	3	8	31	24	91	17

Second division

	P	W	D	L	F	A	Pts
Oxford Utd	42	25	9	8	84	36	84
Birmingham City	42	25	7	10	59	33	82
Manchester City	42	21	11	10	66	40	74
Portsmouth	42	20	14	8	69	50	74
Blackburn Rvrs	42	21	10	11	66	41	73
Brighton	42	20	12	10	54	34	72
Leeds Utd	42	19	12	11	66	43	69
Shrewsbury Town	42	18	11	13	66	53	65
Fulham	42	19	8	15	68	64	65
Grimsby Town	42	18	8	16	72	64	62
Barnsley	42	14	16	12	42	42	58
Wimbledon	42	16	10	16	71	75	58
Huddersfield Town	42	15	10	17	52	64	55
Oldham Athletic	42	15	8	19	49	67	53
Crystal Palace	42	12	12	18	46	65	48
Carlisle Utd	42	13	8	21	50	67	47
Charlton Athletic	42	11	12	19	51	63	45
Sheffield Utd	42	10	14	18	54	66	44
Middlesbrough	42	10	10	22	41	57	40
Notts County	42	10	7	25	45	73	37
Cardiff City	42	9	8	25	47	79	35
Wolves	42	8	9	25	37	79	33

FA Cup final: Manchester United 1, Everton 0.
Milk/League Cup final: Norwich 1, Sunderland 0.
Top scorers (first division): Kerry Dixon (Chelsea) and Gary Lineker (Leicester) 24 goals each.

ARSENAL
Founded: 1886.
Colours: Red/white.
Stadium: Highbury (60,000).
Club address: Arsenal Stadium, Highbury, London N5.
League: 1931, 1933, 1934, 1935, 1938, 1948, 1953, 1971 (8).
F.A. Cup: 1930, 1936, 1950, 1971, 1979 (5).
League Cup: – .
Cup-winners' Cup: Runners-up in 1980.
Fairs' Cup: 1970.

ASTON VILLA
Founded: 1874.
Colours: All claret with blue trimmings.
Stadium: Villa Park (48,000).
Club address: Aston Villa FC, Villa Park, Trinity Road, Birmingham B6 6HE.
League: 1894, 1896, 1897, 1899, 1900, 1910, 1981 (7).
F.A. Cup: 1887, 1895, 1897, 1905, 1913, 1920, 1957 (7 – joint record)
League Cup: 1961, 1975, 1977.
World Club Cup: Runners-up in 1982.
Champions' Cup: 1982.
Super Cup: 1982.

BIRMINGHAM CITY
Founded: 1875.
Colours: Blue/white.
Stadium: St Andrew's (44,500).
Club address: Birmingham City FC, St Andrew's, Birmingham B9 4NH.
League: – .
F.A. Cup: – .
League Cup: 1963.
Fairs' Cup: Runners-up in 1960 and 1961.

BURNLEY
Founded: 1882.
Colours: Claret with light blue trim/white.
Stadium: Turf Moor (23,000).
Club address: Burnley FC, Turf Moor, Burnley BB10 4BX.
League: 1921, 1960.
F.A. Cup: 1914.
League Cup: – .

CHELSEA
Founded: 1905.
Colours: All blue.
Stadium: Stamford Bridge (45,000).
Club address: Chelsea FC, Stamford Bridge, London SW6.
League: 1955.
F.A. Cup: 1970.
League Cup: 1965.
Cup-winners' Cup: 1971.

COVENTRY CITY
Founded: 1883.
Colours: All sky blue.
Stadium: Highfield Road (20,500).
Club address: Coventry City FC, Highfield Road Stadium, King Richard Street, Coventry CV2 4FW.
League: – .
F.A. Cup: – .
League Cup: – .

DERBY COUNTY
Founded: 1884.
Colours: White/blue.
Stadium: Baseball Ground (33,700).
Club address: Derby County, Baseball Ground, Shaftesbury Crescent, Derby DE3 8NB.
League: 1972, 1975.
F.A. Cup: 1946.
League Cup: – .

EVERTON
Founded: 1878.
Colours: Blue/white.
Stadium: Goodison Park (53,419).
Club address: Everton, Goodison Park, Liverpool L4 4EL.
League: 1891, 1915, 1928, 1932, 1939, 1963, 1970, 1985 (8).
F.A. Cup: 1906, 1933, 1966 (3).
League Cup: – .
Cup-winners' Cup: 1985.

IPSWICH TOWN
Founded: 1887.
Colours: Blue/white.
Stadium: Portman Road (37,000).
Club address: Ipswich Town FC, Portman Road, Ipswich, Suffolk IP1 2DA.
League: 1962.
F.A. Cup: 1978.
League Cup: – .
UEFA Cup: 1981.

LEEDS UNITED
Founded: 1919.
Colours: All white.
Stadium: Elland Road (43,900).
Club address: Leeds United AFC, Elland Road, Leeds LS11 OES.
League: 1969, 1974.
F.A. Cup: 1972.
League Cup: 1968.
Champions' Cup: Runners-up in 1975.
Cup-winners' Cup: Runners-up in 1973.
Fairs' Cup: 1968, 1971. Runners-up in 1967.

LEICESTER
Founded: 1884.
Colours: Blue/white.
Stadium: Filbert Street (32,000).
Club address: Leicester City FC, City Stadium, Filbert Street, Leicester LE2 7FL.
League: – .
F.A. Cup: – .
League Cup: 1964.

LIVERPOOL
Founded: 1892.
Colours: All red.
Stadium: Anfield (45,000).
Club address: Liverpool FC, Anfield Road, Liverpool 4.
League: 1901, 1906, 1922, 1923, 1947, 1964, 1966, 1973, 1976, 1977, 1979, 1980, 1982, 1983, 1984 (15 – record).
F.A. Cup 1965, 1974.
League/Milk Cup: 1981, 1982, 1983, 1984 (4).

World Club Cup: Runners-up in 1981.
Champions' Cup: 1977, 1978, 1981, 1984 (4). Runners-up 1985.
Cup-winners' Cup: Runners-up in 1966.
UEFA Cup: 1973, 1976.
SuperCup: 1977. Runners-up in 1978.

MANCHESTER CITY
Founded: 1887.
Colours: All sky blue.
Stadium: Maine Road (52,500).
Club address: Manchester City FC, Maine Road, Moss Side, Manchester M14 7WN.
League: 1937, 1968.
F.A. Cup: 1904, 1934, 1956, 1969 (4).
League Cup: 1970, 1976.
Cup-winners' Cup: 1970.

MANCHESTER UNITED
Founded: 1878.
Colours: Red/white.
Stadium: Old Trafford (58,504).
Club address: Manchester United FC, Old Trafford, Manchester M16 ORA.
League: 1908, 1911, 1952, 1956, 1957, 1965, 1967 (7).
F.A. Cup: 1909, 1948, 1963, 1977, 1983, 1985 (6).
League Cup: – .
World Club Cup: Runners-up in 1968.
Champions' Cup: 1968.

NEWCASTLE UNITED
Founded: 1882.
Colours: Black and white stripes/black.
Stadium: St James' Park.
Club address: Newcastle United FC, St James' Park, Newcastle-upon-Tyne NE1 4ST.
League: 1905, 1907, 1909, 1927 (4)
F.A. Cup: 1910, 1924, 1932, 1951, 1952, 1955 (6).
League Cup: – .

NORWICH CITY
Founded: 1905.
Colours: Yellow/green.
Stadium: Carrow Road (28,500).
Club address: Norwich City FC, Carrow Road, Norwich NR1 1JE.
League: – .
FA Cup: – .
Milk/League Cup: 1962, 1985.

NOTTINGHAM FOREST
Founded: 1865.
Colours: Red/white.

Stadium: City Ground (35,000).
Club address: Nottingham Forest, City Ground, Nottingham NG2 5FJ.
League: 1978.
F.A. Cup: 1898, 1959.
League Cup: 1978, 1979.
World Club Cup: Runners-up in 1980.
Champions' Cup: 1979, 1980.
SuperCup: 1979. Runners-up in 1980.

QUEEN'S PARK RANGERS
Founded: 1885.
Colours: Blue and white hoops/white.
Stadium: Loftus Road (30,000).
Club address: Queen's Park Rangers FC, South Africa Road, London W12 7PA.
League: – .
F.A. Cup: – .
League Cup: 1967.

SHEFFIELD WEDNESDAY
Founded: 1867.
Colours: Blue and white stripes/blue.
Stadium: Hillsborough (50,174).
Club address: Sheffield Wednesday, Hillsborough, Sheffield S6 1SW.
League: 1903, 1904, 1929, 1930 (4).
F.A. Cup: 1896, 1907, 1935 (3).
League Cup: – .

SOUTHAMPTON
Founded: 1885.
Colours: Red and white/black.
Stadium: The Dell (25,000).
Club address: Southampton FC, The Dell, Milton Road, Southampton S09 4XX.
League: – .
F.A. Cup: 1976.
League Cup: – .

STOKE CITY
Founded: 1863.
Colours: Red and white stripes/white.
Stadium: Victoria Ground (35,000).
Club address: Stoke City FC, Victoria Ground, Stoke-on-Trent.
League: – .
F.A. Cup – .
League Cup: 1972.

SUNDERLAND
Founded: 1879.
Colours: Red and white stripes/black.

Stadium: Roker Park.
Club address: Sunderland AFC, Roker Park Ground, Sunderland.
League: 1892, 1893, 1895, 1902, 1913, 1936 (6).
F.A. Cup: 1937, 1973.
League Cup: – .

TOTTENHAM HOTSPUR
Founded: 1882.
Colours: White/blue. In Europe: All white.
Stadium: White Hart Lane.
Club address: Tottenham Hotspur, 748 High Road, Tottenham, London N17.
League: 1951, 1961.
F.A. Cup: 1901, 1921, 1961, 1962, 1967, 1981, 1982 (7 – joint record).
League Cup: 1971, 1973.
Cup-winners' Cup: 1963.
UEFA Cup: 1972, 1984. Runners-up in 1974.

WATFORD
Founded: 1891.
Colours: Yellow/red.
Stadium: Vicarage Road (28,500).
Club address: Watford, Vicarage Road Stadium, Watford WD1 8ER.
League: – .
F.A. Cup: – .
League Cup: – .

WEST BROMWICH ALBION
Founded: 1879.
Colours: Blue and white stripes/white.
Stadium: The Hawthorns (38,600).
Club address: West Bromwich Albion, The Hawthorns, West Bromwich B71 4LF.
League: 1920.
F.A. Cup: 1888, 1892, 1931, 1954, 1968.
League Cup: 1966.

WEST HAM UNITED
Founded: 1900.
Colours: Claret with blue trimmings/white.
Stadium: Upton Park (35,500).
Club address: Boleyn Ground, Green Street, Upton Park, London E13.
F.A. Cup: 1964, 1975, 1980 (3).
League Cup: – .
Cup-winners' Cup: 1965. Runners-up in 1976.

WOLVERHAMPTON WANDERERS
Founded: 1877.
Colours: Old gold/black.
Stadium: Molineux (38,000).
League: 1954, 1958, 1959 (3).

F.A. Cup: 1893, 1908, 1949, 1960 (4).
League Cup: 1974, 1980.
UEFA Cup: Runners-up in 1972.

FINLAND

Finland's domestic football, inspired by the example of neighbours Sweden, is trying to dig itself out of a rut by tinkering with the traditional league championship formula. After years of staying faithful to the simple home-and-away match system applied by virtually everyone else in Europe, the Finns decided this was too predictable. Attendances were falling, and more competitive excitement was needed to bring the fans back.

The problem is, they can't decide on exactly the best system to use. In 1983 the top eight teams in the standard league split away to play off in a championship system, while the bottom four clubs in the first division played off similarly with the top four from the second division. To further complicate matters, clubs took half their points total from the first stage into the second, but half a point was always rounded up.

Ilves of Tampere won that complicated system which appeared to confuse more fans than it attracted. So in 1984 the federation, the SPL (Suomen Palloliitto), decided to simplify matters. Thus at the end of the league stage, the top four clubs played off in knock-out semi-finals, third-place match and final to resolve the title issues.

That proved bad news for one of the country's outstanding clubs, Valkeakosken Haka. In the spring of 1984 they had become the first Finnish club ever to reach the quarter-finals of a European competition. And neither were they disgraced as they went down just 0-1, 0-1 to eventual trophy winners Juventus in the Cup-winners' Cup.

Their problem was in attack. Pertti Nissinen finished as their top scorer in the league, but with just nine goals to his name as they completed the stage on top of the table. But in the play-offs they were notably short of fire-power. They scored just three times in four games, going down to Kuusysi Lahti in the semi-finals and then to Ilves Tampere in the third-place match.

As for Kuusysi they went on to the championship and fell just short of the double when they lost narrowly, by 2-1, to HJK Helsinki in the cup final. Kuusysi are very much a 1980s success story. They first won promotion to the first division in 1981, and then set off on a run of uninterrupted success. In 1982 they won the championship, in 1983 the cup, and then in 1984, of course, the championship again. Their team was built around a nucleus of international players, starting at the back with goalkeeper Ismo Korhonen and continuing with defenders Ilkka Remes, Raimo Kumpulainen – at twenty-nine the 'old man' of the team – and Esa Pekonen, the club's captain. Further forward Kuusysi look to more young players in Ismo Lius and Markus Törnvall for goals. Lius, who was eighteen when he was brought into the team, matched his age with goals last season to finish as the country's second-highest scorer behind Lipponen of TPs. Kuusysi make a habit of producing eighteen-year-olds like rabbits out of a hat. When they won the cup in 1983 it was Törnvall, then eighteen himself, who scored both goals in the final win over Haka.

Kuusysi's coach was Keijo Voutilainen, a forty-nine-year-old who worked well to integrate two English players among his young Finnish products. The two were Keith Armstrong and Kenny Mitchell. Armstrong, now twenty-eight, had played without making much League impression in England with Sunderland, Newport, Scunthorpe and Newcastle. But he had already had one brief spell in Finland with OPs of Oulu before returning to join Kuusysi and winning the third Finnish championship of his career; the previous two were with OPs.

Mitchell is another product of the English north-east. He was born in Sunderland but began his career with Newcastle, for whom he played sixty-six League games, including substitutions, before moving on down the ladder in 1980 to join Darlington. He played only a dozen games there before trying his luck abroad, with some success as far as Voutilainen is concerned. Mitchell had been rated a defender at Newcastle, but Kuusysi pushed him forward into midfield, where his strength complemented the skills of Ilpo Talvio and Jari Rinne. Yet only one of the Kuusysi team played in the Finland team beaten 5-0 at Wembley in the World Cup qualifier in October, 1984, and that was defender Pekonen.

Because of the amateur-based organisation of football in Finland, and the climatic problems, they are unlikely ever to make the sort of international progress achieved by, say, Denmark. It may be significant that Kuusysi have been able to use all-winter indoor training facilities when everyone else had forgotten about football. At least under the sensible guidance of national manager Martti Kuusela, the national team can still produce the odd shock – such as the 1-0 win over Northern Ireland with which Finland began their current World Cup campaign.

Haka did gain some belated consolation for their near misses in 1984. The 1985 cup competition was played at the start of the season and they beat holders HJK in the semi-finals, and then Lahden Reipas 1-0 to claim a record eighth success.

1984 Championship

	P	W	D	L	F	A	Pts
Haka	22	11	9	2	43	26	31
TPs	22	11	7	4	56	21	29
Kuusysi	22	10	8	4	41	24	28
Ilves	22	12	4	6	42	28	28
HJK	22	10	6	6	49	37	26
RoPs	22	9	6	7	33	38	24
KePs	22	7	7	8	35	36	21
KuPs	22	6	7	9	25	32	19
PPT	22	7	3	12	32	42	17
Koparit	22	3	9	10	23	28	15
KPV	22	6	3	13	30	56	15
MP	22	2	7	13	22	53	11

Play-offs: Semi-finals: Kuuysi Lahti bt Valkeakosken Haka 2-0, 1-2 – TPs bt Ilves Tampere 1-2, 4-0. Third place: Ilves bt Haka 2-1, 1-0. Final: Kuusysi bt TPs 4-0, 4-4.
Cup final (1984): HJK 2, Kuusysi Lahti 1.
Cup final (1985): Haka 1, Lahden Reipas 0.
Top scorer: Mikka Liponen (TPs) 24 goals.

H J K
Founded: 1907.
Colours: All blue.
Stadium: Important games in the Olympiastadion (50,000).
Club address: Helsingin Jalkapalloklubi, Stadion 139, 00250 Helsinki 25.
League: 1911, 1912, 1917, 1918, 1919, 1923, 1925, 1936, 1938, 1964, 1973, 1978, 1981 (13).
Cup: 1966, 1981, 1984 (3).

ILVES
Founded: 1931.
Colours: Yellow/green.
Stadium: Ratina (25,000).
Club address: Ilves, Sammonvaltatie 2, 33560 Tampere 56.
League: 1950, 1983.
Cup: 1979.

K T P
Founded: 1927.
Colours: Green and white stripes/white.
Stadium: Urheilukeskus (14,500).
Club address: Kotkan Työväen Palloilijat, Gutzeitintie 10 E 62, 48100 Kotka 10.
League: 1951, 1952.
Cup: 1958, 1961, 1967, 1980 (4).

KOPARIT (K P T)
Founded: 1930.
Colours: All white.
Stadium: Väinölänniemi (10,100).
Club address: Kuopion Pallotoverit (KPT), P L 153, 70101 Kuopie 10.
League: – .
Cup: – .

KuPs
Founded: 1923.
Colours: Yellow/black.
Stadium: Väinölänniemi (10,100).
Club address: Kuopion Palloseura, Niiralankatu 16, 70600 Kuopio 60.
League: 1956, 1958, 1966, 1974, 1976 (5).
Cup: 1968.

KUUSYSI
Founded: 1974.
Colours: All white.
Stadium: Urheilukeskus (10,000).
Club address: Kuusysi, Urheilukeskus, 15110 Lahti 11.
League: 1982, 1984.
Cup: 1983.

LAHDEN REIPAS
Founded: 1891.
Colours: Orange and black stripes/black.
Stadium: Urheilukeskus (10,000).
Club address: Lahden Reipas, Urheilukeskus, 15110 Lahti 11.
League: 1963, 1967, 1970 (3).
Cup: 1964, 1972, 1973, 1974, 1975, 1976, 1978 (7).

M P
Founded: 1929.
Colours: Blue/green.
Stadium: Urheilupuisto (10,000).
Club address: Mikkelin Palloilijat, Kujatie 3, 50100 Mikkeli 10.
League: – .
Cup: 1970, 1971.

O P S
Founded: 1925.
Colours: White/blue.
Stadium: Raatti (10,000).
Club address: Oulun Palloseura, Isokatu 23, 90100 Oulu 10.
League: 1979, 1980.
Cup: – .

T P S
Founded: 1922.
Colours: Black and white stripes/white.
Stadium: Kupittaa (11,000).
Club address: Turun Palloseura, It. Pitkäkatu 54 A 7, 20700 Turku 70.
League: 1928, 1939, 1941, 1945, 1949, 1968, 1971, 1972, 1975 (9).
Cup: – .

VALKEAKOSKEN HAKA
Founded: 1932.
Colours: White/black.
Stadium: Tehtaankentä (5,000).
Club address: Valkeakosken Haka, YPOY, Valke PL 44, 37601 Valkeakoski.
League: 1960, 1962, 1965, 1977 (4).
Cup: 1955, 1959, 1960, 1963, 1969, 1977, 1982, 1985 (8 – record).

FRANCE

The shock relegation of troubled Saint-Etienne in 1984 had apparently left a void in the French first division. Les Verts had dominated for so long that it was hard to believe anyone else could immediately pick up their mantle. But that is exactly what Aime Jacquet's Bordeaux achieved as they not only retained the league title but reached the semi-finals of the European Champions' Cup.

Bordeaux were blessed with several of the key players from the French team who won the European championship in the summer of 1984, defender Patrick

Battiston and midfielders Alain Giresse and Jean Tigana in particular. But they also demonstrated that they had ambition by paying out a French record £1.5 million before the season began for the Portuguese star Fernando Chalana, from Benfica. Chalana had been outstanding in the European finals. So it was ironic that he was one of Bordeaux's few notes of failure in an otherwise outstanding season. Chalana's troubles began when he was injured in a pre-season match. He missed not only the friendly match with his old club Benfica, which was part of the transfer deal, but the entire first half of the season. Then, when he did at last appear, he was soon complaining that the others were refusing to pass him the ball and he would have to get away.

Most championship-winning teams look back on their season and can see that they benefited from suffering little trouble with injuries. But that was certainly not true with Bordeaux. Not only was Chalana's fitness a problem, but injuries robbed them at various stages of the services of both Giresse and Tigana – indeed Tigana was also suspended when the club accused him, wrongly, of faking an injury in protest at their failure to allow him a lucrative transfer to Italy or Spain. Bordeaux's team, however, proved bigger than the sum of its individuals, and so they were well on the way to retaining their title before they met their first defeat – 2-1 away to Lens – in their unlucky thirteenth game of the campaign.

But generally Bordeaux raised their game when faced by a challenge. A typical example was the away match against their most dangerous pursuers, Nantes, at the end of January. Bordeaux had only just returned from a tiring but lucrative trip to Japan. Yet they produced a superb holding performance, and collected both points thanks to a thirty-fifth minute goal from their former West German international spearhead, Dieter Müller. With veteran goal-keeper Dominique Dropsy belying his name at the other end, Bordeaux emerged with their lead enhanced.

A month later Chalana made his league debut in a 1-0 win over Marseille. Equally importantly, that same day Nantes lost 1-0 to Auxerre when under-21 international Basile Boli put in the only goal with his fist with referee Biguet unsighted – much to the fury of Nantes coach Claude Suaudeau.

There was more drama in March, with Bordeaux back at the centre of it. First came a hat-trick for Dieter Müller in the 4-0 league win over Bastia, but then he missed a penalty in the home first leg of the Champions' Cup quarter-final against the Soviet side, Dnepr. The result was a 1-1 draw, and Bordeaux were clearly going to be hard pressed to reach the last four. It would have been a stiff challenge anyway, without all the problems created for the French champions in the Soviet Union. They had upset the authorities by insisting on travelling with an Air France charter flight rather than by using Aeroflot. So, when they got as far as Kiev, they were met by a Soviet refusal to let them fly further because of bad weather.

Dnepropetrovsk is one of those Soviet cities closed to foreigners, and so the match was set for Krivoi Rog in the Ukraine. But it wasn't until after a day of arguments, protests, threats and appeals to UEFA that it was confirmed the match would go ahead. Even then Bordeaux had to travel on to Krivoi Rog on the morning of the match. Football trips to the Soviet Union have become notable over the years for the problems created by local bureaucracy. West Ham, Liverpool and the Greek national team all have tales to tell which rival that of Bordeaux.

The difference in this case was that Bordeaux came away, against all the odds, with a result. A late equaliser by Thierry Tusseau sent the match into extra time at 1-1 and the French then won the penalty shoot-out 5-3. Chalana was the hero for once, converting the fifth Bordeaux penalty with his 'wrong' right foot to send coach Jacquet running into the dressing rooms to find club president Claude Bez, who hadn't dared watch.

In the semi-finals, Bordeaux lost 3-2 on aggregate to Juventus. But their 2-0 victory at home in the rough-and-tumble return match left their pride intact as they surged on to complete their league championship victory. Bordeaux finished three points clear of Nantes, who not only lost out in the title race, but also lost their best player when international defender Maxime Bossis decided, at the season's end, to leave for relegated Racing Club of Paris. They have filled the gap by signing fellow international Yvon Le Roux, whose last game for his old club Monaco saw the Monegasque club beat Paris Saint-Germain 1-0 in the Cup Final. Bernard Genghini scored the only goal in the fourteenth minute, a welcome appearance in the limelight for a fine player whose international career has been restricted because of the presence in the French midfield of the likes of Tigana, Giresse and Michel Platini. Monaco had finished third in the league so their success was good news for Metz. The original French places in the 1985–86 UEFA Cup had gone to Nantes and Monaco. Auxerre were added to fill a gap when English clubs were banned by UEFA, and Monaco's 'defection' to the Cup-winners' Cup thus permitted Metz to take the vacant UEFA Cup place.

At the other end of the table, Racing Paris and Tours went down, along with unlucky Rouen. They took part in a play-off with second division Rennes, and lost their first division place on a penalty shoot-out.

1984–85 League Table

	P	W	D	L	F	A	Pts
Bordeaux	38	25	9	4	70	27	59
Nantes	38	24	8	6	62	32	56
Monaco	38	18	12	8	65	28	48
Auxerre	38	18	11	9	53	39	47
Metz	38	18	9	11	53	39	45
Toulon	38	19	6	13	46	37	44
Lens	38	16	8	14	57	43	40
Sochaux	38	12	14	12	56	43	38
Brest	38	11	14	13	50	51	36
Laval	38	12	12	14	39	52	36
Toulouse	38	11	13	14	43	49	35
Nancy	38	12	10	16	52	54	34
Paris SG	38	13	7	18	58	73	33
Bastia	38	11	10	17	39	68	32
Lille	38	9	13	16	37	45	31
Strasbourg	38	9	13	16	47	57	31
Marseille	38	13	5	20	51	67	31
Rouen	38	8	13	17	28	46	29
Tours	38	9	11	18	44	66	29
RC Paris	38	9	8	21	32	56	26

Cup final: Monaco 1, Paris Saint-Germain 0.
Top scorer: Vahid Halilhodzic (Nantes) 28.

AUXERRE
Founded: 1905.
Colours: White/blue.
Stadium: Abbé-Deschamps (16,500).
Club address: Association de la Jeunesse Auxerroise, Stade Abbé-Deschamps, Route de Vaux, 89000 Auxerre.
League: – .
Cup: – .

BASTIA
Founded: 1963.
Colours: All blue.
Stadium: Furiani (Stade Armand Cesari – 12,000).
Club address: Sporting Étoile Club Bastia, BP 640, 20200 Furiani, Corsica.
League: – .
Cup: 1981.
UEFA Cup: Runners-up in 1978.

BORDEAUX
Founded: 1881.
Colours: Blue/white.
Stadium: Stade Municipal (30,000).
Club address: Girondins de Bordeaux, 347 Bd Wilson, 33200 Bordeaux.
League: 1950, 1984, 1985 (3).
Cup: 1941.

LAVAL
Founded: 1902.
Colours: Orange/black.
Stadium: Francis Le Basser (18,000).
Club address: Stade Lavallois, 51 rue Jeanne d'Arc, 53008 Laval, BP 477.
League: – .
Cup: – .

LENS
Founded: 1906.
Colours: Gold/red.
Stadium: Félix-Bollaert (40,000).
Club address: Racing Club de Lens, Stade Félix-Bollaert, 62300 Lens.
League: – .
Cup: – .

LYON
Founded: 1950.
Colours: Red/blue.
Stadium: Stade Gerland (50,000).
Club address: Olympique Lyonnais, 3 rue Louis Broussas, 69007 Lyon.
League: – .
Cup: 1964, 1967, 1973 (3).

MARSEILLE
Founded: 1899.
Colours: All white.
Stadium: Stade Vélodrome (50,000).
Club address: Olympique Marseille, Stade Vélodrome, 3 Bd Michelet, 13008 Marseille.
League: 1929, 1937, 1948, 1971, 1972 (5).
Cup: 1924, 1926, 1927, 1935, 1938, 1943, 1969, 1972, 1976 (9 – record).

MONACO
Founded: 1924.
Colours: Red and white diagonal halves/white.
Stadium: Stade Louis II (11,000).
Club address: Association Sportive de Monaco, Stade Louis II, Avenue de Fontvieille, MC 98000 Monaco.
League: 1961, 1963, 1978 (3).
Cup: 1960, 1963, 1980, 1982, 1985 (5).

METZ
Founded: 1932.
Colours: Claret/white.
Stadium: Saint-Symphorien (25,000).
Club address: Football Club de Metz, 68 Bl de Saint-Symphorien, 57050 Longeville-les-Metz.
League: – .
Cup: 1984.

NANCY-LORRAINE
Founded: 1967.
Colours: All white with red trimmings.
Stadium: Stade Marcel Picot (37,000).
Club address: Association Sportive Nancy-Lorraine, Parc de Haye, Velaine en Haye, 54840 Gondreville.
League: – .
Cup: 1978.

NANTES
Founded: 1943.
Colours: Yellow/green.
Stadium: Stade de la Beaujoire (51,287 – built for the 1984 European championship finals).
Club address: Football Club de Nantes, Centre Sportif de la Jonelière, 44240 La Chapelle sur Erdre.
League: 1965, 1966, 1973, 1977, 1980, 1983 (6).
Cup: 1979.

NICE
Founded: 1924.
Colours: Red and black stripes/black.
Stadium: Stade Municipal du Ray (30,000).

Club address: Olympique Gymnaste Club de Nice, Parc des Sports de l'Ouest, 181 route de Grenoble, 06200 Nice.
League: 1951, 1952, 1956, 1959 (4).
Cup: 1952 and 1954.

NÎMES
Founded: 1932.
Colours: Red/white.
Stadium: Stade Jean Bouin (14,000).
Club address: Olympique Nîmes, Bar de l'Industrie, 17 Bd Courbet, 30.000 Nîmes.
League: – .
Cup: – .

PARIS SAINT-GERMAIN
Founded: 1973.
Colours: White with red and blue trimmings/red.
Stadium: Parc des Princes (47,700).
Club address: Football Club de Paris Saint-Germain, 30 rue Bergère, 75009 Paris.
League: – .
Cup: 1982, 1983.

REIMS
Founded: 1931.
Colours: Red/white.
Stadium: Stade Auguste Delaune (25,000).
Club address: Stade de Reims, 6 rue Buirette, 51100 Reims.
League: 1949, 1953, 1955, 1958, 1960, 1962 (6).
Cup: 1950, 1958.
Champions' Cup: Runners-up in 1956 and 1959.

RENNES
Founded: 1901.
Colours: Red/black.
Stadium: Stade de la Route de Lorient (25,000).
Club address: Stade Rennes, 111 Route de Lorient, 35000 Rennes.
League: – .
Cup: 1965, 1971.

ROUEN
Founded: 1899.
Colours: Red/white.
Stadium: Robert Diochon (22,000).
Club address: Football Club Rouen, Stade Robert Diochon, 48 Avenue des Canadiens, 76140 Petit Quevilly.
League: – .
Cup: – .

SAINT-ETIENNE
Founded: 1920.
Colours: Green/white.
Stadium: Stade Geoffroy-Guichard (47,836).
Club address: Association Sportive de Saint-Etienne, Stade Geoffroy-Guichard, 32 rue de la Tour, 42000 Saint-Etienne.
League: 1957, 1964, 1967, 1968, 1969, 1970, 1974, 1975, 1976, 1981 (10).
Cup: 1962, 1968, 1970, 1974, 1975, 1977 (6)
Champions' Cup: Runners-up in 1976.

SOCHAUX
Founded: 1928.
Colours: Yellow/blue.
Stadium: Stade Bonal (17,000).
Club address: F C Sochaux-Montbéliard, Bungalow du Stade Bonal, 25200 Montbéliard.
League: 1935, 1938.
Cup: 1937.

STRASBOURG
Founded: 1906.
Colours: Blue/white.
Stadium: Stade de la Meinau (48,969).
Club address: Racing Club de Strasbourg, Stade de la Meinau, 12 rue de l'Extenwoerth, 67100 Strasbourg.
League: 1979.
Cup: 1951, 1966.

TOULOUSE
Founded: 1937.
Colours: Mauve/white.
Stadium: Stadium Municipal (35,000).
League: – .
Cup: 1957.

GREECE

PAOK of Salonika made sure of Greek league title for only the second time in their history when they drew 0–0 away against Panionios on the penultimate day of the season. That same afternoon outgoing champions Panathinaikos were held 2–2 at home by bottom club Pierikos, and thus abandoned all hope of hanging on to their championship. But, looking back, Panathinaikos' Polish coach Jacek Gmoch had no doubt about the turning point in the season: the day in mid–January when halfway leaders PAOK came to Athens and beat the defending champions 1–0 with a goal by Paprica. In the terrace violence and street fighting which followed that game sixteen people were hurt and eleven arrested , but PAOK never looked back. A couple of defeats later on – 3–0 away to Salonika rivals Aris and 2–1 against Olympiakos Piraeus when goalkeeper Steregudias was carried off – set the alarm bells ringing. But

Panathinaikos then obligingly lost 1–0 away to Ethnikos, so PAOK thus remained two points clear.

The problem for Panathinaikos was their inconsistency. They reached the semi–finals of the Champions' Cup, and appeared to possess by far the most talented squad of individuals – with Yugoslav sweeper or midfielder Velimir Zajec, Argentine midfielder Juan Ramon Rocha and new attacking star Dimitrios Saravakos, who cost a Greek record £350,000 from Panionios last year. But they dropped 'silly' points – though one could hardly blame Rocha, who played some superb creative football despite having a prison sentence hanging over him for much of the season. Rocha was born in Buenos Aires, and joined Panathinaikos claiming Greek ancestry which allowed him to evade player import restrictions, in 1979. He took the name of 'Boublis' until rival clubs Olympiakos and AEK protested that Rocha's papers were not in order. After a string of federation and Sports Ministry inquiries, the case eventually came to court in January. Rocha was accused of passport offences and sentenced to fourteen months in jail, suspended pending appeal. This wasn't heard until just before the end of the season when an absolute discharge was substituted for the jail term.

That came too late to lift spirits at Panathinaikos when they faced Liverpool in the Champions' Cup semi-finals, but did mean they gained new heart to beat league title usurpers PAOK in the cup semi-finals. Panathinaikos at one stage boasted average attendances of 36,800, which were topped only by Olympiakos with 40,200. But Olympiakos' fans slipped away as it became clear, towards the end of the season, that they would be out of the frame in both league and cup – where they were beaten 3–1 on aggregate in the eighth-finals by Panathinaikos.

Olympiakos' hero for most of the season was national team goalkeeper Nikos Sarganis. An outspoken character – he criticised many of the foreign imports as being 'paid too much to kick too much' – he also established himself as Olympiakos' penalty-taker. It was Sarganis who scored, from the spot, the match-winner in the 2–1 victory over PAOK in February. He also scored again with a penalty in the cup defeat by Panathinaikos. If only Olympiakos' attack had been as consistent. But the Austrian World Cup forward Kurt Welzl was a disappointment, after whetting the fans' appetite with a hat-trick in a pre-season friendly against PAOK.

The most effective spearhead in the championship was, once again, Tomas Mavros of AEK. For several years AEK have tried, in vain, to give Mavros the sort of support up front which would help restore the championship for the first time since 1979. The solution this past season was to sign Marton Esterhazy, the Hungarian international, from Honved. He cost £110,000 but the AEK fans soon judged it money well spent after he made the winner for Mavros away against Olympiakos in one of his first games. Esterhazy also came close a couple of times, and was unlucky to have a penalty appeal refused when he appeared to be fouled in the box. Not to be outdone, Mavros then scored all five goals in AEK's 5–2 defeat of Egaleo and was unchallenged as top scorer with twenty-seven goals at the end of the season.

Sadly, the Greek game continues to be racked by crowd violence. Apart from the Panathinaikos-PAOK trouble referred to here, there were a string of other incidents. AEK fans went wild after a 4–1 defeat away to Larissa, damaging cars, and in another fracas Panathinaikos' players became embroiled in a fight with OFI fans.

1984–85 League Table

	P	W	D	L	F	A	Pts
PAOK	30	19	8	3	54	26	46
Panathinaikos	30	17	9	4	61	30	43
AEK	30	16	11	3	58	29	43
Olympiakos	30	17	8	5	53	23	42
Iraklis	30	19	3	8	59	33	41
Larissa	30	14	7	9	55	35	35
Aris Salonika	30	8	14	8	38	37	30
Panionios	30	9	12	9	34	40	30
Ethnikos	30	11	5	14	35	47	27
OFI	30	10	6	14	46	49	26
Apollon	30	9	7	14	30	40	25
Kalamaria	30	9	6	15	24	38	24
Doxa	30	8	6	16	33	42	22
Panahaiki	30	8	5	17	26	51	21
Egaleo	30	3	7	20	28	66	13
Pierikos	30	3	6	21	29	77	12

Cup final: Larissa 4, PAOK 1.
Top scorer: Tomas Mavros (AEK) 27 goals.

A E K
Founded: 1924.
Colours: Yellow/black.
Stadium: AEK Stadium (35,000).
Club address: AEK Athens, Heiden 4, Athens.
League: 1939, 1940, 1963, 1968, 1971, 1978, 1979 (7).
Cup: 1932, 1939, 1949, 1950, 1956, 1966, 1978, 1983 (8).

ARIS SALONIKA
Founded: 1914.
Colours: Yellow/black.
Stadium: Harilaon (30,000).
Club address: Aris Salonika, Vas. Olgas 99 A, Salonika.
League: 1928, 1932, 1946 (3).
Cup: 1970.

ETHNIKOS
Founded: 1925.
Colours: Blue/white.
Stadium: Karaiskaki (42,000).
Club address: Ethnikos, Vas. Sofias 105, Piraeus.
League: – .
Cup: 1933.

IRAKLIS
Founded: 1908.
Colours: Blue/white.
Stadium: Kautatzogleou (45,000).
Club address: Iraklis, Pavlou Mela 33, Salonika.

League: – .
Cup: 1976.

LARISSA
Founded: 1964.
Colours: Maroon/white.
Stadium: Alkazar (25,000).
Club address: Larissa FC, Larissa.
League – .
Cup: 1985.

O F I
Founded: 1925.
Colours: Black and white/white.
Stadium: Demotikou (13,500).
Club address: O F I Crete, Iraklion, Crete.
League: – .
Cup: – .

OLYMPIAKOS
Founded: 1925.
Colours: Red and white stripes/white.
Stadium: Karaiskaki (42,000).
Club address: Olympiakos, Konturiotou 138, Piraeus.
League: 1931, 1933, 1934, 1936, 1937, 1938, 1947, 1948, 1951, 1954, 1956, 1957, 1958, 1959, 1966, 1967, 1973, 1974, 1975, 1980, 1981, 1982, 1983 (23 – record).
Cup: 1947, 1951, 1952, 1953, 1954, 1957, 1958, 1959, 1960, 1961, 1963, 1965, 1968, 1971, 1973, 1975, 1980 (17 – record).

PANATHINAIKOS
Founded: 1908.
Colours: Green/white.
Stadium: Panathinaikos (25,000).
Club address: Panathinaikos Armatolon-Klefton 47, Athens.
League: 1930, 1949, 1953, 1960, 1961, 1962, 1964, 1965, 1969, 1970, 1972, 1977, 1984 (13).
Cup: 1940, 1948, 1955, 1967, 1969, 1977, 1982, 1984 (8).
World Club Cup : Runners-up in 1971.
Champions' Cup: Runners-up in 1971.

PANIONIOS
Founded: 1890.
Colours: Red/blue.
Stadium: Neo Smurnis (25,000).
Club address: Panionios, Ioannou Hrisostomou 1, Nea Smyrni, Athens.
League: – .
Cup: 1979.

P A O K
Founded: 1926.
Colours: Black and white/black.
Stadium: Toumpas Stadium (40,000).
Club address: P A O K, Agias Sofias 32, Salonika.
League: 1976, 1985.
Cup: 1972, 1974.

HOLLAND

Ajax Amsterdam won the Dutch league for the twenty-second time in all, the third time in four years, and the fifth time in seven years, despite sacking coach Aad de Mos at a vital stage of the run-in and at a time when PSV Eindhoven and Feyenoord were breathing down their necks. These three giants of the modern Dutch game had all spent heavily last summer. Ajax signed the veteran Belgian sweeper Walter Meeuws, even though a suspension for match-fixing would not expire until the middle of the season; Feyenoord signed one-time Ajax winger Simon Tahamata, another match-fixing culprit from Standard Liège; PSV bought goalkeeper Hans Van Breukelen home from Nottingham Forest, and strengthened their attack with the Danish forward Kenneth Brylle from Anderlecht. With Kees Kist back from France at his old club, AZ'67 Alkmaar, and Johnny Rep lining up for a Feyenoord now deprived of the retired Johan Cruyff, a tight finish to the season was in prospect.

There was also plenty of controversy. Feyenoord set that particular ball rolling after only two months of the season when they parted company with coach Thijs Libregts. A few weeks later they fell further into the doldrums when they lost 3-1 at home to Ajax, and forty-five fans were arrested in scuffles around the stadium and in the centre of Rotterdam.

Ajax were now in the championship driving seat, and underlined the point with the manner of their 7-0 victory over manager-less Roda. Two goals fell to young striker Marco Van Basten, and two more to skipper and midfield general Dick Schoenaker. A fortnight later, however, and it was the turn of Ajax to be caught in disarray as they lost 4-1 at home against PSV. Rene Van der Gijp, the Dutchman brought home only a few weeks earlier from Belgium's Lokeren, scored twice to secure victory. The first PSV goal, however, had been scored by Ernie Brandts, one of Holland's heroes from the 1978 World Cup, and who was being watched by Manchester United manager Ron Atkinson. Thus, at the half-way stage, PSV led Ajax by a whisker. The suspense was to last longer than intended. The holiday break was forcibly extended by bad weather so it wasn't until mid-February that the leaders got back into their stride.

Meeuws made his debut for Ajax in a 4-0 win over Sparta Rotterdam, but was injured after half an hour and substituted; Feyenoord brought Tahamata back into action in an indoor tournament which was, ironically, won by his original club Ajax. Volendam lost coach Leo Beenhakker to the national team after Holland boss Rinus Michels suffered a heart attack. Prodigal son Johan Neeskens signed for Groningen to return to the Dutch scene for the first time in eleven years since setting out on a round-the-world career with Barcelona and New York Cosmos.

Now it was PSV's turn to start throwing away points – in particular a 2-2 draw away to Feyenoord when they were at one stage leading 2-0 until Willy Van de Kerkhof was carried off suffering from concussion. PSV did beat Ajax in the cup, and put seven goals past Haarlem in the league, while Ajax lost at home to Neesken's Groningen. But Ajax were now two points up on PSV, and with a game in hand.

It was at this point that Ajax's internal unrest exploded into public view. Coach de Mos, who had been in charge since 1982, had slowly been losing the confidence of his players. Above all he fell out with the talented Van Basten, who said he would never play another game under de Mos. At the end of April, de Mos caught flu and was away from training for a week. In his absence assistant 'Spitz' Kohn decided to recall both Van Basten and the controversial Meeuws, who had also been axed by de Mos. However, de Mos turned up on the Saturday morning and promptly told Van Basten and Meeuws that they were going straight back among the reserves. It was a bad weekend all round. The club doctor was taken ill and died while out jogging, and the team lost that weekend's game against Haarlem by 1-0. For the players it was the last straw. They asked to meet president Ton Harmsen and were granted permission to vote on the future of de Mos. Only seven of the nineteen first-team squad backed the coach, and once the board were informed a parting of the ways was swiftly arranged.

Such unrest should have opened the way for PSV. But they had lost form since five key players had received letters threatening their families. PSV's agreement of a £230,000 deal to buy Holland star Ruud Gullit was then leaked to the media, which duly took the wind out of Feyenoord's briefly reviving sails. Ajax beat them 4-2, and then celebrated their title with a 5-2 thrashing of Volendam. Van Basten had the last laugh of the season by scoring all five goals.

1984–85 League Table

	P	W	D	L	F	A	Pts
Ajax Amsterdam	34	24	6	4	93	46	54
PSV Eindhoven	34	17	14	3	84	33	48
Feyenoord	34	21	6	7	87	51	48
Sparta Rotterdam	34	17	8	9	62	52	42
Groningen	34	15	11	8	57	43	41
Den Bosch	34	10	16	8	45	32	36
Fortuna Sittard	34	14	6	14	49	48	34
Twente Enschede	34	12	10	12	60	64	34
Haarlem	34	12	9	13	51	57	33
FC Utrecht	34	13	6	15	47	42	32
Roda JC	34	11	10	13	51	59	32
AZ'67 Alkmaar	34	8	14	12	59	70	30
Excelsior	34	9	12	13	47	51	30
MVV Maastricht	34	10	9	15	39	55	29
Go Ahead Eagles	34	11	6	17	46	59	28
Volendam	34	9	7	18	37	67	25
NAC Breda	34	7	5	22	36	67	25
PEC Zwolle	34	4	9	21	34	86	17

Cup final: FC Utrecht 1, Helmond Sport 0.
Top scorer: Marco Van Basten (Ajax) 22 goals.

A Z '67
Founded: 1967.
Colours: Red/white.
Stadium: Sportpark (18,500).
Club address: AZ '67 Alkmaar, Sportpark, Alkmaarderhout, Sportlaan (postbus 104), 1800 AC Alkmaar.
League: 1981.
Cup: 1978, 1981, 1982.
UEFA Cup: Runners-up in 1981.

AJAX AMSTERDAM
Founded: 1900.
Colours: Red and white/white.
Stadium: De Meer (29,380).
Club address: Ajax, Stadion De Meer, Middenweg 401 (postbus 41885), 1098 AV Amsterdam.
League: 1918, 1919, 1931, 1932, 1934, 1937, 1939, 1947, 1957, 1960, 1966, 1967, 1968, 1970, 1972, 1973, 1977, 1979, 1980, 1982, 1983, 1985 (22 – record).
Cup: 1917, 1943, 1961, 1967, 1970, 1971, 1972, 1979, 1983 (9 – record).
World Club Cup: 1972.
Champions' Cup: 1971, 1972, 1973. Runners-up in 1969.
SuperCup: 1972, 1973.

FEYENOORD
Founded: 1908.
Colours: Red and white halves/black.
Stadium: Feyenoord (63,911).
Club address: S C Feyenoord, Feyenoord-stadion, Olympiaweg 50, 3077 AL Rotterdam.
League: 1924, 1928, 1936, 1938, 1940, 1961, 1962, 1965, 1969, 1971, 1974, 1984 (12).
Cup: 1930, 1935, 1965, 1969, 1980, 1984 (6).
World Club Cup: 1970.
Champions' Cup: 1970.
UEFA Cup: 1974.

GO AHEAD EAGLES
Founded: 1971.
Colours: Red/yellow.
Stadium: De Adelaarshorst (18,000).
Club address: Go Ahead Eagles, De Adelaarshorst, Vetkampstraat (postbus 184), 7400 AD Deventer.
League: 1917, 1922, 1930 and 1933 (all as plain Go Ahead).
Cup: – .

GRONINGEN
Founded: 1971.
Colours: White/green.
Stadium: Oosterpark (16,500).
Club address: F C Groningen, Oosterparkstadion, Zaagmuldersweg (postbus 1399), 9701 BJ Groningen.

League: – .
Cup: – .

HAARLEM
Founded: 1889 (Reformed 1980).
Colours: Red/blue.
Stadium: Haarlem-stadion (18,000).
Club address: Haarlem, Haarlem-stadion, Sportweg 8, 2024 CN Haarlem-noord.
League: 1946.
Cup: 1902 and 1912.

P S V EINDHOVEN
Founded: 1913.
Colours: Red/white.
Stadium: PSV-stadion (27,000).
Club address: PSV Eindhoven, PSV-stadion, Frederiklaan 10a, 5615 NH Eindhoven
League: 1929, 1935, 1951, 1963, 1975, 1976, 1978 (7).
Cup: 1950, 1974, 1976 (3).
UEFA Cup: 1978.

RODA
Founded: 1914.
Colours: Yellow/black.
Stadium: Sportpark (25,000).
Club address: Roda JC, Gemeentelijk Sportpark Kerkrade, Parkstraat 4 (postbus 400), 6460 AK Kerkrade.
League: 1956 (as Rapid JC).
Cup: – .

SPARTA ROTTERDAM
Founded: 1888.
Colours: Red, white/black.
Stadium: Spangen (29,687).
Club address: R V & A V Sparta Rotterdam, Spangen-stadion, Spartastraat 7 (postbus 1802), 3000 BV Rotterdam.
League: 1909, 1911, 1912, 1913, 1915, 1959 (6).
Cup: 1958, 1962, 1966 (3).

TWENTE
Founded: 1965.
Colours: All red.
Stadium: Diekman (20,500).
Club address: FC Twente '65, Stadion Diekman, J J van Deinselaan 30, 7541 PE Enschede.
League: – .
Cup: 1977.

UTRECHT
Founded: 1970.
Colours: Red/white.
Stadium: Galgenwaard (20,000).
Club address: F C Utrecht, Galgenwaard-stadion, Herculesplein 331 (postbus 8250), 3584 AA Utrecht.
League: 1958 (as DOS Utrecht – the same year that Velox, the other 1970 merger partners, were amateur champions of Holland).
Cup: 1985.

WILLEM II
Founded: 1896.
Colours: Red, white/blue.
Stadium: Sportpark (20,000).
Club address: S C Tilburg Willem II, Gemeentelijk Sportpark, Goirlseweg 34 (postbus 235), 5000 AE Tilburg.
League: 1916, 1952 and 1955 (3).
Cup: 1944, 1963.

HUNGARY

The 1984–85 season was one of celebration for Hungarian football. After a wretched sequence of seasons in which failure on the pitch at international level was accompanied by match-fixing scandals in domestic competition it appeared that the game had at last emerged from a long, dark tunnel.

The first cause for rejoicing was the achievement of the national team in becoming the first European side to negotiate successfully the qualifying rounds for the 1986 World Cup and ensure their tickets for Mexico. Hungary won all their group matches against Austria, Cyprus and Holland, except for the last one. But even that 1-0 home defeat by the Dutch did little to spoil the new mood of optimism, since the Hungarians had long since known they were bound for the finals.

The second international achievement was that of unfashionable Videoton, from the old capital of Szekesfehrvar, in reaching the final of the UEFA Cup. They were the first Hungarian team to reach a European club final since Ferencvaros lost to Dynamo Kiev in the Cup-winners' Cup showdown a decade earlier. Along the way Videoton collected scalps which became ever more remarkable with each succeeding round. Dukla Prague were the first-round victims, then Paris Saint-Germain, Partizan Belgrade, Manchester United (after a penalty shoot-out) and Zeljeznicar of Yugoslavia in the semi-finals.

Even after Videoton, now rank outsiders, lost 3-0 at home to Real Madrid in the first leg of the final, they refused to give up. In the Estadio Bernabeu, in front of 85,000 Spanish fans who had come only to celebrate, the Hungarians inflicted one of Madrid's rare home defeats in European competition. The score – 1-0 with a late strike from Majer – wasn't enough to overturn the aggregate. But at least Videoton repaired their pride, and coach Ferenc Kovacs admitted: 'I never believed my boys could play so well under so much pressure.' Unfortunately for Videoton, while they were soaking up the pressure all round Europe, the pace had been made too hot for them at home by defending champions Honved. As in the previous campaign of 1983–84, Videoton led the league at half-way, only to see the title slip from their grasp.

Several clubs were still readjusting their personnel after the latest round of match-fixing trials when the season got under way. Chief among the clubs thus afflicted were Csepel. They drafted in former World Cup goalkeeper Jozsef Gelei in place of the disgraced Lajos Puskas (no relation to the fabulous Ferenc), and Gelei had to call up his own son to keep goal in place of suspended former national team keeper, Attila Kovacs.

Videoton's determination to go as far as possible in both domestic and European competition was illustrated as early as October when they came to Budapest to score a 1-0 victory over Honved and establish their league leadership and, at the winter break, they held a two-point advantage over Honved and Debrecen. They began again in the spring with a 3-1 win over Eger but a shock 1-0 home defeat by Pecs and then a 2-1 setback away to Raba ETO in Györ allowed Honved to overtake and move four points clear. That lead had been cut to two points when Honved went to Szekesfehrvar for what would obviously be the decisive match of the season. Detari put Honved ahead from an eleventh-minute penalty; Szabo equalised for Videoton with twenty minutes to go; but then, just when Videoton appeared poised to break through, so Dajka escaped at the other end for Honved's winner.

While Videoton had been bringing some fresh air to the title clashes, some famous old clubs were struggling at the wrong end of the table. Ferencváros sacked coach Geza Vincze after spending most of the season next to bottom, while Vasas Budapest – one-time Champions' Cup semi-finalists – brought old faithful Rudi Illovszky back out of semi-retirement in midseason to take over from Kalman Meszöly. Meszöly, a former World Cup star and national manager, was promptly snapped up as head coach by the Turkish federation.

It was also a season for anniversaries. Ferenc Puskas made one of his

1984–85 League Table

	P	W	D	L	F	A	Pts
Honved	30	20	6	4	63	25	46
Raba ETO Györ	30	15	6	9	57	49	36
Videoton	30	14	8	8	43	28	36
Zalaegerszeg	30	13	8	9	38	31	34
Vasas Budapest	30	10	11	9	56	44	31
Bekescsaba	30	12	6	12	42	53	30
Csepel	30	10	10	10	23	27	30
Debrecen	30	11	8	11	35	33	30
Haladás Szombathely	30	10	9	11	32	34	29
Ujpest Dozsa	30	10	8	12	37	35	28
Pecs	30	9	10	11	33	35	28
Tatabanya	30	11	6	13	44	47	28
Ferencváros	30	11	6	13	34	38	28
MTK/VM	30	11	5	14	44	45	27
Eger	30	10	5	15	26	42	25
Szeged	30	6	2	22	32	73	14

Cup final: Honved 5, Tatabanya 0.
Top scorer: Detari (Honved) and Kiprich (Tatabanya) 18 goals each.

occasional trips home to Budapest to join other past heroes such as Florian Albert at Honved's thirty-fifth birthday celebrations – though the army club clearly has a long way to go to match the hundredth anniversary celebrated by fans and players and officials of Ujpest. They may have been out of the prizes since winning the cup in 1983, but in Andras Töröcsik they still boasted the most gifted player in Hungary, until his summer sale to France.

CSEPEL
Founded: 1912.
Colours: Red/blue.
Stadium: Csepel (16,000).
Club address: Csepel Sport Club, Béké tér 1, 1212 Budapest.
League: 1942, 1943, 1948, 1959 (4).
Cup: – .

DIÓSGYÖR
Founded: 1910.
Colours: Red/white.
Stadium: Karl-Marx stadium (30,000).
Club address: Diósgyöri Vasgyárak Testgyakorló Köre, Pf 515, Marx Károly út 61, 3510 Miskolc.
League: – .
Cup: 1977, 1980.

FERENCVÁROS
Founded: 1899.
Colours: Green/white.
Stadium: Important matches in the Nepstadion (71,000).
Club address: Ferencvárosi Torna Club, Üllöi u. 129, 1091 Budapest.
League: 1903, 1905, 1907, 1909, 1910, 1911, 1912, 1913, 1926, 1927, 1928, 1932, 1934, 1938, 1940, 1941, 1949, 1963 (spring), 1964, 1967, 1968, 1976, 1981 (23 – record).
Cup: 1913, 1922, 1927, 1928, 1933, 1935, 1942, 1943, 1944, 1958, 1972, 1974, 1976, 1978 (14 – record).
Cup-winners' Cup: Runners-up in 1975.
Fairs' Cup: 1965. Runners-up in 1968.

HALADÁS
Founded: 1919.
Colours: Green/white.
Stadium: Szombathely (17,000).
Club address: Haladás Vasutas SE, Rohonci ut 3, 9700 Szombathely.
League: – .
Cup: – .

HONVED
Founded: 1949.
Colours: Red/white.
Stadium: Honved (30,000).
Club address: Budapest Honved SE, Pf.308, 1393 Budapest 62.

League: 1950, 1950 (autumn), 1952, 1954, 1955, 1956, 1980, 1984, 1985 (9).
Cup: 1964, 1985 (2).

M T K / V M
Founded: 1888.
Colours: Blue/white.
Stadium: MTK-stadion (20,000).
Club address: Magyar Testgyakorlók Köre-Vörös Meteor SK, Szánto B.ú. 5a, Pf. 210, 1391 Budapest.
League: 1904, 1908, 1914, 1917, 1918, 1919, 1920, 1921, 1922, 1923, 1924, 1925, 1929, 1936, 1937, 1951, 1953, 1958 (18).
Cup: 1910, 1911, 1912, 1914, 1923, 1925, 1932, 1952, 1968 (9).
Cup-winners' Cup: Runners-up in 1964.

RABA VASAS E T O
Founded: 1904.
Colours: Green/white.
Stadium: Györ (12,000).
Club address: Raba Vasas ETO, Nagy S.J.u. 31, 9027 Györ.
League: 1963, 1982, 1983 (3).
Cup: 1965, 1966, 1967, 1979 (4).

SIÓFOK BANYASZ
Founded: 1921.
Colours: Red/black.
Stadium: Siofok stadium (5,000).
Club address: Siofok Banyasz, Siófok, Aradi vertanuk tere.
League: –.
Cup: 1984

TATABANYA
Founded: 1910.
Colours: Blue/white.
Stadium: Tatabanya (17,000).
Club address: Tatabanyai Banyas SC, Sagvari u. 9, 2800 Tatabanya.
League: – .
Cup: – .

UPJEST
Founded: 1885.
Colours: Lilac/white.
Stadium: Ujpesti-stadion (25,000).
Club address: Ujpesti Dozsa SC, Eötvös u. 7, 1067 Budapest.
League: 1930, 1931, 1933, 1935, 1939, 1945 (spring), 1946, 1947, 1960, 1969, 1970 (spring), 1971, 1972, 1973, 1974, 1975, 1978, 1979 (18).
Cup: 1969, 1970, 1975, 1982, 1983 (5).
Fairs' Cup: Runners-up in 1979.

VASAS
Founded: 1911.

Colours: Red and blue stripes/blue.
Stadium: Vasas-stadion (20,000).
Club address: Vasas Sport Club, Faynu. 58, 1139 Budapest.
League: 1957 (spring), 1961, 1962, 1965, 1966, 1977 (6).
Cup: 1955, 1973.

VIDEOTON
Founded: 1941.
Colours: Red/blue.
Stadium: Sostoi (15,000).
Club address: Videoton Sport Club, Berenyi ut, 8001 Szekesfehervar.
League: – .
Cup: – .
UEFA Cup: Runners-up 1985.

ICELAND

The paths of Icelandic and British football frequently crossed during 1984, starting with the return of former Leicester and Southampton centre-half Tony Knapp as manager of the national team.

The most important administrative meeting of minds was Iceland's decision to copy the English system of three points for a win and two for a draw in league competition. The intention was to increase the emphasis on attacking football with the hope that more goals would result. Its effect in that area was virtually non-existent. The ten league clubs totalled 232 goals compared with 231 the previous year, with the old two-points-for-a-win system.

The second stage of contact with British football was in the World Cup, where Knapp recalled the foreign-based professionals to score a 1-0 win over Wales in Reykjavik. The only goal fell to the West German-based Magnus Bergs, while Icelandic ambition shone through all too clearly. As Wales manager Mike England said: 'There was only one team out there who wanted to win – and it wasn't us.'

Wales later had revenge when they beat Iceland 2-1 at Cardiff and there was also a 3-0 defeat against Scotland at Hampden, again in the World Cup qualifiers.

At European club level KR Reykjavik lost 0-3, 0-4 against Queen's Park Rangers in the first round of the 1984–85 UEFA Cup, and then Sheffield Wednesday manager Howard Wilkinson stole a march on a string of much more fashionable clubs throughout Europe when he signed Sigurdur Jonsson, the talented teenager from IA Akranes. Jonsson, now eighteen, is potentially the finest Icelandic player of all time. He made his league debut at fifteen, and his senior international debut against Malta in the last European championship at the age of sixteen years 251 days.

Certainly his skills have had much to do with the domination of Icelandic domestic football in the past couple of years by IA Akranes. They have won the league-and-cup double for the past two seasons, and the introduction of three-points-for-a-win just increased the gap between IA and the rest of the first division since they ended the 1984 campaign ten points clear of runners-up Valur.

IA conceded eighteen goals in their eighteen league games – a record which at the end of the season earned goalkeeper Bjarni Sigurdsson both the domestic Footballer of the Year award and also a transfer to Norway to join Brann of Bergen. Interestingly, runners-up Valur conceded two fewer goals than IA, but also scored nine fewer. Whereas both clubs lost four games, IA won twelve and drew only two, whereas Valur paid for their weakness up front since they won 'only' seven games, and also drew seven.

The biggest disappointments of the season were KA Akureyri. They had only just earned promotion, but quickly booked a return to the second division. Interestingly, they scored only one goal fewer, twenty-three, than second-placed Valur. But then, in a ten-team league the margin for error is so much smaller.

All-time record champions and cup-winners KR had a quiet season. Few of their players threatened to break into the national squad, and in the league they finished fourth. Even in the cup they suffered a surprise 3-1 defeat against Fram in the semi-finals, while IA Akranes were beating Throttur easily 2-0. Fram, who relied for goals on the league's ten-goal top scorer, Gudmundur Steinsson, finished sixth in the league and though beaten in the cup final, qualified for the Cup-winners' Cup by virtue of that IA Akranes 'double'.

1984 League Table

	P	W	D	L	F	A	Pts*
IA Akranes	18	12	2	4	33	18	38
Valur	18	7	7	4	24	16	28
IBK Keflavik	18	8	3	7	19	22	27
KR Reykjavik	18	6	7	5	20	23	25
Vikingur	18	6	6	6	29	28	24
Fram Reykjavik	18	6	4	8	23	22	22
Thor	18	6	4	8	25	25	22
Throttur	18	5	7	6	19	19	22
UBK Breidabliks	18	4	8	6	17	20	20
KA Akureyri	18	4	4	10	23	29	16

Cup final: IA Akranes 2, Fram 1.
Top scorer: Gudmundur Steinsson (Fram) 10 goals.
* Three points for a win.

FRAM
Founded: 1908.
Colours: Blue/white.
Stadium: Important games in the Laugardalsvöllur (14,800).
Club address: Fram FC, c/o Nökkvavogi 24, 104 Reykjavik.
Championship: 1913, 1914, 1915, 1916, 1917, 1918, 1921, 1922, 1923, 1925, 1939, 1946, 1947, 1962, 1972 (15).
Cup: 1970, 1973, 1979, 1980 (4).

I A AKRANES
Founded: 1946.
Colours: Orange/black.
Stadium: Akranessvöllur (3,000) but important matches in the Laugardals-völlur (Reykjavik – 14,800).

98

Club address: Idróttabandalap Akraness, c/o Vesturgötu 32, 300 Akranes.
Championship: 1951, 1953, 1954, 1957, 1958, 1960, 1970, 1974, 1975, 1977, 1983, 1984, (12).
Cup: 1978, 1982, 1983, 1984 (4).

I B K
Founded: 1956.
Colours: Yellow/blue.
Stadium: Keklavíkurvöllur (5,000).
Club address: Idróttabandalap Keflavíkur, c/o Heidarbraut 10, 230 Keflavik.
Championship: 1964, 1969, 1971, 1973 (4).
Cup: 1975.

I B V
Founded: 1946.
Colours: All white.
Stadium: Vestmannaeyjavöllur (2,000).
Club address: Idrottabandalap Vestmannaeyja FC, c/o Asbyrgi, 900 Vestmannaeyjar.
Championship: 1979.
Cup: 1968, 1972, 1981 (3).

K R
Founded: 1899.
Colours: Black and white stripes/black.
Stadium: Important matches in the Laugardalsvöllur (14,800).
Club address: Knattspyrnufélag Reykjavikur, c/o Laugalaek 12, 105 Reykjavik.
Championship: 1912, 1919, 1926, 1927, 1928, 1929, 1931, 1932, 1934, 1941, 1948, 1949, 1950, 1952, 1955, 1959, 1961, 1963, 1965, 1968 (20 – record).
Cup: 1960, 1961, 1962, 1963, 1964, 1966, 1967 (7 – record).

VALUR
Founded: 1911.
Colours: Red/white.
Stadium: Important matches in the Laugardalsvöllur (14,800).
Club address: Knattspyrnufelagid Valur, c/o P O Box 839, 101 Reykjavik.
Championship: 1930, 1933, 1935, 1936, 1937, 1938, 1940, 1942, 1943, 1944, 1945, 1956, 1966, 1967, 1976, 1978, 1980 (17).
Cup: 1965, 1974, 1976, 1977 (4).
Centre-forward Albertsson was the league's top scorer in the 1983 season with fourteen goals.

VIKINGUR
Founded: 1908.
Colours: Red and black stripes/black.
Stadium: Important matches in the Laugardalsvöllur (14,800).
Club address: Knattspyrnufelagid Vikingur, c/o Vesturbergi 63, 109 Reykjavik.
Championship: 1920, 1924, 1981, 1982 (4),
Cup: 1971.

ISRAEL

Maccabi of Haifa finished well in command of the 1984–85 Israeli league championship, with a five-point lead over runners-up Beitar Jerusalem. But early in the campaign the finishing order appeared likely to be the other way round, particularly after Beitar took over at the top of the table in mid-December. Maccabi Haifa lost 1–0 at home and Beitar seized their opportunity to squeeze a 1–0 victory away to Maccabi Petah-Tikvah.

Beitar's move perhaps did not receive the attention it might otherwise have gained because of events at around the same time at second division Hapoel Ramat Gan. They had not paid up several players transferred during the summer, and one obtained a court order – turning up at training along with two sequestration officials and collected shirts, boots, footballs and even goal nets in lieu of payment.

That was a further demonstration of the financial crisis afflicting Israeli domestic football – not that Maccabi Haifa had too many problems on this front. Their main problem was to reassert themselves in the league, which they quickly did. Beitar crashed 3–0 to Shimshon of Tel-Aviv, and Maccabi were back in the driving seat and moving four points clear. Beitar now began to falter, dropping points at home to make Haifa's task easier. Haifa did not always take advantage, though. Before the last game they had allowed Beitar within two points of the top, which threatened all their efforts since the Israelis now use the English system with three points for a victory to try to encourage a greater emphasis on attacking football.

In the end Haifa won their last match 2–0 at home to finish with sixty-five points from thirty games which – allowing of course for the change in the points system – was a record. Beitar finished as runners-up, with Shimshon Tel-Aviv slipping into third place ahead of Maccabi Petah-Tikvah. Maccabi Petah-Tikvah lost a lot of momentum in the closing rounds after stringing together half a dozen consecutive victories to turn themselves into an outside threat to the leaders during the spring.

Final Table

	P	W	D	L	F	A	Pts
Maccabi Haifa	30	20	5	5	57	20	65
Beitar Jerusalem	30	17	9	4	52	27	60
Shimshon Tel-Aviv	30	13	10	7	29	20	49
Maccabi P-T.	30	13	9	8	45	31	48
Hapoel Haifa	30	11	11	8	30	26	44
Hapoel P-T.	30	11	10	9	30	27	43
Maccabi Tel-Aviv	30	9	15	6	34	23	42
Maccabi Nathanya	30	9	11	10	54	40	38
Hapoel Tel-Aviv	30	9	11	10	31	32	38
Maccabi Yavne	30	8	12	10	34	38	36
Hapoel Kfar Saba	30	6	15	9	26	33	33
Maccabi Yaffo	30	8	9	13	30	40	33
Hapoel Beer Sheva	30	6	14	10	26	30	32
Beitar Tel-Aviv	30	7	10	13	28	43	31
Hapoel Lud	30	5	8	17	15	55	23
Hakoah Maccabi RG	30	2	13	15	17	52	19

Cup final: Beitar Jerusalem 1, Maccabi Haifa 0.
Top scorer: David Lavie (Maccabi Nathanya) 18 goals.

The clubs' rivalries failed to enthuse a majority of sports fans in Israel. Many clubs had difficulties putting together attendances of more than 1,000. A frequent attempt to boost crowds in the past had been the use of double-headers – two matches played one after the other in a major stadium. Several clubs have now gone further, with FA permission, and have experimented with triple-headers. The image of the game was not enhanced, either, by controversies over refereeing standards. In one notable incident a referee abandoned a cup tie after he was injured and, for reasons best known to himself, refused to allow either linesman to take his place. The referees' association supported him in a 'wise decision', but everyone else was highly critical.

As for the cup, the sixteen first division teams enter at a late stage of competition and are never, initially, drawn against each other. Ironically the one team to fail to make it beyond the first round proper were cup-holders Hapoel Lud (Lyd) who lost in a replay. Beitar took happy consolation for their league failure when they spoiled Maccabi Haifa's double bid with a 1–0 win in the final.

BEITAR JERUSALEM
Founded: 1924.
Colours: Yellow/black.
Stadium: YMCA (8,000).
Club address: Beitar Jerusalem, Mazia 2 st., Jerusalem 94563.
League: – .
Cup: 1976, 1979, 1985 (3).

HAPOEL TEL-AVIV
Founded: 1924.
Colours: All red.
Stadium: Bloomfield (20,000).
Club address: Hapoel Tel-Aviv, Brener 4 st., Tel-Aviv 61040.
League: 1934, 1935, 1936, 1938, 1943, 1957, 1966, 1969, 1981 (9).
Cup 1928, 1935, 1936, 1938, 1943, 1957, 1966, 1969, 1981 (9).

MACCABI HAIFA
Founded: 1924.
Colours: Green/white.
Stadium: Kyriat Haeem (20,000).
Club address: Maccabi (Haifa), P O Box 4109, Haifa 31040.
League: 1984, 1985.
Cup: 1962.

MACCABI NATANYA
Founded: 1939.
Colours: Yellow/black.
Stadium: Maccabi (10,000).
Club address: Maccabi (Natanya), P O Box 2242, Natanya 42122.
League: 1971, 1974, 1978, 1980, 1983 (5).
Cup: 1978.

MACCABI TEL-AVIV
Founded: 1906.
Colours: Yellow/black.
Stadium: Bloomfield (20,000).
Club address: Maccabi (Tel-Aviv), Hayarkon 291 st., Tel-Aviv 63504.
League: 1937, 1939, 1941, 1947, 1950, 1952, 1954, 1956, 1958, 1968, 1970, 1972, 1977, 1979 (14 – record).
Cup: 1929, 1930, 1933, 1941, 1946, 1947, 1954, 1955, 1958, 1959, 1964, 1965, 1967, 1970, 1977 (15 – record).

ITALY

For almost thirty years the millionaire Agnelli family, owners of Fiat, had dreamed of the day when 'their' club, Juventus, would be acclaimed champions of Europe, when the European Cup would be brought home to Turin. That dream, of course, became a nightmare on the evening of 29 May in the Heysel Stadium in Brussels after English hooligans rampaged across the terracing sending thirty-eight fans, thirty of them Italian, to their awful deaths. Some were asphyxiated in the crush, some were trampled underfoot. In view of the scenes which live television carried around Europe and the world, millions were shocked that the European Cup final should have been played.

The decision will forever remain controversial. But it is worthy of note that while the majority of television viewers appeared to find the playing of the match deplorable, most of those in the Heysel Stadium believed the decision to go ahead correct. Cancellation would have unleashed an even more terrible explosion of malevolence; by playing the final the authorities gained time to bring in police and army reinforcements; the crowd was kept in the ground and emergency services were comparatively unhindered. Also, the vast majority of the 50,000 crowd were kept in ignorance of the scale of the disaster until much, much later.

The Juventus players, French superstar Michel Platini in particular, were reluctant to go ahead with the match. But of course they played in the end and won with a penalty converted by the Frenchman after Liverpool defender Gary Gillespie had brought down Zbigniew Boniek. Television re-runs showed that the foul took place outside the penalty box. But it was what one might term a 'moral' penalty. Referee André Daina, a former Swiss international forward, later denied Liverpool a penalty for a trip on Ronnie Whelan. And so Juventus collected the European Champions' Cup. But there was no triumphant homecoming. The players and officials were all too well aware as they returned to Turin of the supporters who had gone out to watch a football match, and would never come back. Tarnished glory indeed.

The Juventus players were innocent pawns in the events in Brussels – a disaster which cast a long shadow back over what had been an eventful season in terms of 'mere' football. The summer of 1984 had seen top clubs engaged in a major spending spree to beat the incoming ban on foreign signings. Juventus had Platini and Boniek and were happy to stay with them. But Internazionale splashed out £3 million on the West German Karl-Heinz Rummenigge, Napoli paid a world record £6 million for Argentina's Diego Maradona (from Barcelona), and they were followed in by a host of other top names.

'Don't talk to me about some project for a European or world league,' said Milan's executive vice-president and former star Gianni Rivera. 'It's been organised already and it's called the Italian championship.'

Not all the big-money deals paid off. Brazil's World Cup captain Socrates was a major disappointment at Fiorentina; Scotland's Graeme Souness spoiled a superb season at Sampdoria by collecting a two-match ban right at the end for petulantly throwing down his shirt after being substituted; Mark Hateley began strongly for Milan, but then faded after injury and a contract dispute; Brazil's Zico, on the books of Udinese, was sentenced to eight months in jail plus a hefty fine – all imposed in his absence – for breaking currency export regulations.

Maradona took a while to adjust too, even though Naples is regarded as the 'most South American' of Italian cities. But the fans didn't have to wait long to see that massive fee justified – nor did the club, much to the delight of president Corrado Ferlaino.

When he set up the Maradona deal a string of leading banks shied clear of providing the initial funding. Clearly, they didn't know the Italian fan. Napoli's home attendances averaged well over 70,000 to bring in receipts of more than £11 million: almost twice the Maradona transfer fee. Napoli's 3-1 league win over Internazionale produced record league match takings of a staggering £550,000.

Inter, with Rummenigge and Irishman Liam Brady in the ranks, dropped points unnecessarily at inconvenient times. Thus they lost out to surprise packet Verona in the championship race, and were defeated controversially by Real Madrid in the UEFA Cup semi-finals. Inter's protest that international defender Giuseppe Bergomi had been forced out of the match after being struck by a marble, was virtually ignored.

Everyone had problems. Juventus suffered through the poor form of goalkeeper Stefano Tacconi early in the season, and centre-forward Paolo Rossi towards the end; Roma were without injured Brazilian schemer Paolo Roberto Falcao for virtually the entire term; and neighbours Lazio couldn't put together performances to match the ambition of president Giorgio Chinaglia and were therefore relegated.

With the big names all dropping points, unfashionable Verona came through to win the championship for the first time in their history. They made certain with one game to go in their thirty-match programme. In the vital twenty-ninth round of the first division schedule, Verona were away to Atalanta in Bergamo. Eugenio Perico put the hosts ahead just before the interval. But a few minutes after the break, Verona pulled level with a goal from Denmark's Preben Elkjaer. Toriho, their closest pursuers, were being held goal-less away to Fiorentina the same day, which provided Verona with an impregnable four-point advantage. It was a success which would have been impossible without the shrewd signings – almost unnoticed in the summer of 1984 – of Elkjaer and the powerful West German, Hans-Peter Briegel. Verona beat Tottenham to Elkjaer's signature, and though he scored only six goals in the league they were vital – one, against Juventus, being scored after Elkjaer had lost a boot in a scramble to get the ball into the net.

As for Briegel, he had been relegated to a full-back's role in the West German national team. But coach Osvaldo Bagnoli at Verona switched the former decathlete back into his original role in midfield, and was instantly rewarded. In the very first match of the season, Verona beat Napoli 3-1 and Briegel not only scored the opening goal but played Maradona out of the game. Briegel would go on to enjoy what he considers one of his best-ever seasons, which included the scoring of nine goals, and led to a return to Franz Beckenbauer's West German national squad. Asked for Verona's secret, coach Bagnoli said: 'Lack of tension and great friendship among the players. We always felt free to play the way we wanted. But then, when you're outsiders that's comparatively easy. Maybe next season, as champions, we'll find things very different.'

Bagnoli's rapport with the players was one obvious factor of their success, clearly demonstrated by the way he had revived the careers of Juventus cast-offs Giuseppe Galderisi and Pietro Fanna. Galderisi was Verona's top scorer with ten goals, earning a national squad recall for the end-of-season trip to Mexico. He wasn't the only man to impress national boss Enzo Bearzot. In defence Bagnoli turned skipper Roberto Tricella into an Italian international, and Antonio Di Gennaro in midfield promised to fill the national team gap left by the serious leg injury suffered more than a year earlier by Fiorentina's 'Golden Boy' Giancarlo Antognoni.

Finally, to return to Juventus, Platini was the league's top scorer with eighteen goals, providing him with the accolade of leading marksman for the third successive year. Such a hat-trick had been secured only once before, by Sweden's Gunnar Nordahl in the early 1950s.

1984–85 League Table

	P	W	D	L	F	A	Pts
Verona	30	15	13	2	42	19	43
Torino	30	14	11	5	36	22	39
Internazionale	30	13	12	5	42	28	38
Sampdoria	30	12	13	5	36	21	37
Juventus	30	11	14	5	48	33	36
Milan	30	12	12	6	31	25	36
Roma	30	10	14	6	33	25	34
Napoli	30	10	13	7	34	29	33
Fiorentina	30	8	13	9	33	31	29
Atalanta	30	5	18	7	20	32	28
Udinese	30	10	5	15	43	46	25
Avellino	30	7	11	12	27	33	25
Como	30	6	13	11	17	27	25
Ascoli	30	4	14	12	24	40	22
Cremonese	30	4	7	19	22	48	15
Lazio	30	2	11	17	16	45	15

Cup final: Sampdoria bt Milan 1-0, 2-1.
Top scorer: Michel Platini (Juventus) 18 goals.

BOLOGNA
Founded: 1909.
Colours: Red and blue halves/white.
Stadium: Stadio Comunale (46,000).
Club address: Bologna Football Club, Via Testoni 5, 40123 Bologna.
League: 1925, 1929, 1936, 1937, 1939, 1941, 1964 (7).
Cup: 1970, 1974.

CAGLIARI
Founded: 1920.
Colours: Red and blue/blue.
Stadium: Stadio Santa Elia (60,000).
Club address: Cagliari Calcio, Via Tola 30, 09100 Cagliari, Sardinia.
League: 1970.
Cup: – .

FIORENTINA
Founded: 1926.
Colours: All mauve.
Stadium: Stadio Comunale (68,800).
Club address: Fiorentina Associazione Calcio, Via del Parione 11, 50100 Florence.
League: 1956, 1969.
Cup: 1940, 1961, 1966, 1975 (4).
Champions' Cup: Runners-up in 1957.
Cup-winners' Cup: 1961. Runners-up in 1962.

GENOA
Founded: 1893.
Colours: Red and blue halves/blue shorts.
Stadium: Stadio Luigi Ferraris (55,773).
Club address: Genoa 1893, Piazza della Vittoria 11, 16121 Genoa.
League: 1898, 1899, 1900, 1902, 1903, 1904, 1915, 1923, 1924 (9).
Cup: 1937.

INTERNAZIONALE
Founded: 1908.
Colours: Black and blue stripes/black shorts.
Stadium: Stadio Giuseppe Meazza, San Siro (83,141).
Club address: Internazionale Football Club, Foro Buonaparte 70, 20121 Milano.
League: 1910, 1920, 1930, 1938, 1940, 1953, 1954, 1963, 1965, 1966, 1971, 1980 (12).
Cup: 1939, 1978, 1982 (3).
World Club Cup: 1964, 1965.
Champions' Cup: 1964, 1965. Runners-up in 1967 and 1972.

JUVENTUS
Founded: 1897.
Colours: Black and white stripes/white.
Stadium: Stadio Comunale (71,160).
Club address: Juventus Football Club, Galleria San Federico 54, 10121 Turin.
League: 1905, 1926, 1931, 1932, 1933, 1934, 1935, 1950, 1952, 1958, 1960, 1961, 1967, 1972, 1973, 1975, 1977, 1978, 1981, 1982, 1984 (21 – record).
Cup: 1938, 1942, 1959, 1960, 1965, 1979, 1983 (7 – record).
World Club Cup: Runners-up in 1973.
Champions' Cup: 1985. Runners-up in 1973 and 1983.
Cup-winners' Cup: 1984.

Fairs' Cup Runners-up in 1965 and 1971.
UEFA Cup: 1977.
Super Cup: 1984.

LAZIO
Founded: 1900.
Colours: Sky blue with white trimmings/white.
Stadium: Stadio Olimpico (66,341).
Club address: Lazio Società Sportiva, Via Col di Lana 9, 00195 Rome.
League: 1974.
Cup: 1958.

MILAN
Founded: 1899.
Colours: Black and red stripes/white.
Colours: Black and red stripes/white.
Stadium: Stadio Giuseppe Meazza, San Siro (83,141).
Club address: Milan Associazione Calcio, Via Turati 3, 20121 Milan.
League: 1901, 1906, 1907, 1951, 1955, 1957, 1959, 1962, 1968, 1979 (10).
Cup: 1967, 1972, 1973, 1977 (4).
World Club Cup: 1969. Runners-up in 1963.
Champions' Cup: 1963, 1969. Runners-up in 1958.
Cup-winners' Cup: 1968, 1973. Runners-up in 1974.
SuperCup: Runners-up in 1973.

NAPOLI
Founded: 1926.
Colours: All sky blue.
Stadium: Stadio San Paolo (85,012).
Club address: Napoli Società Sportiva Calcio, Via Vicinale Paradiso, Soccava, 80126 Naples.
League: – .
Cup: 1962, 1976.

ROMA
Founded: 1927.
Colours: All red with yellow trimmings.
Stadium: Stadio Olimpico (66,341).
Club address: Roma Associazione Sportiva, Via del Circo Massimo 7, 00153 Rome.
League: 1942, 1983.
Cup: 1964, 1969, 1980, 1981, 1984 (5).
Champions' Cup: Runners-up in 1984.
Fairs' Cup: 1961.

SAMPDORIA
Founded: 1946.
Colours: Blue with two white, one red and one black hoop/white.
Stadium: Stadio Luigi Ferraris (55,773).

Club address: Sampdoria Union Calcio, Via XX Settembre 33, 16121 Genoa.
League: – .
Cup: 1985.

TORINO
Founded: 1906.
Colours: Red/white.
Stadium: Stadio Comunale (71,160).
Club address: Torino Calcio, Corso Vittorio Emanuele II 77, 10128 Turin.
League: 1927 (revoked), 1928, 1943, 1946, 1947, 1948, 1949, 1976 (7).
Cup: 1936, 1943, 1968, 1971 (4).

UDINESE
Founded: 1896.
Colours: White with one broad black stripe/white.
Stadium: Stadio Friuli (52,000).
Club address: Udinese Calcio, Via Cotonificio 94, 33100 Udine.
League: – .
Cup: – .

VERONA
Founded: 1959.
Colours: All blue.
Stadium: Stadio Marc'Atonio Bentegodi (36,000).
Club address: Hellas-Verona Associazione Calcio, Piazzale Olimpia, Cancello E, 37138 Verona.
League: 1985.
Cup: – .

JAPAN

Yomiuri, who won the league-and-cup double, are setting a new trend in Japanese football, which is leading the game there towards professionalism. The biggest problem with the game's development over the years has been that the Japanese Soccer League – founded on the advice of the then FIFA coach Dettmar Cramer – has been based on amateur players and company clubs.

Until recently Yomiuri were the only non-company club in the first division, and they remain the only one to have finished among the prizes. The company clubs draw their players from among their employees. They work for a few hours in the morning then train in the afternoon. But there is no difference in their pay whether they win or lose because they are paid as 'employees' not as footballers. When they finish playing they can work in the company until retiring in their mid-fifties, so it's not surprising that no one makes enormous efforts – not even the coaches and administrators. After all, they are employees of the same company.

But Yomiuri are breaking that tradition. They are sponsored by the huge Yomiuri group, which includes a newspaper and a television network, and they are organised on European lines. That is, they organise a pioneering youth policy, and although their players are not considered professionals there is a bonus system based on where they finish in the league. Also, the Yomiuri players are not drawn just from the Yomiuri company. Some are teachers, some students and some shopkeepers.

The improvement in standards which the Yomiuri development has encouraged means that league attendances now average around 3,600. This is less than half the average of the late 1960s, when enthusiasm knew no bounds after the excitement of winning the bronze medal in the Olympic finals in 1964 in Tokyo. But it is fifty per cent up on average attendances during the last few years. And already some of the company clubs, impressed by Yomiuri's achievements, have announced their own bonus systems. These clubs include Nissan and Fujita.

As for Yomiuri's successful 1984 campaign, that was masterminded by the controversial wandering West German coach, Rudi Gutendorf. For years Yomiuri had been considered a team who put too many eggs in an attacking basket. Now, with Gutendorf's coaching know-how and the experience of national team sweeper Hisashi Kato, Yomiuri have tightened up.

In attack, Gutendorf made an important change by bringing in Steve Paterson, a Scottish-born forward who had played three league games with Manchester United in the late 1970s. It was Paterson who scored the second goal on New Year's Day 1985, which assured Yomiuri their defeat of Furukawa in the Emperor's Cup Final. The other goal came from key player Tosuka. Earlier the two clubs had played a far less peaceful match in the league. Tosuka and the Brazilians Ramos and Yonashiro were all handed heavy suspensions by the federation for incidents during a game.

Ironically, when it came to the last game of the season with Yomiuri level on points with Yamaha, it took an eighty-second-minute penalty to bring victory. Yomiuri thus became the first side to win the title two years in a row since Yanmar in 1974 and 1975. They might have had a tougher time landing the title, however, if early pacemakers Nissan hadn't lost star player Kimura, injured against South Korea, midway through the season.

1984 League Table

	P	W	D	L	F	A	Pts
Yomiuri	18	11	4	3	41	20	26
Nissan	18	11	3	4	40	23	25
Yamaha	18	10	4	4	28	16	24
Furukawa	18	8	5	5	28	20	21
Honda	18	7	5	6	26	24	19
Fujita	18	6	6	6	25	25	18
Mitsubishi	18	6	3	9	22	33	15
NKK	18	4	6	8	17	23	14
Yanmar	18	5	4	9	15	28	14
Hitachi	18	2	0	16	11	41	4

Cup final: Yomiuri 2, Furukawa 0.

FUJITA
Founded: 1968.
Colours: Yellow/green.
Stadium: Komazawa (20,000) but important matches in National Stadium (62,000).

Club address: Fujita Football Club, Sendagaya 4–6–15, Shibuya-ku, Tokyo 151.
League: 1977, 1979, 1981 (3).
Cup: 1977, 1979 (2).
League Cup: 1973.

FURUKAWA
Founded: 1946.
Colours: White/blue.
Stadium: Nishigaoka (10,000) but important matches in National Stadium.
Club address: Furukawa Football Club, Marunouchi 2–6–1, Chiyoda-ku, Tokyo 100.
League: 1976.
Cup: 1960, 1961, 1974, 1976 (4).
League Cup: 1977, 1982.

MITSUBISHI
Founded: 1951.
Colours: Red/white.
Stadium: Nishigaoka (10,000), but top games in National Stadium.
Club address: Mitsubishi Football Club, Marunouchi 2–5–1, Chiyoda-ku, Tokyo 100.
League: 1969, 1973, 1978, 1982 (4).
Cup: 1971, 1973, 1978, 1980 (4).
League Cup: 1978, 1981.

NISSAN
Founded: 1972.
Colours: Blue/white.
Stadium: Mitsuzawa (14,000) but top games in National Stadium.
Club address: Nissan Football Club, Takara-cho 2, Kanagawa-ku, Yokohama-shi, Kanagawa 21.
League: – .
Cup: 1983.
League Cup: – .

YAMAHA
Founded: 1972.
Colours: All blue.
Stadium: Yamaha (8,000).
Club address: Yamaha Football Club, Shinkai 2500, Iwata-ski, Shizuoka 438.
League: – .
Cup: 1982.
League Cup: – .

YANMAR
Founded: 1957.
Colours: All red.
Stadium: Kobe (20,000).

Club address: Yanmar Football Club, Chaya-cho 1–32, Kita-ku, Osaka-shi, Osaka 530.
League: 1971, 1974, 1975, 1980 (4).
Cup: 1968, 1970, 1974 (3).
League Cup: 1973, 1983, 1974 (3).

YOMIURI
Founded: 1969.
Colours: Green/white.
Stadium: Kawasaki (10,000) but top games in National Stadium.
Club address: Yomiuri Soccer Club, Yomiuri Land, Yanokuchi 3294, Inagi-shi, Tokyo 206.
League: 1983, 1984.
Cup: 1984.
League Cup: – .

KUWAIT

Kuwait football was never more highly rated than when the national team, having reached the Olympic quarter-finals in Moscow, followed up by reaching the finals of the 1982 World Cup. Their performance in the initial 1–1 draw against Czechoslovakia drew further admirers. But then the Kuwaitis – both players and officials – spoiled it all with their high-handed petulance during the 4–1 defeat by France.

From that point Kuwait football appears to have slipped back. A 1–0 defeat by Iraq in the 1982 Asian Games final should have served as a warning that they dared not stand still, given the massive enthusiasm and financial commitment being invested in football in many other Middle East countries. A further two years and the Kuwaitis found themselves left in the shadows of the qualifying round to the Los Angeles Olympics, while Iraq, Qatar and Saudi Arabia went through instead.

A further setback came when it was time for Kuwait to defend the Asian Cup in the finals in Singapore in late 1984. They beat Qatar 1–0 and Syria 3–1, were held 0–0 by South Korea and lost 1–0 to Saudi Arabia in their first round group. That was not a decisive defeat, since two teams went on to the semi-finals, and Kuwait had finished second behind the Saudis. But in the semi-finals they lost 1–0 after extra time against China, and salvaged third place only thanks to a 6–5 victory over Iran in a penalty shoot-out after a 1–1 draw in the 'consolation final'.

The Kuwaitis appear to be specialists in such penalty deciders. Their domestic cup final even went to a shoot-out, in which Kuwait Club defeated Kasmah 4–2 after a 2–2 draw. To win the cup was a reward for Kuwait's efforts through the season when they had failed, by just two points, to disturb the current domestic reign of Al-Arabi – who owe their continued success to the foundations laid by the former Tottenham and Scotland star, Dave Mackay. Al-Arabi have won the championship for the past four years in a row, and five times in the last six seasons. They have also won the cup twice in that time thanks to the dedication of players who work at their daily jobs from 6 a.m. until 1 p.m. then turn up for training and coaching from four o'clock onwards.

Such devotion to the game was not, however, enough when it came to the qualifying rounds for the 1986 World Cup finals in Mexico. While league top scorer Faisal Al Dakhil remains one of the most admired players in the Middle East – he was placed third in the 1984 Asian Footballer of the Year poll – he cannot continue to carry his country forever. The need to rebuild the national team was underlined in the World Cup qualifiers where Kuwait dropped three decisive points to eventual sub-group winners Syria. Kuwait lost 1–0 away and were held goal-less at home. Their 3–1 victory away to Yemen AR was too little, too late.

Final Points Totals

1 Al-Arabi 42. 2 Kuwait Club 40. 3 Kasmah 34. 4 Salmiya 29. 5 Tadhamon 27. 6 Qadsia 25. 7 Yarmouk 25. 8 Al-Jahra 24. 9 Fahaheel 21. 10 Al-Shabab 20. 11 Khitan 11. 12 Al-Nasr 10. 13 Sulaibikhat 4. 14 Sahel 0.
Cup final: Kuwait by Kasmah 4–2 on penalties after a 2–2 draw.
Top scorer: Faisal Al-Dakhil (Qadsia) 22 goals.

AL-ARABI
Founded: 1960.
Colours: Green/white.
Stadium: Sabah Al-Salem (25,000).
Club address: Al-Arabi Sporting Club, c/o Kuwait FA, Udailiya Plot 4, Al-Ittihad Street, PO Box 2029, Al-Safat, Kuwait.
League: 1962, 1963, 1964, 1966, 1967, 1970, 1980, 1982, 1983, 1984, 1985 (11 – record).
Cup: 1962, 1963, 1964, 1966, 1969, 1971, 1981, 1983 (8).

QADSIA
Founded: 1961.
Colours: Yellow/blue.
Stadium: Al-Qadsia (25,000).
Club address: Al-Qadsia Sporting Club, c/o Kuwait FA, Udailiya Plot 4, Al-Ittihad Street, PO Box 2029, Al-Safat, Kuwait.
League: 1967, 1971, 1973, 1975, 1976, 1978 (6).
Cup: 1965, 1967, 1968, 1972, 1974, 1975, 1979 (7 – record).

KASMAH
Founded: 1964.
Colours: Orange/white.
Stadium: Kasmah (25,000).
Club address: Kasmah Sporting Club, c/o Kuwait FA, Udailiya Plot 4, Al-Ittihad Street, PO Box 2029, Al-Safat, Kuwait.
League: – .
Cup: 1982, 1984.

KUWAIT
Founded: 1960.
Colours: All white.
Stadium: Kuwait (25,000).

Club address: Kuwait Sporting Club, c/o Kuwait FA, Udailiya Plot 4, Al-Ittihad Street, PO Box 2029, Al-Safat, Kuwait.
League: 1965, 1968, 1972, 1974, 1977, 1979 (6).
Cup: 1976, 1977, 1978, 1980, 1985 (5).

SALMIYA
Founded: 1964.
Colours: All sky blue.
Stadium: Thamer (10,000).
Club address: Salmiya Sporting Club, c/o Kuwait FA, Udailiya Plot 4, Al-Ittihad Street, PO Box 2029, Al-Safat, Kuwait.
League: 1981.
Cup: – .

LUXEMBOURG

Luxembourg is one of those backwaters of European football where the game is still a part-time occupation and where playing for one's country remains a matter of personal pride: how else can one explain a willingness to submit to defeat with such monotonous regularity?

But the 1984–85 season saw the calm waters of football in the Grand Duchy disturbed by a number of controversies. The major upset involved the national team management. For years this had been the sole preserve of the former Standard Liège defender Louis Pilot. He had now been lured back to the Belgian club and his place filled by a former Standard team-mate in one-time full-back Jef Vliers. It would not prove a happy appointment. Luxembourg began their season with a 7-0 home defeat against the West German club Bayer Leverkusen, and then suffered two rather more important home reverses in the World Cup qualifiers: losing 4-0 to France and 5-0 to East Germany.

The first cracks began to appear. Veteran defender Romain Michaux decided to retire from the international scene after the defeat by France, and forward Roby Langers – one of the few Luxembourg players to have spent any serious length of time abroad, in his case with Borussia Mönchengladbach – was axed from the national squad after squabbling with Vliers. The last straw was Vliers's decision to substitute Langers during the defeat by the East Germans. Those departures from the scene upset some of the other players, and it was hardly surprising that Luxembourg should then lose 4-0 in Bulgaria in a World Cup qualifier at the start of December. What was surprising was that skipper Herbert Meunier, who had become one of the most patient of defenders, was sent off during the second half.

Vliers took his men on a rare three-match tour in December. The results were narrow defeats away to Cyprus, Israel and Turkey, and a request from the federation's executive committee when Vliers returned home, that he step down as national boss. He had, it was suggested, lost the confidence of the players. Vliers disagreed and tried to resist, though to no avail.

At the start of February Josy Kirschens was handed the job of caretaker national manager before the job proper was handed over to the Avenir Beggen coach, Paul Philipp. Avenir, under Philipp, had won the league-and-cup double in 1984. They had won the cup by defeating Union Sportive 4-1 in the final. Yet Avenir lost to Union by that same margin in the Luxembourg Super Cup with which the 1984–85 season began. This was one of the last games in senior competition for veteran forward Nico Braun, who retired in mid-season.

By then it was clear that neither Union nor Avenir were going to get much of a say in the current championship. Record champions Jeunesse Esch were out in front thanks to the defensive security provided by the prodigal thirty-two-year-old centre-back Chico Rohmann, who had returned from the crisis-hit game in the United States. Jeunesse didn't lose a match until March, when they went down 3-2 at home to Eischen. They even allowed pursuing Red Boys to move level on points at one stage before pulling away to complete the season with a lead of five points over the Differdange club.

1984–85 League Table

	P	W	D	L	F	A	Pts
Jeunesse Esch	22	17	3	2	65	20	37
Red Boys	22	13	6	3	41	22	32
Avenir Beggen	22	12	4	6	51	25	28
Progres Niedercorn	22	11	6	5	45	30	28
Spora Luxembourg	22	9	6	7	34	28	24
Union Luxembourg	22	9	5	8	45	39	23
Aris Bonnevoie	22	6	6	10	36	44	18
Olympique Eischen	22	8	2	12	27	42	18
Stade Dudelange	22	5	6	11	26	48	16
Alliance Dudelange	22	6	3	13	20	50	15
FC Wiltz	22	6	1	15	45	55	13
US Rumelange	22	4	4	14	19	51	12

Cup final: Red Boys 1, Jeunesse Esch 0.
Top scorers: Krings (Avenir) and Guillot (Jeunesse) 16 goals each.

ARIS
Founded: 1922.
Colours: White/black.
Stadium: Important matches in the Stade Municipal de la Ville de Luxembourg (15,100).
Club address: FC Aris Bonnevoie, c/o 194 route de Thionville, 1016 Luxembourg.
League: 1964, 1966, 1972 (3).
Cup: 1967.

AVENIR BEGGEN
Founded: 1915.
Colours: Yellow/black.
Stadium: Important matches in the Stade Municipal de la Ville de Luxembourg (15,100).
Club address: FC Avenir Beggen, BP 382, 2013 Luxembourg.
League: 1969, 1982, 1984 (3).
Cup: 1983, 1984.

JEUNESSE D'ESCH
Founded: 1907.
Colours: Black/white.

Stadium: Stade Emile Mayrisch, Esch (10,800). Important matches in the Stade Municipal de la Ville de Luxembourg (15,100).
Club address: Association Sportive la Jeunesse d'Esch-sur-Alzette, BP 45, 4001 Esch-sur-Alzette.
League: 1921, 1937, 1951, 1954, 1958, 1959, 1960, 1963, 1967, 1968, 1970, 1973, 1974, 1975, 1976, 1977, 1980, 1983, 1985 (19 – record).
Cup: 1935, 1937, 1946, 1954, 1973, 1974, 1976, 1981 (8).

PROGRÈS NIEDERCORN
Founded: 1919.
Colours: Yellow/black.
Stadium: Stade Progrès (2,650). Important matches in the Stade Municipal de la Ville de Luxembourg (15,100).
Club address: Progrès Niedercorn FC, c/o 25 rue Prinzenberg, 4650 Niedercorn.
League: 1953, 1978, 1981 (3).
Cup: 1933, 1945, 1977, 1978 (4).

RED BOYS
Founded: 1907.
Colours: Red/white.
Stadium: Stade Municipal (10,000).
Club address: FA Red Boys Differdange, BP 38, 4501 Differdange.
League: 1923, 1926, 1931, 1932, 1933, 1979 (6).
Cup: 1925, 1926, 1927, 1929, 1930, 1931, 1934, 1936, 1952, 1953, 1958, 1972, 1979, 1982 (14 – record).

STADE DUDELANGE
Founded: 1913.
Colours: White/black.
Stadium: Important matches in the Stade Municipal de la Ville de Luxembourg (15,100).
Club address: CS le Stade Dudelange, c/o 146 rue RP Jacques Thiel 3572 Dudelange.
League: 1939, 1940, 1945, 1946, 1947, 1948, 1950, 1955, 1957, 1965 (10).
Cup: 1938, 1948, 1949, 1956 (4).

UNION SPORTIVE
Founded: 1908.
Colours: White/blue.
Stadium: Important matches in the Stade Municipal de la Ville de Luxembourg (15,100).
Club address: FC Union Sportive Luxembourg, BP 1614, 1016 Luxembourg I.
League: 1912, 1914, 1915, 1916, 1917, 1927, 1962, 1971 (8).
Cup: 1947, 1959, 1963, 1964, 1969, 1970 (6).

U S RUMELANGE
Founded: 1908.
Colours: Blue/white.
Stadium: Stade Municipal (3,000).

Club address: Union Sportive Rumelange, BP 3, 3701 Rumelange.
League: – .
Cup: 1968, 1975.

MALTA

In football terms a 'striker' has generally been accepted as an attacking player, a forward, a goal-scorer. Now, however, there appears to be an ever-increasing number of players willing to employ a 'strike' in its other meaning, i.e., a withdrawal of labour. Malta has not escaped such sporting industrial unrest. At least clubs and players on the George Cross island are in good company. In Argentina players went on strike over freedom of contract; in Spain players went on strike over social security benefits and overdue back pay; in Italy the start of league matches has occasionally been delayed by players making an industrial point.

But in the case of Malta it was the clubs who took action in a clash over where real control in the domestic game lies.

At the start of January, four leading clubs refused to stage their scheduled league fixtures at the Ta Qali national stadium to draw attention to the association's failure to satisfy them on a number of demands. The first was that a larger percentage of gate receipts from the Ta Qali – where all Maltese league games are staged – should be released for division among the clubs. A second demand was for permission to switch league matches from Saturday to Sunday in an attempt to increase attendances. The FA's immediate response was to fine all the striking clubs £250 each. The clubs had announced in advance of the FA's emergency meeting that they were ready to resume playing as a sign of goodwill. But that didn't prevent MFA president George Abela laying down the law. He said: 'We want the clubs to declare publicly that they were mistaken in calling a strike. They will have to promise their loyalty to the association. And if they can't bring themselves to do that, then there is no place for them in the MFA.' Further financial penalties were inflicted on the original four clubs, plus the others who supported them. But although the league duly swung back into action it was hard to believe that this was the end of the row with the government-backed MFA.

When the strike began it was Hamrun Spartans who were leading the league from Valletta – the respective cup-winners and champions from the 1983–84 season – well in control. But by the end of the campaign everything had changed, and it was Rabat Ajax who landed the league title for the first time in their history. Rabat made it by one point after a dramatic last couple of games. In the penultimate round of matches they drew 2-2 with Hamrun, and in the last game they were held 0-0 by Sliema Wanderers. Hamrun could have pulled level on points, but they too were held, goal-less away to Zurrieq.

Valletta fell away badly at the end, losing their last match 2-0 against Floriana – not that this result was much use to Floriana. The island's record champions (twenty-four titles) were relegated for the first time in their eighty-five year history. But then, Malta's small, eight-club league can produce some odd features. Relegated Floriana actually totalled just four points fewer than champions Rabat!

1984–85 League Table

	P	W	D	L	F	A	Pts
Rabat Ajax	13	5	6	2	19	12	17
Hamrun Spartans	13	4	8	1	18	8	16
Sliema Wanderers	13	5	5	3	13	10	15
Valletta	13	6	2	5	18	15	14
Zurrieq	13	5	4	4	17	13	14
Hibernians	13	5	4	4	14	12	14
Floriana	13	4	5	4	11	11	13
Marsa	13	0	1	12	6	35	1

Cup final: Zurrieq bt Valletta 2-1 in replay after 0-0 draw.

FLORIANA
Founded: 1900.
Colours: Green and white stripes/white.
Stadium: Important matches in the Ta'Qali Stadium (40,000).
Club address: Floriana FC, 28 St Anne Street, Floriana.
League: 1910, 1912, 1913, 1921, 1922, 1925, 1927, 1928, 1929, 1931, 1935, 1937, 1950, 1951, 1952, 1953, 1955, 1958, 1962, 1968, 1970, 1973, 1975, 1977 (24 – record).
Cup: 1938, 1945, 1947, 1949, 1950, 1953, 1954, 1955, 1957, 1958, 1961, 1966, 1967, 1972, 1976, 1981 (16).

HAMRUN SPARTANS
Founded: 1907.
Colours: Red/black.
Stadium: Important matches in the Ta'Qali Stadium (40,000).
Club address: Hamrun Spartans FC, 42 Broad Street, Hamrun.
League: 1914, 1918, 1947, 1983 (4).
Cup: 1983, 1984.

HIBERNIANS
Founded: 1932.
Colours: White/black.
Stadium: Important matches in the Ta'Qali Stadium (40,000).
Club address: Hibernians FC, Paola Square, Paola.
League: 1961, 1967, 1969, 1979, 1981, 1982 (6).
Cup: 1962, 1970, 1971, 1980, 1982 (5).

RABAT AJAX
Founded: 1946.
Colours: Black and white stripes/black.
Stadium: Important matches in the Ta'Qali Stadium (40,000).
Club address: Rabat Ajax FC, Civic Centre, Parish Street, Rabat.
League: 1985.
Cup: – .

SLIEMA WANDERERS
Founded: 1909.
Colours: Sky blue/blue.

Stadium: Important matches in the Ta'Qali Stadium (40,000).
Club address: Sliema Wanderers FC, 21 Tower Road, Sliema.
League: 1920, 1923, 1924, 1926, 1930, 1933, 1934, 1936, 1938, 1939, 1940, 1949, 1954, 1956, 1957, 1964, 1965, 1966, 1971, 1972, 1976 (21).
Cup: 1935, 1936, 1937, 1940, 1946, 1948, 1951, 1952, 1956, 1959, 1963, 1965, 1968, 1969, 1974, 1979 (16 – record).

VALLETTA
Founded: 1910.
Colours: All white.
Stadium: Important matches in the Ta'Qali Stadium (40,000).
Club address: Valletta City FC, 126 St Lucia Street, Valletta.
League: 1915, 1932, 1945, 1946, 1948, 1959, 1960, 1963, 1974, 1978, 1980, 1984 (12).
Cup: 1960, 1964, 1975, 1977, 1978 (5).

ZURRIEQ
Founded: 1949.
Colours: Red/white.
Stadium: Important matches in the Ta'Qali Stadium (40,000).
Club address: Zurrieq FC, Republic Square, Zurrieq.
League: – .
Cup: 1985.

MEXICO

Just as European football was mourning the dead of Bradford and Brussels so Mexico – venue for the 1986 World Cup – was suffering a crowd tragedy of its own. The occasion was the second leg of the championship final between UNAM and América in the Estadio Olimpico '68 in Mexico City. A crowd of 90,000 – some 20,000 beyond the capacity approved for the game – was estimated to have burst through the police and security cordons. The stadium gates were shut but still the crowds outside pressed forward, in particular in Entry 29. Those at the front of the crowd were, as in Brussels, asphyxiated and trampled as panic broke out. No one in the stadium – the crowd included Italy's national manager Enzo Bearzot – realised anything was amiss because the noise drowned out the sounds of the police and emergency service sirens. Some seventy-four people were hurt, and later it was announced that families of victims intended to join in a legal action against the police for a failure to maintain safety – even though 7,000 officers, many on horseback, were present outside the stadium.

As for the match itself, that ended in a 0–0 draw – América surviving thanks to the outstanding form in goal of Argentine-born Hector Miguel Zelada. The first leg of the final had finished 1–1, but the winning team in the Mexican play-off is the team with most points. Since both América and UNAM had shared the points, they went on to a play-off in the new World Cup stadium at Queretaro. Again there was trouble, with around seventy fans hurt in scuffles and brawls which erupted during and after América's 3–1 victory in front of a 40,000 crowd. América's hero was former Argentine international Daniel Brailovsky, who opened the scoring with a first-half penalty, and then made it 2–0 early in the second half. UNAM's Brazilian Tuca Ferretti pulled one goal back with just over a quarter of an hour to play, but three minutes later América's Mexican international, Hermosillo, made the final score 3–1. América thus retained their title.

The Mexican championship is a complex affair. Four groups of five teams compete, playing all the other teams home and away. Two-leg knock-out quarter- and semi-finals then take place between the top two teams from each group. But all that domestic detail will be forgotten, of course, at the end of May next year when world champions Italy open the 1986 World Cup finals in the Estadio Azteca in Mexico City.

Colombia were the original choice as 1986 hosts. But as soon as FIFA decided to expand the number of finalists to twenty-four from sixteen, it became clear that all the Colombian federation's plans had been thrown awry. During the 1982 finals in Spain, rumour and report gathered pace on Colombian doubts and on the ambitions of Brazil and the United States to take over. Outsiders in the substitute race were Mexico. The Colombians stalled for a while, pleading for a return to the old sixteen-team format on the one hand, and trying to ensure support from their own government on the other. At the end of October 1982, the Colombians announced that they were pulling out, leaving the field clear for the Brazilians and Americans, while Mexico began coming up strongly on the rails.

The late Artemio Franchi, then president of UEFA, put in a good word for the Mexicans on the grounds of the infrastructure created for 1970, and Brazil's claim began to fade. Their greatest-ever player, Pele, shocked his fellow countrymen by backing the United States on the strength of his career revival with the New York Cosmos. Then the war of words between FIFA head João Havelange and the president of the Brazilian federation, Giulite Coutinho, burst into the open. On top of that, it emerged that there were government doubts about financing the World Cup at a time when Brazil was one of the world's top debtor nations.

Havelange threw his hat into the ring in Mexico's favour in January 1983. In February Canada confirmed their interest in staging the finals, and in March FIFA's World Cup panel began to examine the rival candidatures. On 31 March they decided to recommend Mexico – to an outraged reaction from the Americans. Too late, the Americans, who had, apparently, hardly bothered to address themselves to FIFA's initial investigation questionnaire, brought the weight of Henry Kissinger to join the fight. It was even suggested that Kissinger's involvement was more of a publicity move, organised by the United States Soccer Federation, to cover their embarrassment at having lost out to their southern neighbours.

At the decisive meeting in Stockholm the Americans were given little more than half an hour in committee to state their case. It was too late. Mexico, their bid backed by the financial power of the Televisa television chain, were home and dry.

Now attention on Mexico and in Mexico altered its focus: away from the politicians and administrators and onto the national team. Although Mexico have appeared in the World Cup finals on eight occasions, their achievements run to one appearance in the quarter-finals – and that was when they were hosts in 1970 and benefited from some generous refereeing decisions to reach even that stage.

This time, Mexico want to make a far better impression, and the man in the hot seat as manager is a Yugoslav, Bora Milutinovic – a member of one of Yugoslavia's most famous footballing families. Milutinovic played for Partizan Belgrade and then Nice and Monaco in France before emigrating to Mexico to play for the UNAM club. He retired in 1975 and was appointed club coach, guiding UNAM twice to the Mexican championship and twice to the Central American Club Cup. That success earned him the national team post in 1982, long before the chance to become World Cup hosts had been appreciated. Security is no part of a national manager's job, and Milutinovic came close to an unheralded departure in the spring of 1984 when he took his rebuilt national team to Italy for a friendly, coming home chastened by a 5–0 defeat which could have been heavier.

1984–85 League Tables

Group 1	P	W	D	L	F	A	Pts
América	38	17	12	9	53	40	46
Leon	38	12	18	8	56	46	42
UN Leon	38	13	9	16	41	45	35
Neza	38	8	12	18	44	58	28
Necaxa	38	5	15	18	33	58	25

Group 2	P	W	D	L	F	A	Pts
UNAM	38	25	5	8	71	38	55
Atlas	38	17	9	12	65	58	43
Tampico Madero	38	17	8	13	65	58	42
Oaxtepec	38	12	11	15	54	61	35
Morella	38	6	18	14	37	55	30

Group 3	P	W	D	L	F	A	Pts
Un. Guadalajara	38	16	15	7	60	44	47
Cruz Azul	38	17	13	8	53	38	47
Atlante	38	17	10	11	51	44	44
Potosino	38	10	14	14	49	60	34
Monterrey	38	10	12	16	51	67	32

Group 4	P	W	D	L	F	A	Pts
Guadalajara	38	16	13	9	49	30	45
Puebla	38	13	11	14	53	43	37
UA Guadalajara	38	12	12	14	52	50	36
Toluca	38	8	14	16	34	53	30
Zacatepec	38	10	7	21	31	54	27

Relegation play-off: Necaxa bt Zacatepec 2–1, 1–0.
Championship quarter-finals: América bt Guadalajara 2–0, 1–0 – Leon bt Un. Guadalajara 1–0, 0–1 (7–6 pens) – Atlas bt Cruz Azul 1–1, 3–1 – UNAM bt Puebla 0–2, 2–0 (7–6 pens).
Semi-finals: América bt Atlas 1–1, 2–0 – UNAM bt Leon 3–3, 2–0.
Final: América bt UNAM 1–1, 0–0, 3–1 (play-off).
Top scorer: Cabinho (Leon) 23 goals.

In the autumn of 1984 Mexico came to Europe again, and this time fared much better – drawing with the Republic of Ireland, East Germany and Sweden, losing 3–0 to the Soviet Union, but winning against both Finland and Hungary. A South American tour followed, including a 1–1 draw away to South American champions Uruguay and, slowly, Mexican fans began to believe in their team at long last. When Milutinovic's men marked the opening of the new Queretaro World Cup stadium in February 1985 with a 5–0 thrashing of Poland – placed third in Spain in 1982 – there was virtually a national celebration.

Milutinovic has spread his eye around all the major Mexican teams in the search for the right players. But unlike current World Cup-holders Italy, who had six players from the Juventus club in their 1982 winning team, Mexico's manager is suspicious of relying too much on any one club. He reasons that if the 'core' team should hit a bad patch, the national team will suffer and the solution is out of his hands. Thus Milutinovic's tour squad in 1984 was drawn from nine clubs, who supplied the nineteen players. The strongest representation came from Universidad de Mexico, with five players – defenders Rafael Amador and Felix Cruz, midfielders Miguel Espana and Manuel Negrete, and star striker Luis Flores – the latter nicknamed the new golden boy of Mexican football.

Milutinovic demanded – and was granted – virtually a year to prepare his team for the finals; a year in which his needs take precedence over the clubs. Thus the 1985–86 domestic season sees members of the national squad barred to their clubs altogether. It had been considered fielding the national team in the championship but this was later rejected because it was hoped to arrange a full schedule of friendly internationals against foreign national team and club sides.

AMÉRICA
Founded: 1906
Colours: Yellow/blue.
Stadium: Estadio Azteca (108,499).
Club address: Club de Fútbol América SA, Toro 100, México 22 DF.
League: 1925, 1926, 1927, 1928, 1966, 1971, 1976, 1984, 1985 (9).
Interamerican Cup: 1978.
Cup: 1938, 1955, 1964, 1965, 1974 (5).
CONCACAF Cup: 1977. Runners-up in 1966.

ATLANTE
Founded: 1916 (as Sinaloa).
Colours: Red and blue stripes/blue.
Stadium: Ciudad los Deportes (Mexico City; 45,000).
Club address: Club de Futbol Atlante, Instituto Mexicano de Seguro Social, México DF.
League: 1932, 1941, 1947, (3).
Cup: 1942, 1951, 1952 (3).
Interamerican Cup: 1984.
CONCACAF Cup: 1983.

CRUZ AZUL
Founded: 1932.
Colours: White with blue trimmings/white.
Stadium: Estadio Azteca (108,499).
Club address: Club Deportivo Social y Cultural Cruz Azul, Cda Perpetua 7, Mexico DF 19.
League: 1970, 1972, 1973, 1974, 1979, 1980, 1982, (7).
Cup: 1969.
Interamerican Cup: Runners-up in 1972.
CONCACAF Cup: 1969, 1970 (shared), 1971 (3).

GUADALAJARA
Founded: 1906.
Colours: Red and white stripes/blue.
Stadium: Jalisco (70,951).
Club address: Guadalajara FC, Estadio de Jalisco, Guadalajara.
League: 1951 (shared), 1957, 1959, 1960, 1961, 1962, 1964, 1965, 1969, 1970 (10).
Cup: 1963, 1970 (2).
CONCACAF Cup: 1963, 1964, 1965 (3).

LEON
Founded: 1944.
Colours: Green/white.
Stadium: Nou Camp (39,000).
Club address: Club Social y Deportivo Leon, c/o Federación Mexicana de Fútbol Asociación, A González 74, Colona Juárez, Mexico DF ZP6.
League: 1948, 1949, 1952, 1956 (4).
Cup: 1949, 1958, 1967, 1971, 1972 (5).

NECAXA
Founded: 1925.
Colours: Red and white stripes/white.
Stadium: Aztec (108,499).
Club address: Necaxa, c/o Federación Mexicana de Fútbol Asociación, A González 74, Colona Juárez, Mexico DF ZP6.
League: 1933, 1935, 1937, 1938.
Cup: 1933, 1936, 1960, 1966 (4).
Interamerican Cup: Runners-up in 1976 (as Atletico Español).
CONCACAF Cup: 1975.

PUEBLA
Founded: 1944.
Colours: White with a sky blue sash/white.
Stadium: Cuauhtemoc (40,000).
Club address: 'Puebla', c/o Federación Mexicana de Fútbol Asociación, A González 74, Colona Juárez, Mexico DF ZP6.

League: 1983.
Cup: 1945, 1953 (2).

TAMPICO-MARERO
Founded: 1945 (from a merger of the two clubs whose colours remain in use: Marero's yellow and black stripes/black for home games; Tampico's sky blue/white for away games).
Stadium: Tamaulipas (35,000).
Club address: 'Tampico-Marero', c/o Federación Mexicana de Fútbol Asociación, A González 74, Colona Juárez, Mexico DF ZP6.
League: 1953.
Cup: 1961.

TOLUCA
Founded: 1925.
Colours: Red and white/white.
Stadium: Luis Dosal (30,512).
Club address: Club Deportivo Toluca, Estadio Luis Dosal, Toluca.
League: 1967, 1968, 1975.
Cup: 1956.
Interamerican Cup: Runners-up in 1979.
CONCACAF Cup: 1978.

U N A M
Founded: 1940.
Colours: All blue with a puma face on the shirt, the university emblem.
Stadium: Mexico '68 (65,000).
Club address: Universidad Nacional Autónoma de Mexico, Avenida Universidad, Mexico 20 DF.
League: 1977, 1981 (2).
Cup: 1975.
Interamerican Cup: 1981.
CONCACAF Cup: 1980, 1982.

NEW ZEALAND

Gisborne City, comparative newcomers to the Rothmans National League, carried almost all before them. Having given advance notice of their improvement by finishing runners-up in the 1983 Chatham Cup final, Gisborne won the league with a clear fourteen-points advantage over Papatoetoe, and again reached the cup final.

Once again, however, they lost out in the cup. In 1983 it was Mount Wellington who beat them; this time it was Manurewa, the club who have emerged so powerfully in the 1980s thanks to the hard work of John Adshead, the English-born coach who guided New Zealand's Kiwis to the 1982 World Cup finals.

It was Adshead's former national team assistant, Kevin Fallon, who master-minded the Gisborne success. But the team was built around a five-man nucleus of internationals in Sam Byrne (former League of Ireland player), Peter Simonsen, record international Grant Turner, Kenny Cresswell and the League's top scorer, Colin Walker. The former Barnsley and Doncaster professional finished the season with sixteen of Gisborne's fifty-nine goals, and also collected the Footballer of the Year award.

The turning point in the campaign came right at mid-season. Gisborne were early leaders, but then appeared to falter when they lost to defending champions Manurewa. But while Manurewa then lost their next game 4-1 to Miramar Rangers, Gisborne roared back to form with a 6-0 thrashing of Dunedin City. McLoughlin (two), Owen, Byrne, Meacock and Walker (penalty) ran up the goals – four of them in the first half. Gisborne eventually finished well clear of Papatoetoe, who surprised the league by improving one place on their previous season's placing – and that had been upset enough. Christchurch United, second for much of the time, slipped back to third place ahead of Manurewa, who had their success this time in the Chatham Cup.

The competition is so named because of its presentation to members of the New Zealand FA back in December, 1922, by the company of the visiting British ship, HMS *Chatham*. The commander, Captain Prickett, said that the ship's crew had requested permission to present a cup for football competition in return for the kindness and hospitality shown during their visit. Sir Charles Skerret, for the New Zealand FA – which had been founded back in 1891 – received the cup, and rules were immediately drawn up on lines similar to the English FA Cup. Seacliff of Otago were the first winners, in 1923, and Manurewa added their name to this prestige list when they defeated league champions Gisborne 2-1 in the 1984 final.

Gisborne came to the game in Auckland having also won the pre-season Air Zealand Cup, and looking for the treble. But a game which had promised so much proved a disappointment. Steve Sumner, one of the stars of New Zealand's 1982 World Cup effort, snatched goals in the twelfth and twenty-eighth minutes to give Manurewa a half-time lead. It was only then that

1984 League Table

	P	W	D	L	F	A	Pts*
Gisborne City	22	15	6	1	59	16	51
Papatoetoe	22	10	7	5	35	26	37
Christchurch Utd.	22	10	5	7	37	32	35
Manurewa	22	9	6	7	40	42	33
Miramar Rangers	22	8	7	7	40	46	31
Wellington Diamond U.	22	7	9	6	31	26	30
Dunedin City	22	8	4	10	34	39	28
Napier City Rovers	22	7	5	10	38	53	26
North Shore Utd.	22	7	4	11	27	31	25
Mount Wellington	22	5	9	8	28	36	24
Nelson United	22	5	6	11	25	42	21
University	22	5	4	13	31	36	19

Cup final: Manurewa 2, Gisborne City 1.
Top scorer: Colin Walker (Gisborne City) 16 goals.
*Three points for a win.

Gisborne began to press forward with any serious intent. They did pull one goal back, through midfielder Cresswell, in the eighteenth minute. But their desperate last attempts to force the goal which would bring extra time were foiled by Manurewa goalkeeper Rudi Feitsma.

CHRISTCHURCH UNITED
Founded: 1970.
Colours: All blue.
Stadium: English Park (12,000) and Queen Elizabeth II Park (40,000).
Club address: Christchurch United, c/o New Zealand FA, PO Box 18296, Glen Innes, Auckland 6.
League: 1973, 1975.
Cup: 1972, 1974, 1975, 1976.

DUNEDIN CITY
Founded: 1909 (as High School Old Boys).
Colours: Gold/blue.
Stadium: Caledonian Ground (8,300).
Club address: Dunedin City, c/o New Zealand FA, PO Box 18296, Glen Innes, Auckland 6.
League: – .
Cup: 1981.

GISBORNE CITY
Founded: 1939 (as Eastern Union).
Colours: All sky blue.
Stadium: Childers Road (8,000).
Club address: Gisborne City FC, c/o New Zealand FA, PO Box 18296, Glen Innes, Auckland 6.
League: 1984.
Cup: – .

MANUREWA
Founded: 1960.
Colours: Yellow/blue.
Stadium: Gallagher Park, Auckland (3,000).
Club address: Manurewa FC, c/o New Zealand FA, PO Box 18296, Glen Innes, Auckland 6.
League: 1983.
Cup: 1978, 1984.

MOUNT WELLINGTON
Founded: 1952.
Colours: All red.
Stadium: Bell McKinlay Park, Auckland (7,000).

Club address: Mount Wellington FC, c/o New Zealand FA, PO Box 18296, Glen Innes, Auckland 6.
League: 1972, 1974, 1979, 1980, 1982 (5).
Cup: 1973, 1980, 1982, 1983 (4).

NORTH SHORE UNITED
Founded: 1894.
Colours: All maroon.
Stadium: Fuji Film Stadium, Auckland (3,000).
Club address: North Shore United FC, c/o New Zealand FA, PO Box 18296, Glen Innes, Auckland 6.
League: 1977.
Cup: 1952, 1960, 1963, 1967, 1979 (5).

WELLINGTON DIAMOND UNITED
Founded: 1893.
Colours: Orange/blue.
Stadium: Basin Reserve (12,000).
Club address: Wellington Diamond Utd., c/o New Zealand FA, PO Box 18296, Glen Innes, Auckland 6.
League: 1976, 1981.
Cup: – .

NORTHERN IRELAND

Linfield, for all their domination of Northern Ireland football, have yet to beat Belfast rivals Glentoran in a cup final. Their chances this past season of ending that jinx looked particularly bright. Linfield had again run away with the league title, leaving Coleraine trailing three points behind as runners-up and Glentoran down in thrid place, at a distance of five points. In lorry driver Martin McGaughey, Linfield boasted one of the most effective strikers in domestic competition in Eurpoe. For weeks he had been dueling with Fernando Gomes of FC Porto as to who could run up the most league goals in Europe. Then, a couple of weeks before the end of the season, McGaughey was injured. With thirty-four goals he was beyond catching by any other Northern Irish goalscorers, but Gomes was able to get clean away to land the Golden Boot prize.

As for Linfield, the injury significantly reduced their chances against Glentoran in the cup final at The Oval, Glentoran's home ground. Linfield are a club whose name and tradition lie very much on the Protestant side of the Irish divide. But Glentoran are proud of their record for constructing 'mixed' teams; the suburban hooliganism of both sets of fans – which started outside the stadium well before kick-off – reflected the political, social and religious gap.

The game matched the mood. It was a hard, rugged match, with few chances once it had got going, eight minutes late because a linesman needed attention after being struck by a missile thrown from the crowd just before the scheduled start time. Headers by Mullan and Gibson – after twenty-three and forty-one minutes respectively – provided the only goals in a 1–1 draw which was described afterwards as 'a war', by Glentoran manager Billy Johnston. But he had a smile on his face when his team won the replay 1–0, earning the right to enter the Cup-winners' Cup as holders.

For football in general in Northern Ireland this had been a watershed season, the first without the financial back-up of a couple of British championship internationals. That particular lifeline had ended with the 1–1 draw against Wales in Swansea on 22 May, 1984. Players and officials insisted that the ending of the British championship against their wishes would only make them all the more determined, in a World Cup qualifying group which featured England as well as Rumania, Finland and Turkey. That bubble of confidence was punctured when the Irish lost their first qualifying tie by 1–0 away to a Finland team which had been dismissed as the minnows of the group. But home victories over Rumania, the Finns and Turkey revived hope to a pitch not even defeat in Belfast by England could quell.

The 2–0 victory over Turkey in Belfast was Pat Jennings's 110th appearance for Northern Ireland, making him the most-capped British player of all time and putting him behind only Bjorn Nordqvist (Sweden, 115) and Dino Zoff (Italy, 112) in the European, if not world, rankings.

1984–85 League Table

	P	W	D	L	F	A	Pts
Linfield	26	17	5	4	67	22	39
Coleraine	26	14	8	4	55	30	36
Glentoran	26	14	6	6	54	27	34
Portadown	26	13	5	8	34	29	31
Cliftonville	26	10	8	8	37	35	28
Crusaders	26	9	9	8	32	37	27
Glenavon	26	11	4	11	45	53	26
Ballymena	26	9	7	10	36	35	25
Distillery	26	8	8	10	35	41	24
Larne	26	10	2	14	37	47	22
Ards	26	8	5	13	32	40	21
Newry	26	7	6	13	39	57	20
Bangor	26	5	9	12	24	39	19
Carrick	26	3	6	17	24	62	12

Cup final: Glentoran 1, Linfield 0 (after 1–1 draw).
Top scorer: McGaughey (Linfield) 34 goals.

ARDS
Founded: 1902.
Colours: Red/white.
Stadium: Castlereagh Park (10,000).
Club address: Ards, c/o 27 Chesterbrook Cres, Newtownards, Co Down BT23 392.
League: 1958.
Cup: 1927, 1952, 1969, 1974 (4).

BALLYMENA UNITED
Founded: 1928 (as Ballymena).
Colours: All sky blue.
Stadium: The Showgrounds (8,000).
Club address: Ballymena United, c/o 17 Rock Mount, Doury Road, Ballymena BT43.
League: – .
Cup: 1929, 1940, 1958, 1981, 1984 (5).

CARRICK RANGERS
Founded: 1939.
Colours: Yellow/black.
Stadium: Taylors Avenue, Carrickfergus (5,000).
Club address: Carrick Rangers, c/o 68 North Road, Carrickfergus, Co Antrim BT38 8LZ.
League: – .
Cup: 1976.

CLIFTONVILLE
Founded: 1879.
Colours: Red/white.
Stadium: Cliftonville (21,000).
Club address: Cliftonville, c/o 8 Seamount Parade, Belfast BT15 3NT.
League: 1906 (shared), 1910.
Cup: 1883, 1888, 1897, 1900, 1901, 1907, 1909, 1979 (8).

DISTILLERY
Founded: 1880.
Colours: White/black.
Stadium: Lambeg (14,000).
Club address: Distillery, c/o 22 Slievedarragh Park, Belfast BT14 8JA.
League: 1896, 1899, 1901, 1903, 1906, 1963 (6).
Cup: 1884, 1885, 1886, 1889, 1894, 1896, 1903, 1905, 1910, 1925, 1956, 1971 (12).

COLERAINE
Founded: 1927.
Colours: Blue and white/white.
Stadium: The Showgrounds, Coleraine (8,000).
Club address: Coleraine, c/o 15 King's Road, Coleraine, Co Londonderry BT51 3LN.
League: 1974.
Cup: 1965, 1972, 1975, 1977 (4).

CRUSADERS
Founded: 1909.
Colours: Red and black stripes/black.
Stadium: Shore Road, Belfast (10,000).
Club address: Crusaders, c/o 15 Waveney Avenue, Belfast BT15 4FR.
League: 1973, 1976.
Cup: 1967, 1968.

GLENAVON
Founded: 1889.
Colours: Blue/white.
Stadium: Mourneview (8,000).
Club address: Glenavon, c/o 34 Greenhill Pk, Lurgan, Craigavon BT66 8LS.
League: 1952, 1957, 1960 (3).
Cup: 1957, 1959, 1961 (3).

GLENTORAN
Founded: 1883.
Colours: Red and green stripes/white.
Stadium: The Oval, Belfast (40,000).
Club address: Glentoran FC, The Oval, Mersey Street, Belfast BT4 1EW.
League: 1894, 1897, 1905, 1912, 1913, 1921, 1925, 1931, 1951, 1953, 1964, 1967, 1968, 1970, 1972, 1977, 1981 (17).
Cup: 1914, 1917, 1921, 1932, 1933, 1935, 1951, 1966, 1973, 1983, 1985 (11).

LINFIELD
Founded: 1886.
Colours: Blue/white.
Stadium: Windsor Park (45,000).
Club address: Linfield FC, Windsor Park, Donegall Avenue, Belfast BT12 6LW.
League: 1891, 1892, 1893, 1895, 1898, 1902, 1904, 1907, 1908, 1909, 1911, 1914, 1922, 1923, 1930, 1932, 1934, 1935, 1949, 1950, 1954, 1955, 1956, 1959, 1961, 1962, 1966, 1969, 1971, 1975, 1978, 1979, 1980, 1982, 1983, 1984, 1985 (37 – record).
Cup: 1891, 1892, 1893, 1895, 1898, 1899, 1902, 1904, 1912, 1913, 1915, 1916, 1919, 1922, 1923, 1930, 1931, 1934, 1936, 1939, 1942, 1945, 1946, 1948, 1950, 1953, 1960, 1962, 1963, 1970, 1978, 1980, 1982 (33 – record).

PORTADOWN
Founded: 1924.
Colours: Red/white.
Stadium: Shamrock Park (20,000).
Club address: Portadown, c/o 30 Clanbrassil Drive, Portadown, Craigavon BT63 5EH.
League: – .
Cup: – .

NORWAY

Vålerengen carrried off the 1984 league title – just as they had apparently intended right from the start of the campaign. Even when they weren't playing well the Oslo club picked up points. They lost only three of their twenty-two games, and conceded just fourteen goals to land the crown after taking advantage of the slip-ups of long-time pursuers Bryne and Lillestrøm.

Somehow there wasn't a lot of excitement about Vålerengen's success. It was due to a well-drilled team in which the defenders made few mistakes, and the midfielders and strikers severely punished any errors in the opposing penalty box. None of their domestic rivals ever outplayed them and they were not even thrown out of their stride when experienced Norway goalkeeper, Tom R. Jacobsen, was injured in mid-season. New signing, Geir Mediaas from Steinkjer, stepped in and produced some faultless performances.

Also, in defence, Vålerengen were fortunate to line up the discovery of the season in nineteen-year-old Per Edmund Mordt. He had been playing in the Norwegian fourth division a year earlier, yet within months of securing a first-team spot with Vålerengen, Mordt was playing for his country, and had an excellent game in the 1-0 World Cup win over the Republic of Ireland in Oslo in October last year.

Championship-winners are usually those teams who have the good fortune to avoid injuries. But in Vålerengen's case this wasn't true. Apart from goalkeeper Tom R. Jacobsen, they suffered several other injury problems in midfield and attack, but overcame them. They also survived a scandal over breaches of the amateur regulations which govern Norwegian league football still. Auditors discovered that Vålerengen had been paying their players real money instead of the 'prize cards' issued by the federation.

In addition, star striker Pål Jacobsen had been granted an interest-free loan. Jacobsen later paid back the cash, and declared the loan to the income tax authorities! He was suspended for two weeks by the federation, and fined. Also punished for these offences, which dated back to the 1983 season, were three senior officials of Vålerengen and two other players – one of whom, Morten Haugen, had in the meantime been transferred to Frigg of Oslo.

At the wrong end of the league, Strindheim, after sitting in mid-table for half the season, suddenly collapsed into the relegation zone, and duly finished bottom. Down with them went Fredrikstad, who won the cup, but paid the penalty for sacking Englishman Tony Knapp before the season, when they became the first Norwegian cup-winners ever to suffer relegation in the same season.

Fredrikstad's cup final opponents were Viking, who had finished runners-up in the league. The first match was drawn 3-3 after extra time, but while Fredrikstad managed another three superb goals in the replay, Viking

1984 League Table

	P	W	D	L	F	A	Pts*
Vålerengen	22	13	6	3	40	14	32
Viking	22	7	7	6	33	23	25
Start	22	10	5	7	33	29	25
Bryne	22	7	10	5	37	36	24
Lillestrøm	22	8	7	7	39	30	23
Rosenborg	22	8	7	7	36	37	23
Kongsvinger	22	9	8	5	29	32	23
Molde	22	7	7	8	36	41	21
EIK	22	8	3	11	30	36	19
Moss	22	4	9	9	26	30	17
Fredrikstad	22	5	7	10	23	35	17
Strindheim	22	5	5	12	18	37	15

Cup final: Fredrikstad 3, Viking 2 (replay after 3-3 draw).
Top scorer: Sverre Brandhaug (Rosenborg) 13 goals.

managed only two. Fredrikstad were two-up in eighteen minutes through Jørn Andersen and Per Egil Ahlsen (penalty) and though Kjell Lundal pulled one back in the sixty-third minute, it was only five minutes more before Terje Jensen secured the cup for Fredrikstad. Andersen, Ahlsen, Vidar Hansen, Hans Deunk and goalkeeper Jan Erik Olsen were Fredrikstad's best players.

BRANN
Founded: 1908.
Colours: All red.
Stadium: Brann Stadion (25,200).
Club address: Sportsklubben Brann, Boks 161, 5032 Minde.
League: 1962, 1963.
Cup: 1923, 1925, 1972, 1976, 1982 (5).

BRYNE
Founded: 1926.
Colours: Red/white.
Stadium: Bryne Stadion (8,000).
Club address: Bryne Idrettslag Fotballgruppa, Boks 257, 4341 Bryne.
League: – .
Cup: – .

FREDRIKSTAD
Founded: 1903.
Colours: White/red.
Stadium: Fredrikstad Stadion (15,000).
Club address: Fredrikstad Fotballklub, Boks 300, 1601 Fredrikstad.
League: 1938, 1939, 1949, 1951, 1952, 1954, 1957, 1960, 1961 (9 – record).
Cup: 1932, 1935, 1936, 1938, 1940, 1950, 1957, 1961, 1966, 1984 (10).

LILLESTRØM
Founded: 1917.
Colours: Yellow/black.
Stadium: Lillestrøm Stadion (8,000).
Club address: Lillestrøm Sportsklubb, Boks 196, 2001 Lillestrøm.
League: 1959, 1976, 1977 (3).
Cup: 1977, 1978, 1981 (3).

MOLDE
Founded: 1911.
Colours: Blue/white.
Stadium: Molde Stadion (6,000).
Club address: Molde Fotballklubb, Boks 316, 6401 Molde.
League: – .
Cup: – .

MOSS
Founded: 1906.
Colours: Yellow/black.
Stadium: Moss Stadion (6,000).

Club address: Moss Fotballklub, Boks 47, 1501 Moss.
League: – .
Cup: 1983.

ROSENBORG TRONDHEIM
Founded: 1917.
Colours: White/black.
Stadium: Lerkendal Stadion (30,000).
Club address: Rosenborg Ballklubb, Boks 592, 7001 Trondheim.
League: 1967, 1969, 1971 (3).
Cup: 1960, 1964, 1971 (3).

START
Founded: 1905.
Colours: Yellow/black.
Stadium: Kristiansand Stadion (6,000).
Club address: Idrettsklubben Start, Marvikveien 94, 4600 Kristiansand.
League: 1978, 1980.
Cup: – .

VALERENGEN
Founded: 1913.
Colours: Blue/white.
Stadium: Important matches in the Ullevål Stadium (24,500).
Club address: Vålerengen Idrettsforening, Boks 6016, Etterstad, Oslo 6.
League: 1965, 1981, 1983, 1984 (4).
Cup: 1980.

VIKING STAVANGER
Founded: 1899.
Colours: Blue/white.
Stadium: Stavanger Stadion (19,800).
Club address: Vikings Fotballavdeling, Boks 587, 4001 Stavanger.
League: 1958, 1972, 1973, 1974, 1975, 1979, 1982 (7).
Cup: 1953, 1959, 1979 (3).

PARAGUAY

Guarani, who featured in the first official football match organised in Paraguay seventy-nine years ago, returned to the headlines after nearly two decades in the doldrums to win the championship for the eighth time. And a complicated affair it was – not so much for any reason created by Guarani, but because of the sheer nature of the Paraguayan championship.

First the top ten clubs competed in two mini-leagues, with the two leading clubs then playing off to decide the overall first round winner. In this case that meant Olimpia, champions for the six previous years, who defeated Guarani 6-3 in the first stage decider. Olimpia – who had been Guarani's opponents in that first match long ago – collected four bonus points for their success. Guarani collected three – and vital points they would turn out to be at the end of the championship.

Next came yet another stage, involving matches in two mini-leagues. Total points were then added together from first and second rounds, with the bonus points teams automatically qualifying for the final stage of the championship. Through with them went Sol de America and Atletico Colegiales.

Then each club played the others once. If a simple system of points gained in this final stage had decided the champions, then Cerro Porteno would have landed the crown for the twentieth time in their seventy-two-year history. They had, after all, won more games (three) in the final round than anybody else, and conceded fewer goals (two in five games). But they had collected only one bonus point in that first round, compared with three for Guarani. And those bonus points edged Guarani one point ahead of Cerro to the title and a triumph for Cayetano Re, the one-time Paraguayan international centre-forward who had returned home after a successful playing career in Spain, which included spells at Elche and Barcelona.

Guarani won the first Paraguayan title back in 1906, but reached probably their finest era in the 1960s. Then they colllected the title in 1964 and 1967, and once reached the semi-finals of the South American Club Cup. In 1966 they lost out to River Plate of Argentina at the penultimate stage, but returned two years later to progress as far as the quarter-final groups before having to make do with runners-up spot – and elimination – behind Palmeiras of Brazil.

If Cayetano Re's ambitions stretched to the South American Club Cup, he kept it a secret. Hardly had the championship ended than he handed in his notice at Guarani to take over as Paraguay's national team manager for the World Cup qualifiers against Bolivia and three-times champions Brazil. Re was succeeded at Guarani by Juan Angel Romero.

This was not the only off-field controversy in which Guarani were involved. Another made headlines during the first round of the championship, when Luis Garcia Siani of struggling Nacional, claimed he had been offered 400 dollars to play badly against Guarani. He named two former Guarani players as the men who tried to buy his assistance in a game which Guarani did win by 2-1. An inquiry to discover whether the two former players still had any connection with Guarani proved a waste of time.

Olimpia had a bitterly disappointing season. The upsets began in the South American Club Cup. In their first round group they started their last match – against the once-infamous Argentines of Estudiantes de la Plata – needing to win by five clear goals to pip Independiente at the top on goal difference. When the score was still 0-0 at half-time, Olimpia knew it was hopeless. They had given up on a miracle to such an extent that when they were awarded a penalty, goalkeeper Almeida was summoned the full length of the pitch to despatch what proved to be the winning goal past Luis Islas.

Back in domestic competition, Olimpia rallied their supporters with the first round play-off win by 6-3 over Guarani. Olimpia believed that winning the first round guaranteed a place in the 1985 South American Club Cup. In fact it didn't. In the final round of the championship, Olimpia lost one of their early matches by 3-0 to struggling Atletico Colegiales. With that defeat went their hopes of a seventh consecutive championship – and also Uruguayan coach Angel Castelnoble.

He was replaced by another Uruguayan, Luis Cubilla. A roly-poly right-winger in the 1960s who wandered to River Plate in Argentina and Barcelona in Spain before he returned to help Uruguay to fourth place in the 1970 World

Cup, Cubilla was no stranger to Olimpia. It was he who had masterminded their shock triumphs in 1979 in both the South American Club Cup, and then the World Club Cup (albeit against Sweden's Malmo in the latter showdown – not the most awkward of opponents). That success had taken Cubilla on to coach Uruguay's Peñarol and then Argentina's River Plate. But similar success eluded him, and he returned to Olimpia after being sacked both by Peñarol and then by River Plate.

One piece of sad news: the death after a street accident in Spain of Eulogio Martinez, a Barcelona star in the early 1960s, and perhaps Paraguay's greatest post-war player.

1984 Championship

First round final placings: 1 Olimpia* 12 pts. 2 Guarani 12 pts. 3 Cerro Porteño 11 pts. 4 Libertad 10 pts. 5 Sol de America 10 pts. 6 River Plate 8 pts. 7 Colegiales 8 pts. 8 Sportivo Luqueño 6 pts. 9 Nacional 6 pts. 10 Tembetary 6 pts.

*Olimpia beat Guarani 6-3 in a play-off for first place.

Second round final placings: Group A: 1 Libertad 14 pts. 2 Olimpia 14 pts. 3 Colegiales 12 pts. 4 Tembetary 7 pts. 5 Nacional 5 pts. Group B: 1 Sportivo Luqueno 12 pts. 2 River Plate 12 pts. 3 Sol de America 10 pts. 4 Cerro Porteno 9 pts. 5 Guarani 4 pts.

Third Round

	P	W	D	L	F	A	Bns	Pts
Guarani	5	2	3	0	10	6	3	10
Cerro Porteno	5	3	2	0	7	2	1	9
Olimpia	5	1	1	3	5	7	4	7
Libertad	5	1	3	1	2	4	1	6
Sol de America	5	1	3	1	6	6	0	5
Colegiales	5	0	2	3	2	7	0	2

CERRO PORTENO
Founded: 1912.
Colours: Red and white stripes/white.
Stadium: Dr Adriano Irala (30,000).
Club address: Cerro Porteno, Avenida de las Américas 828, Asunción.
League: 1913, 1915, 1918, 1919, 1935, 1939, 1940, 1941, 1944, 1950, 1954, 1961, 1963, 1966, 1970, 1972, 1973, 1974, 1977 (19).

GUARANI
Founded:1903.
Colours: Black and yellow stripes/black.
Stadium: Lorenzo Livieres (20,000).
Club address: Guarani, Av. Dr E. Ayala y Centenario, Asunción.
League: 1906, 1907, 1921, 1923, 1949, 1964, 1967, 1984 (8).

LIBERTAD
Founded: 1905.
Colours: Black and white stripes/white.
Stadium: Alfredo Stroessner (45,000; under construction).

Club address: Libertad, Av. Artigas y Cusmanich, Asunción.
League: 1910, 1917, 1920, 1930, 1943, 1945, 1955, 1976 (8).

NACIONAL
Founded: 1904.
Colours: White with red trimming/blue.
Stadium: Arsenio Erico (10,000).
Club address: Nacional FC, Caballero y Cerro León, Asunción.
League: 1909, 1911, 1924, 1926, 1942, 1946 (6).

OLIMPIA
Founded: 1902.
Colours: All white with black hoop.
Stadium: Estadio Manuel Ferreira (40,000), but important matches in the Estadio Defensores del Chaco (national stadium – 60,000).
Club address: Olimpia, Avenida Mariscal López 1499, Asunción.
League: 1912, 1914, 1916, 1927, 1928, 1929, 1931, 1936, 1937, 1938, 1947, 1948, 1956, 1957, 1958, 1959, 1960, 1962, 1965, 1968, 1969, 1971, 1975, 1978, 1979, 1980, 1981, 1982, 1983 (29 – record).
World Club Cup: 1979.
S. American Club Cup: 1979. Runners-up in 1960.
Interamerican Cup: 1980.

SOL DE AMERICA
Founded: 1909.
Colours: All blue.
Stadium: Estadio Sol (8,000).
Club address: Sol de America, Av. A. de Figueroa y Tacuary, Asunción.
League: – .

SPORTIVO LUQUEÑO
Founded: 1921.
Colours: Blue and yellow stripes/blue.
Stadium: Feliciano Caceres (38,000).
Club address: Sportivo Luqueño, Calle Rodriguez de Francis, Luque.
League: 1951, 1953.

PERU

Sport Boys from the Lima port of Callao, one of the outstanding clubs in the early days of organised league football in Peru, returned to their former glories by landing the 1984 championship. But it was close. At the end of the season, which involved them in forty-three matches spread across two league programmes, they finished up one point ahead of Colegio Nacional Iquitos – another surprise packet in a season which saw traditional giants such as Alianza, Sporting Cristal and Universitario take a back seat.

Peruvian football has many problems, most of them stemming from finance, or the lack of it. Several times in recent years the championship has been suspended because of rows between the Lima-based clubs and the provincial

1984 Championship
First Round – Metropolitan Zone

	P	W	D	L	F	A	Pts
Universitario	18	10	6	2	28	14	26
Alianza Lima	18	8	8	2	28	16	24
Sporting Cristal	18	9	4	5	37	26	22
Sport Boys	18	8	5	5	31	22	21
C.N.I.	18	6	4	8	15	21	16
Union Huaral	18	6	4	8	17	22	16
Dep. Municipal	18	4	7	7	23	26	15
Atletico Chalaco	18	3	9	6	21	28	15
Juventud La Palma	18	3	7	8	17	34	13
Octavio Espinoza	18	3	6	9	10	18	12

Southern Zone

	P	W	D	L	F	A	Pts
Melgar	16	8	3	4	21	14	21
Diablos Rojos	16	9	2	5	22	12	20
Coronel Bolognesi	16	6	4	6	16	15	16
Cienciano	16	4	4	8	8	20	12
Alfonso Ugarte	16	5	1	10	24	30	11

Northern Zone

	P	W	D	L	F	A	Pts
Atletico Torino	16	8	4	4	28	21	20
Sport Pilsen	16	7	5	4	28	25	19
Univ. de Catamarja	16	7	4	5	30	20	18
Carlos Manucci	16	4	4	8	19	28	12
Jose Galvez	16	3	5	8	24	35	11

Central Zone

	P	W	D	L	F	A	Pts
Dep. Tarma	16	9	4	3	25	12	22
Huancayo	16	6	5	5	18	15	17
Defensor Anda	16	7	3	6	14	15	17
Dep. Hospital	16	7	1	8	18	20	15
Hostal Rey	16	2	5	9	15	28	9

*Top five clubs from the Metropolitan (Lima) zone and the three from each of the other three zones qualified for the final championship round.

Final Round

	P	W	D	L	F	A	Pts
Sport Boys	26	13	9	4	34	15	35
Colegio Nacional Iquitos	26	13	8	5	41	21	34
Alianza Lima	26	10	9	7	34	17	29
Melgar	26	9	10	7	25	32	28
Sporting Cristal	26	8	12	6	35	24	28
Universitario	26	11	5	10	41	32	27
Atletico Torino	26	11	5	10	44	30	27
Coronel Bolognesi	26	9	8	9	26	28	26
Huancayo	26	9	8	9	21	34	26
Deportiva Tarma	26	6	11	9	15	28	23
Union Huaral	26	9	4	13	14	37	22
Universidad Catamarja	26	8	5	13	24	27	21
Sport Pilsen	26	6	7	13	27	50	19
Diablos Rojos	26	5	9	12	13	32	19

teams about fixture arrangements and travel costs. The Lima clubs always protest that whereas they pull in big crowds in the provinces, the provincial clubs, in return, are no attraction in Lima.

Consider the attendances. In May 1984, while a good crowd (by Peruvian championship standards) of 12,285, turned out to see one of the main Lima derbies, between Sporting Cristal and Universitario, across the city only 526 fans went along to see Alianza – sixteen times champions and one of the oldest and most popular clubs in the country – play at home to unrated, unfashionable Octavio Espinoza.

It's hardly any wonder that the metropolitan clubs felt they couldn't afford the fares for flights up and down the country. Indeed, it's because of these problems that – with the exception of the great central defender Hector Chumpitaz – Peru has never held on to its star players.

Over the last twenty-five years, outstanding men such as Juan Seminario (Zaragoza, Barcelona and Fiorentina), Victor Benitez (Milan and Roma), Miguel Loayza (River Plate of Buenos Aires), Juan Gallardo (Milan and Cagliari), and more recently World Cup stars such as Teofilo Cubillas, Cesar Cueto and Guillermo La Rosa, have been sold abroad.

The clubs and federation are so deeply in debt, that both for the qualifying rounds of the 1982 and 1986 World Cups it was only thanks to the cash provided by a television corporation that Peru's leading foreign-based players were able to be recalled. The outcome for domestic competition was the reorganisation in 1984. The first round consisted of home and away matches being played in four regional zones with the pious hope that this would supply the finance to subsidise the second round, which involved the top teams from all four sections.

The season began with bad news. Chumpitaz, now well over forty and the unofficial world record-holder with 127 international appearances claimed on his behalf, announced that this would be his last season. His club, Sporting Cristal, as if in sympathy, hit a bad patch and duly let Universitario escape at the top of the metropolitan league. Sporting Cristal also lost a controversial first-round play-off by 2-1 against Universidad de los Andes of Venezuela in the South American Club Cup and missed out on the anticipated cash bonanza of two lucrative home matches in the semi-finals.

It was a bad year for Peruvian clubs in the international tournament. The other Peruvian entry, Melgar, were banned from the event for a year for fielding an ineligible player. That proved to be immaterial anyway, for Melgar finished in fourth place, seven points behind Sport Boys in the second round of the championship. Sport Boys were unstoppable, and not even a couple of witch doctors – hired by opponents Atletico Torino on a visit to Callao – had any effect. Sport Boys won 3-0.

Finally, Alianza, who finished third, set a championship record with the size of their 11-0 win over Sport Pilsen. Veteran Cubillas, recalled from the North American Soccer League, hit a hat-trick.

ALFONSO UGARTE
Founded: 1929.
Colours: White with red sash/black.
Stadium: Estadio Torres Belón de Puno (25,000).
Club address: Club Alfonso Ugarte, Puno, Prov. de Puno.
League: – .

ALIANZA
Founded: 1901.
Colours: Blue and white stripes/blue.
Stadium: Alejandro Villanueva (38,000).
Club address: Club Alianza de Lima, Puerta 4, Estadio Alianza, Alejandro Villanueva, Lima.
League: 1927, 1928, 1931, 1932, 1933, 1934, 1948, 1952, 1954, 1955, 1957, 1962, 1963, 1965, 1977, 1978 (16).

ATLÉTICO CHALACO
Founded: 1902.
Colours: Red and white stripes/white.
Stadium: Telmo Carbajo (15,000).
Club address: Atlético Chalaco, 585 V. Fajardo, Callao, Lima.
League: 1930, 1947.

ATLETICO TORINO
Founded: 1952.
Colours: All white with two black stripes on the right.
Stadium: Campeonisimo (10,000).
Club address: Club Atlético Torino, Estadio Campeonisimo, Talaca, Prov. Piura.
League: – .

DEPORTIVO MUNICIPAL
Founded: 1935.
Colours: White with red sash/black.
Stadium: Important matches in the Estadio Nacional (45,000).
Club address: Club Deportivo Municipal, Estadio Nacional, Puerta No 4, Calle Jose Diaz, Lima.
League: 1938, 1940, 1943, 1949 (4).

MELGAR
Founded: 1915.
Colours: Red and black/black.
Stadium: Mariano Melgar (15,000).
Club address: Melgar FC, Sto Domingo 313, Arequipa,
League: 1981.

SPORT BOYS
Founded: 1927.
Colours: Pink/black.
Stadium: Telmo Carbajo (15,000).
Club address: Sport Boys, Estadio Telmo Carbajo, Callao, Lima.
League: 1935, 1937, 1942, 1951, 1958, 1984 (6).

SPORTING CRISTAL
Founded: 1922.
Colours: Sky blue/white.
Stadium: Alejandro Villanueva (50,000).

Club address: Club Sporting Cristal, Puerta 4, Estadio Alianza, Alejandro Villanueva, Lima.
League: 1926, 1956, 1961, 1968, 1970, 1972, 1973, 1979, 1980, 1983 (10).

UNION HUARAL
Founded: 1947.
Colours: Red and white stripes/black.
Stadium: Estadio Huaras (12,000).
Club address: Union Huaral, Estadio Huaras, Huaral, Lima.
League: 1976.

UNIVERSITARIO
Founded: 1924.
Colours: All cream.
Stadium: Lolo Fernandez (20,000).
Club address: Club Universitario de Deportes, 04 J. Chavez, Lima.
League: 1929, 1939, 1941, 1945, 1946, 1959, 1960, 1964, 1966, 1967, 1969, 1971, 1975, 1982 (14).
S. American Club Cup: Runners-up in 1972.

POLAND

Górnik of Zabrze, the only Polish team ever to have reached a European final, are back among the continental elite. Some thirteen years after their last league success, and fifteen years since they lost to Manchester City in the Cup-winners' Cup final in Vienna, they stand as champions of Poland. Górnik managed to cling onto a narrow lead for most of the second half of the season, but underlined the strength of their title claim in the very last match when they won 2–1 to Widzew Lodz – who would themselves have won the championship instead if they had taken the match by a three-goal margin. Legia Warsaw might also have stolen the title on the last day but lost their chance when they were held 1–1 away by Pogoń Szczecin.

Górnik did not begin the season in particularly happy fashion because of a row over their transfer dealings, and it was Legia, the Polish army team, who were the early leaders and maintained their advantage at half-way and the winter break. The second half of the season got under way in March, and saw two important meetings between Legia and Górnik. The first was in a cup quarter-final first leg, which Górnik won 3–1 on their way towards the semi-finals. The second match was in the league; again Górnik ran up three goals to leapfrog to the top of the table. Another week and they were alone no longer. Now Górnik, Legia and Lech Poznań all stood on twenty-six points – and then Górnik were held 0–0 away by Górnik Walbrzych and slipped back to third place, though not for long. One more week and it was all change again. This time Legia and Widzew both lost, so Górnik went back into the league leadership, thanks to their 1–0 success over Baltyk Gdynia. Lech's challenge was now eliminated as Górnik beat them 5–0, and the stage was set for the dramatic run-in and its decisive last match.

At the other end of the table there was also plenty of drama right at the end when no fewer than seven clubs began their last-round matches knowing that one mistake could be enough to send them down to the second division along with six-times former champions Wisla Krakow. They had been bottom of the table at the winter break and failed to show any spark of revival. Also down there struggling were former champions Slask Wroclaw and the last-match dog-fight involved, along with them, Radomiak, Baltyk, Pogoń, Lechia, GKS and Motor Lublin. After an anxious flurry of action it was Radomiak who were pushed into the other relegation place.

Polish football has appeared comparatively unaffected by the social and political unrest of the last couple of years, possibly because control is so central. But there have been problems – notably with relation to transfers encouraged by a system of under-the-counter payments. There was also the player revolt during the last European championship qualifiers in support of goalkeeper Jozef Mlynarczyk, who had been turned off a flight abroad after arriving at Warsaw airport having had a few drinks too many.

The latest episode to prove that everything is not as it seems, involved Widzew's international midfielder Jerzy Wijas towards the end of the season. The matter came into the open – and into the Polish newspapers too – after Wijas was selected, then dropped, from the national team's squad to face Belgium in a World Cup qualifier. Wijas, it turned out, had been refused an exit visa by the passport authorities on the grounds that he was refusing to undertake his compulsory stint of national service.

The reasons are simple. For a long time Wijas had been the envy of Legia, the army club. They have in recent years been deprived of many of their old powers to dragoon other club's stars into the ranks. But the security of an army life plus the certainty of a career beyond the game can make joining an army team an attractive proposition for an Eastern European player. Wijas didn't agree. What's more, his club, Widzew didn't agree. Legia couldn't make any formal approaches until Wijas had enlisted as a conscript. Thus, with the support of the Widzew club president, he did not enlist, and because he didn't enlist he ran into hot water with the authorities. Wijas had played well in the

1984–85 League Table

	P	W	D	L	F	A	Pts
Górnik Zabrze	30	16	10	4	38	16	42
Legia Warsaw	30	17	7	6	36	19	41
Widzew Lódź	30	13	12	5	34	16	38
Lech Poznań	30	14	10	6	41	31	38
Zaglebie	30	11	9	10	37	38	31
L K S Lódź	30	11	8	11	31	32	30
Ruch Chorzow	30	10	9	11	28	28	29
Górnik Walbrzych	30	8	13	9	32	35	29
Motor Lublin	30	9	9	12	30	36	27
G K S Katowice	30	7	12	11	22	28	26
Lechia Gdansk	30	8	10	12	23	24	26
Pogoń Szczecin	30	9	8	13	24	36	26
Baltyk Gdynia	30	9	8	13	22	35	26
Slask Wroclaw	30	8	9	13	34	36	25
Radomiak Radom	30	8	9	13	29	32	25
Wisla Krakow	30	7	7	16	19	32	21

Cup final: Widzew bt GKS 3-1 on pens after 0-0 draw.
Top scorer: Leszek Iwaricki (Motor Lublin) 14 goals.

previous 2-1 home win over Finland in a friendly in Opole but his skill and perception were badly missed in Brussels where Poland lost 2–0 and also, later in the month, in Tirana, even though Poland managed a 1–0 victory there over Albania. He then faced not only disciplinary proceedings through the federation, angry and embarrassed by his 'neglect of duty' but legal action for non-enlistment.

CRACOVIA
Founded: 1906.
Colours: Red and white stripes/white.
Stadium: Cracovia (12,000).
Club address: Klub Sportowy Cracovia, 31–111 Krakow, ul. Manifestu Lipcowego 27.
League: 1921, 1930, 1932, 1937, 1948 (5).
Cup: – .

G K S KATOWICE
Founded: 1964.
Colours: Red/white.
Stadium: Katowice (18,000).
Club address: Gorniczy Klub Sportowy Katowice, 40-952 Katowice, ul. Ceglana 68.
League: – .
Cup: – .

GORNIK ZABRZE
Founded: 1948.
Colours: Blue/white.
Stadium: Gornik (25,000).
Club address: Klub Sportowy Gornik, 41–800 Zabrze, ul. Roosevelta 81.
League: 1957, 1959, 1961, 1963, 1964, 1965, 1966, 1967, 1971, 1972, 1985 (11).
Cup: 1965, 1968, 1969, 1970, 1971, 1972 (6).
Cup-winners' Cup: Runners-up in 1970.

GWARDIA
Founded: 1948.
Colours: All blue.
Stadium: Gwardia (12,000).
Club address: Warszawski Klub Sportowy Gwardia, 02–634 Warsaw, ul. Raclawicka 132.
League: – .
Cup: 1954.

LECH
Founded: 1922.
Colours: Blue/white.
Stadium: Lech (35,000).
Club address: Kolejowy Klub Sportowy Lech, 61–875 Poznan, ul. Marchlewskiego 142.
League: 1983.
Cup: 1982, 1984.

LEGIA
Founded: 1916.
Colours: All white.
Stadium: Legia (35,000).
Club address: Centralny Wojskowy Klub Sportowy Legia, 00–950 Warsaw, ul. Lazienkowska 3.
League: 1955, 1956, 1969, 1970 (4).
Cup: 1955, 1956, 1964, 1966, 1973, 1980, 1981 (7).

L K S
Founded: 1908.
Colours: Red/white.
Stadium: Lodz (40,000).
Club address: Lódzki Klub Sportowy, 90-420, Lódź, ul. Piotrkowska 76.
League: 1958.
Cup: 1957.

RUCH
Founded: 1920.
Colours: Blue/white.
Stadium: Ruch (40,000). Important matches in the Slaski stadium (93,000).
Club address: Klub Sportowy Ruch, 41–506 Chorzow, ul. Cicha 6.
League: 1933, 1934, 1935, 1936, 1938, 1939 (unfinished), 1947, 1952, 1953, 1960, 1968, 1974, 1975, 1979 (14 – record).
Cup: 1951, 1974.

SLASK WROCLAW
Founded: 1946.
Colours: White/green.
Stadium: Olimpijski (45,000).
Club address: Wojskowy Klub Sportowy Slask, 54–434 Wroclaw, ul. Oporowska 62.
League: 1977.
Cup: 1976.

STAL MIELEC
Founded: 1939.
Colours: Blue/white.
Stadium: Stal (30,000).
Club address: Fabryczny Klub Sportowy Stal, 39–300 Mielec, ul. Soskiego.
League: 1973, 1976.
Cup: – .

SZOMBIERKI BYTOM
Founded: 1919.
Colours: White/green.
Stadium: Szombierki (35,000).
Club address: Gorniczy Klub Sportowy Szombierki, 41–907 Bytom, ul. Frycza Modrzewskiego 3.
League: 1980.
Cup: – .

WIDZEW LODZ
Founded: 1910.
Colours: White/red.
Stadium: Widzew (25,000).
Club address: Robotnicze Towarzystwo Sportowe Widzew, 92–230 Lodz, ul.
Armii Czerwonej 80.
League: 1981, 1982.
Cup: 1985.

WISLA
Founded: 1906.
Colours: All red.
Stadium: Wisla (45,000).
League: 1927, 1928, 1949, 1950, 1951, 1978 (6).
Cup: 1967.

ZAGLEBIE
Founded: 1906.
Colours: Red/white.
Stadium: Ludowy (34,000).
Club address: Gorniczy Klub Sportowy Zaglebie, 41–200 Sosnowiec, Stadion
Ludowy.
League: – .
Cup: 1962, 1963, 1977, 1978 (4).

PORTUGAL

Porto carried almost everything before them in Portugal to win the league
championship and domestic Super Cup before finishing runners-up to Benfica
in the cup final. Skipper Fernando Gomes finished the season with thirty-nine
goals, which not only left him unchallenged as the league's top scorer, but also
meant regaining the Golden Boot as the most lethal striker in Europe. The key
to the outcome of the season's campaign was to be found in the close-season
transfer dealings of 1984. Porto lost international midfielders Jaime Pacheco
and Sousa to Sporting of Lisbon but hit back with interest in whisking away
Sporting's Paolo Futre, the most outstanding young player in Portuguese
football.

Benfica, meanwhile, the third 'great', were having all sorts of problems.
Swedish coach Sven-Goran Eriksson had left for Roma, closely pursued
by midfielder Glenn Stromberg, who signed for Atalanta. Also, Fernando
Chalana, the midfielder-cum-winger who had starred in the finals of the
European championship, had been the subject of a string of bids and an offer
of £1.5 million – a record for a Portuguese player – from Bordeaux had been
impossible to refuse. Benfica's fans expected some compensatory signings to
fill all those gaps – in vain. President Fernando Martins insisted that the money
had to go towards the expansion and development of Benfica's stadium and
other sports facilities.

As if that wasn't enough to provoke unrest, Benfica had trouble replacing
Eriksson as coach. Yogoslav Tonislav Ivic was eventually taken on, and quit

after a fortnight because Benfica refused to pay him in German marks, only escudos. Pal Csernai, the Hungarian-born former Bayern Munich coach, was quickly hired. But he proved totally the wrong choice, upsetting both players and the media. Long before the season had finished it was known he was on his way back to West Germany, to Borussia Dortmund. In fact, if Benfica hadn't won the cup he would have become the first coach in more than twenty years to have failed to win at least one trophy for the Eagles of Lisbon.

Sporting also had managerial problems, though theirs didn't surface until the closing weeks of the season, significantly after it became clear they had no hope of catching Porto at the top of the table. Welshman John Toshack had been appointed by Sporting in the hope that he could recreate the success of fellow Briton Malcolm Allison, under whom they had won the league-and-cup double in 1982. But Toshack was dogged by problems. Sporting suffered a string of injuries to key players early in the season, yet by the half-way mark were doing well to stay in contention with Porto at the top.

Along the way they had provided Toshack with a 2-0 victory over the Belenenses side run by Jimmy Melia, an 8-1 thrashing of Braga (Manuel Fernandes scored three in Sporting's biggest win in eleven years), and a goalless draw away to Porto. The match in the Antas stadium in the northern city was a tough affair. There were seven bookings – one of them for Toshack for a touchline protest – and a star display from Sporting's veteran goalkeeper, Victor Damas.

But later would come a shock cup defeat against struggling Rio Ave, a controversial television interview in which the tone of Toshack's criticisms of his players was misunderstood, and finally a swingeing attack on the Welshman by Sporting's (reserve) Bulgarian international midfielder, Kostov. A couple of days later – and with two matches remaining in the league campaign – it was announced that Sporting and Toshack had parted company. The premature end to his stay did nothing to reduce the reputation of British managerial ability, however, as Benfica demonstrated by bringing back from

1984–85 League Table

	P	W	D	L	F	A	Pts
FC Porto	30	26	3	1	78	13	55
Sporting Lisbon	30	19	9	2	72	26	47
Benfica	30	18	7	5	65	28	43
Boavista	30	13	11	6	37	26	37
Portimonense	30	14	8	8	51	41	36
Belenenses	30	11	8	11	40	46	30
Académica Coimbra	30	12	5	13	45	47	29
Sporting Braga	30	9	10	11	46	43	28
Victoria Guimaraes	30	9	7	14	33	39	25
Peñafiel	30	7	11	12	25	42	25
Victoria Setúbal	30	7	11	12	35	50	25
Salgueiros	30	8	7	15	40	56	23
Río Ave	30	7	9	14	27	43	23
Farense	30	7	8	15	21	49	22
Varzim	30	2	13	15	23	49	17
Vizela	30	4	7	19	31	71	15

Cup final: Benfica 3, FC Porto 1.
Top scorer: Fernando Gomes (FC Porto) 39.

Southampton John Mortimore, who had previously impressed in Lisbon before becoming assistant to Lawrie McMenemy.

Benfica's players were delighted by the appointment, and duly turned on one of their best displays of the season to defeat Porto 3-1 in the cup final in Lisbon. Nunes put Benfica ahead after just fourteen minutes of the final in the National Stadium, and Danish striker Michael Manniche – badly missed in mid-season when sidelined by knee trouble – increased that lead twenty minutes later. Two minutes into the second half the tall, lanky Manniche made it 3-0 from the penalty spot. Porto's only goal also came from the penalty mark, converted in the sixty-seventh minute by Futre. But that was much too late to prevent Porto going down to what was their seventh defeat on the eight occasions they have met Benfica in the final.

ACADÉMICA COIMBRA
Founded: 1914.
Colours: All black.
Stadium: Estadio Municipal (30,000).
Club address: Clube Academicá de Coimbra, Rua Alexandre Herculano 37, 3000 Coimbra.
League: – .
Cup: 1939.

BRAGA
Founded: 1921.
Colours: Red/white.
Stadium: Estadio 1° Maio (37,172).
Club address: Sporting Clube de Braga, Praça Conde de Agrolongo 126–1°, 4700 Braga.
League: – .
Cup: 1966.

BELENENSES
Founded:1919.
Colours: Blue/white.
Stadium: Estadio do Restelo (35,000).
Club address: Clube Futebol Os Belenenses, Estadio do Restelo, 1400 Lisbon.
League: 1946.
Cup: 1942, 1960.

BENFICA
Founded: 1904.
Colours: Red/white.
Stadium: Estádio da Luz (70,000).
Club address: Sport Lisboa e Benfica, Estádio da Luz, Apartado 21111, 1128 Lisbon Codex.
League: 1936, 1937, 1938, 1942, 1943, 1945, 1950, 1955, 1957, 1960, 1961, 1963, 1964, 1965, 1967, 1968, 1969, 1971, 1972, 1973, 1975, 1976, 1977, 1981, 1983, 1984 (26 – record).
Cup: 1930, 1931, 1935, 1940, 1943, 1944, 1949, 1951, 1952, 1953, 1955, 1957, 1959, 1962, 1964, 1969, 1970, 1972, 1980, 1981, 1985 (21 – record).

World Club Cup: Runners-up in 1961 and 1962.
Champions' Cup: 1961, 1962. Runners-up in 1963, 1965, 1968.
UEFA Cup: Runners-up in 1983.

BOAVISTA
Founded: 1903.
Colours: Black and white check/black.
Stadium: Estadio do Bessa (27,000).
Club address: Boavista Futebol Clube, Avenida da Boavista 1083, 4100 Oporto.
League: – .
Cup: 1975, 1976, 1979 (3).

PORTO
Founded: 1906.
Colours: Blue and white stripes/blue.
Stadium: Estadio das Antas (64,336).
Club address: Futebol Clube do Porto, Avenida Fernão de Magalhaes, 4300 Oporto.
League: 1935, 1939, 1940, 1956, 1959, 1978, 1979, 1985 (8).
Cup: 1922, 1925, 1932, 1937, 1956, 1958, 1968, 1977, 1984 (9).
Cup-winners' Cup: Runners-up in 1984.

SPORTING
Founded: 1906.
Colours: Green and white hoops/black.
Stadium: Estadio Jose Alvalade (49,089).
Club address: Sporting Clube de Portugal, Estadio Jose Alvalade, 1699 Lisbon Codex.
League: 1941, 1944, 1947, 1948, 1949, 1951, 1952, 1953, 1954, 1958, 1962, 1966, 1970, 1974, 1980, 1982 (16).
Cup: 1923, 1934, 1936, 1938, 1941, 1945, 1946, 1948, 1954, 1963, 1971, 1973, 1974, 1978, 1982 (15).
Cup-winners' Cup: 1964.

VARZIM
Founded: 1915.
Colours: All black.
Stadium: Estadio Varzim (25,000).
Club address: Varzim Sport Clube, Rua Santos Minho 28–1°, 4490 Póvoa de Varzim.
League: – .
Cup: – .

VITORIA GUIMARAES
Founded: 1922.
Colours: All white.
Stadium: Estadio Municipal (28,000).
Club address: Vitoria Sport Clube, Rua Joao I 83, 4800 Guimaraes.
League: – .
Cup: – .

VITORIA SETÚBAL
Founded: 1910.
Colours: Green and white stripes/white.
Stadium: Estadio do Bonfim (32,520).
Club address: Vitoria Futebol Clube, Rua do Bocage 4, 2902 Setúbal Codex.
League: – .
Cup: 1965, 1967.

REPUBLIC OF IRELAND

Shamrock Rovers became the first club in twelve years to retain the league title. In fact they went one better than in 1984, because this time they brought off the league-and-cup double for the first time in twenty-one years and their fourth double overall. Thus Shamrock manager Jim McLaughlin became the first to win the double with two different clubs, having already done so in 1979 with Dundalk. Shamrock won the famous Fried Chicken League of Ireland Championship – to give it the official title – early in April when a 3-1 victory over Cork City at Milltown added up to their twelfth title since they joined the league in 1922.

Goals from Noel King, Noel Larkin and Mick Byrne did the trick against Cork and it was Larkin – whom McLaughlin had rescued from virtual retirement after a long spell with Athlone Town – whose goal won the cup. It came in the fifty-seventh minute of a rain-soaked final against Galway United at Dalymount Park, providing a record twenty-second cup success.

McLaughlin was born in Derry, and played his early club football with Derry City – who created a precedent with their application to cross the border from the North and play in the League of Ireland's new first division. He moved to Birmingham in 1958 and then went on to play for Shrewsbury, Swansea and Peterborough – making a total of 456 Football League appearances, with 126 goals. He also played twelve times for Northern Ireland, but moved south when it came to entering management, taking over at Dundalk in November, 1974. The league-and-cup double in 1979 was the pinnacle of his achievement with the county Louth club, and he moved to Shamrock Rovers in 1983. His success has been instant. In 1984 Shamrock won the league title for the first time in twenty years and reached the cup final, and now they are double-holders.

Not that McLaughlin alone deserves all the credit. Among the regular players to make their mark were goalkeeper Jody Byrne – who followed McLaughlin from Dundalk – assistant manager Noel King in midfield along-side club captain Pat Byrne, and centre-forward Mick Byrne, who was Shamrock's top scorer with eleven goals.

Among the other clubs Bohemians finished as league runners-up, six points behind Shamrock, with Athlone third and University College Dublin fourth. The students were elected to the league only six years ago, and struggled until they allowed outsiders to play for them in 1983 – promptly surprising Shamrock Rovers in the 1984 cup final and performing creditably against Everton in the Cup-winners' Cup when they lost 'only' 0-0, 0-1 in the first round. Galway United are also comparative newcomers to the LOI, having joined in 1977. They came close to emulating UCD last season. They reached the cup final only to lose, of course, to Shamrock but their reward was a place in Europe.

Longford Town were relegated at the end of their first season in the top flight, but the other newcomers, Cork City, finished in mid-table despite parting with manager Bobby Tambling early in the season.

1984–85 League Table

	P	W	D	L	F	A	Pts
Shamrock Rovers	30	22	5	3	63	21	49
Bohemians	30	19	5	6	57	29	43
Athlone Town	30	17	6	7	54	28	40
U.C.D.	30	12	14	4	41	26	38
Limerick City	30	16	5	9	61	40	37
Galway Utd.	30	9	11	10	49	42	29
Waterford Utd	30	11	7	12	44	41	29
Dundalk	30	9	10	11	34	39	28
Cork City	30	10	8	12	30	39	28
Home Farm	30	11	5	14	43	47	27
St Patrick's Ath	30	10	7	13	36	45	27
Shelbourne	30	9	8	13	39	46	26
Sligo Rovers	30	7	12	11	34	47	26
Drogheda Utd.	30	7	10	13	43	60	24
Finn Harps	30	6	7	17	38	71	19
Longford Town	30	3	4	23	27	71	10

Cup final: Shamrock Rovers 1, Galway United 0.
Top scorers: O'Conner (Athlone Town) and Gaynor (Limerick City) each 17 goals.

ATHLONE
Founded: 1892.
Colours: Sky blue and black stripes/black.
Stadium: St Mel's Park (15,000).
Club address: Athlone Town AFC, St Mel's Park, Athlone, Westmeath.
League: 1981, 1983.
Cup: 1924.

BOHEMIANS
Founded: 1890.
Colours: Red and black stripes/black.
Stadium: Dalymount Park (45,000).
Club address: Bohemians FC, Dalymount Park, Phibsboro, Dublin 7.
League: 1924, 1928, 1930, 1934, 1936, 1975, 1978 (7).
Cup: 1928, 1935, 1970, 1976 (4).

DROGHEDA
Founded: 1919.
Colours: All claret with blue sleeves.
Stadium: United Park (15,000).
Club address: Drogheda United, United Park, Windmill Road, Drogheda.
League: – .
Cup: – .

DUNDALK
Founded: 1919.
Colours: White/black.
Stadium: Oriel Park (18,000).
Club address: Dundalk FC, Oriel Park, Dundalk.
League: 1933, 1963, 1967, 1976, 1979, 1982 (6).
Cup: 1942, 1949, 1952, 1958, 1977, 1979, 1981 (7).

FINN HARPS
Founded: 1954.
Colours: White/blue.
Stadium: Finn Park (10,000).
Club address: Finn Harps FC, Finn Park, Ballybofey, Co Donegal.
League: – .
Cup: 1974.

HOME FARM
Founded: 1928.
Colours: Sky blue and white hoops/white.
Stadium: Tolka Park (20,000).
Club address: Home Farm FC, Tolka Park, Richmond Road, Dublin.
League: – .
Cup: 1975.

LIMERICK CITY
Founded: 1983.
Colours: Yellow and green/green.
Stadium: Rathbane (15,000).
Club address: Limerick City FC, Rathbane, Limerick.
League: 1960 and 1980.
Cup: 1971 and 1982.

ST PATRICK'S ATHLETIC
Founded: 1929.
Colours: All red.
Stadium: Richmond Park (15,000).
Club address: St Patrick's Athletic FC, Emmet Road, Inchicore, Dublin 8.
League: 1952, 1955, 1956 (3).
Cup: 1959, 1961.

SHAMROCK ROVERS
Founded: 1899.
Colours: Green and white hoops/green.
Stadium: Glenmalure Park (25,000).
Club address: Shamrock Rovers FC, Glenmalure Park, Milltown Road, Dublin 6.
League: 1923, 1925, 1927, 1932, 1938, 1939, 1954, 1957, 1959, 1964, 1984, 1985 (12 – record).
Cup: 1925, 1929, 1930, 1931, 1932, 1933, 1936, 1940, 1944, 1945, 1948, 1955, 1956, 1962, 1964, 1965, 1966, 1967, 1968, 1969, 1978, 1985 (22 – record).

SHELBOURNE
Founded: 1895.
Colours: Red/white.
Stadium: Harold's Cross Stadium (10,000).
Club address: Shelbourne FC, Harold's Cross Stadium, Dublin 6.
League: 1926, 1929, 1931, 1944, 1947, 1953, 1962 (7).
Cup: 1939, 1960, 1963 (3).

SLIGO ROVERS
Founded: 1908.
Colours: Red and white stripes/red.
Stadium: The Showgrounds, (6,000).
Club address: Sligo Rovers FC, The Showgrounds, Sligo.
League: 1937, 1977.
Cup: 1983.

UNIVERSITY COLLEGE DUBLIN
Founded: 1895.
Colours: All blue.
Stadium: Belfield Park (10,000).
Club address: University College Dublin FC, Belfield, Dublin 4.
League: – .
Cup: 1984.

WATERFORD
Founded: 1921.
Colours: All blue.
Stadium: Kilcohan Park (10,000).
Club address: Waterford United FC, Kilcohan Park, Waterford.
League: 1966, 1968, 1969, 1970, 1972, 1973 (6).
Cup: 1937, 1980.

RUMANIA

Dinamo Bucharest did not, for once, have things all their own way, although they reached the last match of the season still with faint hopes of overhauling neighbours Steaua. Steaua had no intention, however, of slipping up. A goal from veteran international midfielder Ladislau Bölöni after twenty-six minutes was enough to defeat SC Bacău and ensure that the army team – as Steaua are – collected their tenth league title. The same afternoon Dinamo were beating FC Baia Mare 2-0 with goals from Orac, a forty-third-minute penalty, and Dragnea nine minutes from the end. It was a victory which ensured 'merely' a place in the 1985-86 UEFA Cup.

Steaua's triumph was created by the guiding hand of coach Florin Halagian, a forty-five-year-old who was once a useful forward with Dinamo Bucharest and then Arges Pitesti in the 1960s. Halagian believed in Steaua's league title chance to a greater extent than any of his players at the start of the season. But then, he probably saw better than they did how the signing of Bölöni from

Tirgu Mureş would make all the difference both in midfield control and in attacking penetration.

Steaua are the club backed by the Ministry of Defence, with Colonel Ion Popescu as president, and with a former Rumanian federation general secretary, Ion Alexandrescu, as head of the multi-sports club's football section. Alexandrescu played for Steaua in the 1950s when the club was known as CCA and building the reputation which has been duly maintained since their foundation after the war of never having been relegated. The current players' monthly pay of around £400 basic may seem poverty-line compared with the superstars of western Europe. But the advantages, particularly, of playing for Steaua are also to be found in an ideal way to pass the compulsory spell of national service and in the assurance of a job for life in the army, or other defence institutions. While on the subject of defence, it's worth noting that this was the very area in which Steaua had the advantage on the rest of the league. Their defence conceded twenty-four goals in thirty-four games, by far the best record around. Yet in mid-November few of their fans would have given much for Steaua's chances of improving on their second place behind Dinamo in the 1983–84 season.

The cause for pessimism was a 2-1 home defeat by Dinamo which left Steaua's greatest rivals two points clear of them at the top of the table. To Halagian's fury, his men had allowed Dinamo to snatch the points despite falling behind early on and despite having forward Suciu sent off twenty-five minutes from the final whistle.

The attack had failed. But there were few other failures after that. A fortnight after the defeat by Dinamo, Steaua revived their fans' faith with a 4-1 home victory over Politechnica Timisoara. Majaru scored a hat-trick – a rare feat in the Rumanian first division but one which was emulated just a week later by team-mate Piturca in the 3-1 away win over Bihor. The significance of that victory was that Dinamo were held 0-0 the same day by the Timisoara outfit so roundly beaten the previous week by Steaua. Thus the two Bucharest clubs were now level on points, but Steaua eased ahead to claim the halfway lead as the winter break arrived, thanks to a 4-1 win over Craiova. A bruising game saw Steaua striker Piturca and Craiova's sweeper and national team captain Stefanescu sent off eight minutes from the end.

Despite this narrow lead at the top, few people took Steaua seriously as championship challengers. They had been second too often. Voting in the Footballer of the Year poll underlined how underrated they remained, as not one Steaua player managed to get into the top five of a contest topped by Silviu Lung, the national team goalkeeper from Craiova. But Craiova were out of the title race – and Dinamo found Steaua's pace hard to match as well when the league restarted in March. The decisive matches came on 17 March in a double-header played before a Rumanian league record crowd of 100,000 in the August 23 stadium. Dinamo surprisingly lost 2-1 to Sportul Studentesc but Steaua moved four points clear at the top with a 2-0 victory over Rapid Bucharest. After that they never looked back. In the last couple of weeks Steaua began to give away silly points and allowed Dinamo faint hope of a miracle. But when the chips were down on the last day Steaua made sure of the points, and went on to complete the league-and-cup double by defeating Craiova in the cup final.

But if Steaua took the team honours, the individual who outshone all others was young winger Gheorghe Hagi, whose top-scoring twenty goals lifted Sportul Studentesc to third place in the table. Already in eastern Europe, they were calling him the 'Rumanian Maradona'.

1984–85 League Table

	P	W	D	L	F	A	Pts
Steaua	34	23	8	3	71	24	54
Dinamo Bucharest	34	21	10	3	59	31	52
Sportul Studentesc	34	20	8	6	71	28	48
Un. Craiova	34	17	5	12	61	46	39
Gloria Buzau	34	13	8	13	51	51	34
ASA Tirgu Mureş	34	13	7	14	32	32	33
Argeş Pitesti	34	12	8	14	44	35	32
Corvinul Hunedoara	34	15	2	17	51	52	32
Poli Timisoara	34	12	8	14	35	52	32
FC Bihor	34	13	5	16	39	43	31
Rapid Bucharest	34	10	10	14	36	43	30
FCM Brasov	34	13	4	17	33	41	30
FC Olt	34	13	4	17	34	52	30
Chimia Rm. Vilcea	34	11	7	16	26	50	29
SC Bacău	34	11	6	17	36	41	28
Jiul	34	11	6	17	36	58	28
FC Baia Mare	34	11	4	19	30	46	26
Poli Iasi	34	8	8	18	36	56	24

Cup final: Steaua Bucharest 2, Universitatea Craiova 1.
Top scorer: Gheorghe Hagi (Sportul Studentesc) 20 goals.

ARGEŞ PITESTI
Founded: 1953.
Colours: All blue.
Stadium: 1 Mai (15,000).
Club address: F C Argeş Pitesti, Pitesti, str Horia, Cloşca şi Crişan 15.
League: 1972, 1979.
Cup: – .

A S A
Founded: 1962.
Colours: Red/blue.
Stadium: 23 August (12,500).
Club address: A S A, Tirgu Mures, str Lenin 5.
League: – .
Cup: – .

BACAU
Founded: 1950.
Colours: Blue/red.
Stadium: 23 August (20,000).
Club address: S C Bacau, str Pictor Aman 94.
League: – .
Cup: – .

BAIA MARE
Founded: 1948.
Colours: Yellow/blue.
Stadium: 23 August (13,000).
Club address: F A Baia Mare, Baia Mare, str Minerilor 11.
League: – .
Cup: – .

CORVINUL
Founded: 1921.
Colours: All blue.
Stadium: Corvinul (15,000).
Club address: Corvinul, Hunedoara, Bd Mihai Viteazul 10.
League: – .
Cup: – .

CHIMIA
Founded: 1946.
Colours: White/blue.
Stadium: 1 Mai (13,000).
Club address: Chimia RV, Ramnicul Vilcea, str Avram Iancu 7.
League: – .
Cup: 1973.

DINAMO BUCHAREST
Founded: 1948.
Colours: White/red.
Stadium: Dinamo Stadion (18,000) but important matches in the 23 August national stadium (95,000).
League: 1955, 1962, 1963, 1964, 1965, 1971, 1973, 1975, 1977, 1982, 1983, 1984 (12 – record).
Cup: 1959, 1964, 1968, 1982, 1984 (5).

JIUL PETROSANI
Founded: 1919.
Colours: White/black.
Stadium: Jiul (20,000).
Club address: Petroşani, str Enăchită Văcărescu 8.
League: – .
Cup: 1974.

PETROLUL
Founded: 1952.
Colours: Yellow/blue.
Stadium: Petrolul (25,000).
Club address: Petrolul, Ploeşti, str Stadionului 26.
League: 1958, 1959, 1966 (3).
Cup: 1963.

RAPID
Founded: 1923.
Colours: White/orange.
Stadium: Republicii (30,000).
Club address: Rapid, Bucharest, Calea Giuleşti 18.
League: 1941, 1942, 1967 (3).
Cup: 1935, 1937, 1938, 1939, 1940, 1941, 1942, 1972, 1975 (9).

SPORTUL STUDENŢESC
Founded: 1916.
Colours: White/black.
Stadium: Sportul Studenţesc (15,000).
Club address: Sportul Studenţesc, Bucharest, str Ştefan Furtuña 140.
League: – .
Cup: – .

STEAUA
Founded: 1947.
Colours: Red/blue.
Stadium: Steaua (30,000).
Club address: Steaua, Bucharest, Calea Plevnei 114.
League: 1951, 1952, 1953, 1956, 1960, 1961, 1968, 1976, 1978, 1985 (10).
Cup: 1949, 1950, 1951, 1952, 1955, 1962, 1966, 1967, 1969, 1970, 1971, 1976, 1979, 1985 (14).

UNIVERSITATEA CRAIOVA
Founded: 1948.
Colours: White/blue.
Stadium: Central (30,000).
Club address: FC Universitatea, Craiova, str Gheorghe Doja 24.
League: 1974, 1980, 1981 (3).
Cup: 1977, 1978, 1981, 1983 (4).

SAUDI ARABIA

Saudi Arabia's self-congratulations over their victory in the Asian Cup in Singapore at the end of 1984 did not last long. The national team defeated Kuwait and Syria in their first-round group, then squeezed past Iran by virtue of a 5–4 victory in a penalty shoot-out after a 1–1 draw after extra time in the semi-finals.

In the final the Saudis beat China 2–0 with goals from Shaye Al-Nafisah and star striker Majid Mohammad – a powerful forward compared by many 'in the know' in the Middle East with the 1982 Brazilian World Cup leader Serginho. The other key Saudi player was goalkeeper Abdullah Al-Diayye. He provided the crucial penalty save which won the semi-final against Iran and collected the Asian Cup Best Goalkeeper trophy. He also finished fourth in the Asian Footballer of the Year poll, despite playing his domestic football with second division Al Tayee, while the award itself went to Majid Mohammad.

The Saudis have spent heavily on European and Brazilian football knowhow, and have proved impatient to see a return on their investment. For example, in 1978 top club Al Hilal sacked veteran Brazilian coach Paolo Amaral – once in charge with Juventus of Italy – after only three days. There was a prolonged diplomatic row between Saudi Arabia and Brazil as the luckless coach struggled for a cash settlement and the return of his passport.

Later that year, coincidentally, Al Hilal won the championship, though clearly Amaral can have had little influence on the players. They have been the dominant club over the last few years on the domestic scene, winning the championship three times since its inception in 1978–79. They retained the league title in 1985, under Ladislao Kubala, after overtaking Shabab and seeing off the added challenge of an Ittihad club who then collapsed and slipped from third place into a mid-table position by the season's end. Third place at the close went to Al Ahli, who had been making headlines in sports pages around the world for their role in the Brazilian confederation's attempt to regain the services of Tele Santana to run their World Cup qualifying campaign.

Santana had gone out to Saudi Arabia after the 1982 World Cup, vowing never again to manage the Brazilian national team. But the CBF approached him at the end of November 1984, asking if he would think again. Santana was quickly persuaded, but Al Ahli were not so happy. They agreed to release him at the end of the championship in March, but that was too late for the Brazilians – who appointed Evaristo de Macedo. He proved not to possess the magic wand for which Brazil's fans had hoped and so, belatedly, the CBF came back for Santana on the eve of Brazil's first World Cup qualifier in Bolivia at the start of June. The Saudi season having ended he was now free to take up the appointment on the understanding that the job would last only as long as the qualifying matches. Once Santana had seen Brazil secure their ticket for Mexico at the start of July he was, in theory, due back with Al Ahli. How the Brazilian confederation cope with that remains to be seen.

Final Points Totals

1 Hilal Club 37. 2 Shabab 34. 3 Ahli 29. 4 Ittifak 29. 5 Nasr 25. 6 Ittihad 22. 7 Riyadh 19. 8 Qadsia 19. 9 Nahdah 18. 10 Wehdah 14. 11 Gabalin 11. 12 Ohod 7.
Cup final: Ittifak bt Hilal 5–4 on penalties after 0–0 draw.

AL-AHLY
Founded: 1957.
Colours: Green and white/white.
Stadium: Al-Ahly (25,000).
Club address: Al-Ahly Club, Medina Road, Jeddah.
League: 1984.
Cup: 1962, 1965, 1969, 1970, 1971, 1972, 1973, 1977, 1978, 1979, 1983 (11).

AL-HILAL
Founded: 1957.
Colours: Blue and white/white.
Stadium: Al-Hilal (20,000).
Club address: Club Al-Hilal, Riyadh.
League: 1979, 1985.
Cup: 1961, 1964, 1980, 1984 (4).

AL-ITTIFAK
Founded: 1944.
Colours: Green and red/green.
Stadium: Al-Ittifak (20,000).
Club address: Club Al-Ittifak, Dammam, Eastern Province.
League: 1983.
Cup: 1968, 1985.

AL-ITTIHAD
Founded: 1947.
Colours: Black and yellow/yellow.
Stadium: Al-Ittihad (40,000).
Club address: Al-Ittihad, Al-Sahafa Street, Al-Medina, Jeddah.
League: 1982.
Cup: 1958, 1959, 1960, 1963, 1967, 1982 (6).

AL-NASR
Founded: 1955.
Colours: Yellow and blue/yellow.
Stadium: Al-Nasr (25,000).
Club address: Club Al-Nasr, Riyadh.
League: 1980, 1981.
Cup: 1974, 1976, 1981 (3).

SCOTLAND

Aberdeen's success in retaining the Scottish league title may look, from afar, like an oil-fired repeat of the dominance Celtic and/or Rangers used to exert. But closer examination reveals a different story, and also underlines the sterling achievement and ability of their managerial mastermind, Alex Ferguson.

Aberdeen began the 1984–5 season with a string of handicaps. Clubs who win championships usually keep their key players, who are only too happy to stay around for a tilt at the Champions' Cup. But that, in Aberdeen's case, was far from the truth. Gordon Strachan, their flame-haired midfield inspiration, has gone to Manchester United after a transfer wrangle in which West Germany's Köln also tried to secure the player. West Germany's Bundesliga was the destination, however, for another Aberdeen stalwart, striker Mark McGhee, their sixteen-goal top scorer in the 1984 championship. Also on his way was defender Doug Rougvie to Chelsea, while long-term injuries to Neale Cooper and Peter Weir left Ferguson with virtually half a team.

Some managers are shrewd operators in the transfer market but not such good coaches. Some managers are good coaches but lack judgement when it comes to buying and selling. The two are widely differing 'arts' but Ferguson has mastered both. Having proved the one by his achievements in terms of titles – including the 1983 Cup-winners' Cup – Ferguson reminded Aberdeen's fans that he can be equally adept in the marketplace. Thus he paid £40,000 to Clyde for Tom McQueen to fill the gap left at the back for Rougvie's departure, and splashed £100,000 on Frank McDougall from St Mirren.

McDougall, a Glasgow-born twenty-seven-year-old, was handed the responsiblity of taking over from McGhee up front, and accomplished the task with such style and verve that he finished the campaign as the league's leading scorer with twenty-one goals.

Aberdeen's reshaped team dominated the premier division from start to finish. Only Celtic kept up any sort of challenge. Remarkably, Aberdeen took only three out of a possible eight points from their four games against Celtic. But David Hay's team spoiled the effect by dropping points wastefully against Hibernian, bottom Club Morton and Dundee.

Ironically it was against Celtic that Aberdeen made sure of the title, in front of their own fans in the Granite City at Pittodrie. The score was 1-1 at the final whistle, but Celtic fans still have their doubts about the result because of a controversial incident in the eighty-sixth minute. Celtic's Murdo MacLeod swung a long centre into the Aberdeen goalmouth, Tom McAdam outjumped Aberdeen's Scotland goalkeeper Jim Leighton, and Frank McGarvey shot home. It looked a good goal to the Celtic fans and to many neutrals. But referee George Smith disallowed it for a foul on the goalkeeper.

That was the third controversial decision by the referee. The first was in awarding Celtic a first-half penalty against Aberdeen's Billy Stark for a supposed foul on Celtic striker Mo Johnston. Roy Aitken converted the penalty to give Celtic a lead they held into the second half when referee Smith awarded Aberdeen a free kick for a challenge by MacLeod on Stewart McKimmie. Celtic were still puzzling over the validity of the award while Aberdeen got on with the game and Willie Mercer headed the equaliser.

But if Celtic lost out in the league they had some consolation in the Scottish cup – though they left it late. There were thirteen minutes remaining in the final against Dundee United when Davie Provan scored direct from a free kick to pull Celtic level at 1-1. United's heads went down, and, with six minutes to go, McGarvey steered in Aitken's cross for the winner. It was a second cup final defeat for Dundee United, who had been defeated 1-0 by Rangers earlier in the season in the League Cup decider.

But while Rangers were celebrating that success at the end of October so Celtic were becoming embroiled in international controversy. The scene was their second round Cup-winners' Cup tie against the Austrians of Rapid

1984–85 League Table

	P	W	D	L	F	A	Pts
Aberdeen	36	27	5	4	89	26	59
Celtic	36	22	8	6	77	30	52
Dundee United	36	20	7	9	67	33	47
Rangers	36	13	12	11	47	38	38
St Mirren	36	17	4	15	51	56	38
Dundee	36	15	7	14	48	50	37
Hearts	36	13	5	18	47	64	31
Hibernian	36	10	7	19	38	61	27
Dumbarton	36	6	7	23	29	64	19
Morton	36	5	2	29	29	100	12

Cup final: Celtic 2, Dundee United 1.
League cup final: Rangers 1, Dundee United 0.
Top scorer: Frank McDougall (Aberdeen) 21 goals.

Vienna. A rugged first leg in Vienna saw Celtic lose substitute Jim McInally because of a sending-off, and lose the match 3-1 after a tough tussle. The return, at Parkhead, was even more unpleasant. Celtic won 3-0, but Rapid had defender Reinhard Kienast sent off and defender Rudi Weinhofer helped off, claiming he had been hit by a missile thrown from the crowd. UEFA ultimately ordered a replay at Old Trafford which Celtic lost in traumatic circumstances as two Rapid players were attacked on the pitch by hooligans; 1984–5 will not go down in the Parkhead records as one of Celtic's happiest seasons.

ABERDEEN
Founded: 1903.
Colours: All red.
Stadium: Pittodrie (24,000).
Club address: Aberdeen FC, Pittodrie Stadium, Aberdeen AB2 1QH.
League: 1955, 1980, 1984, 1985 (4).
S.F.A. Cup: 1947, 1970, 1982, 1983, 1984 (5).
League Cup: 1956, 1977.
Cup-winners' Cup: 1983.
SuperCup: 1983.

CELTIC
Founded: 1888.
Colours: Green and white hoops/white.
Stadium: Celtic Park (67,500).
Club address: Celtic, Celtic Park, Parkhead, Glasgow G40 3RE.
League: 1893, 1894, 1896, 1898, 1905, 1906, 1907, 1908, 1909, 1910, 1914, 1915, 1916, 1917, 1919, 1922, 1926, 1936, 1938, 1954, 1966, 1967, 1968, 1969, 1970, 1971, 1972, 1973, 1974, 1977, 1979, 1981, 1982 (33).
S.F.A. Cup: 1892, 1899, 1900, 1904, 1907, 1908, 1911, 1912, 1914, 1923, 1925, 1927, 1931, 1933, 1937, 1951, 1954, 1965, 1967, 1969, 1971, 1972, 1974, 1975, 1977, 1980, 1985 (27 – record).
League Cup: 1957, 1958, 1966, 1967, 1968, 1969, 1970, 1975, 1983 (9).
World Club Cup: Runners-up in 1967.
Champions' Cup: 1967. Runners-up in 1970.

DUNDEE
Founded: 1893.
Colours: Dark blue/white.
Stadium: Dens Park (22,381).
Club address: Dundee FC, Dens Park, Dundee DD1 1RQ.
League: 1962, 1979.
S.F.A. Cup: 1910.
League Cup: 1952, 1953, 1974 (3).

DUNDEE UNITED
Founded: 1909.
Colours: Tangerine/black.
Stadium: Tannadice Park (22,250).
Club address: Dundee United, Tannadice Park, Dundee DD3 7JW.
League: 1983.

S.F.A. Cup: – .
League Cup: 1980, 1981.

DUNFERMLINE
Founded: 1885.
Colours: Black and white stripes/black.
Stadium: East Den Park (27,500).
Club address: Dunfermline Athletic, Dunfermline, Fife KY12 7RB.
League: – .
S.F.A. Cup: 1961, 1968.
League Cup: – .

HEARTS
Founded: 1874.
Colours: Maroon/white.
Stadium: Tyneside Park (23,450).
Club address: Heart of Midlothian, Tyneside Park, Gorgie Road, Edinburgh EH11 2NL.
League: 1895, 1897, 1958, 1960 (4).
S.F.A. Cup: 1891, 1896, 1901, 1906, 1956 (5).
League Cup: 1955, 1959, 1960, 1963 (4).

HIBERNIAN
Founded: 1875.
Colours: Green/white.
Stadium: Easter Road (29,464).
Club address: Hibernian, Easter Road Park, Edinburgh EH7 5QG.
League: 1903, 1948, 1951, 1952 (4).
S.F.A. Cup: 1887, 1902.
League Cup: 1973.

KILMARNOCK
Founded: 1869.
Colours: Blue and white hoops/blue.
Stadium: Rugby Park (18,500).
Club address: Kilmarnock, Rugby Park, Kilmarnock KA1 2DP.
League: 1965.
S.F.A. Cup: 1920, 1929.
League Cup: – .

MORTON
Founded: 1874.
Colours: Blue and white hoops/white.
Stadium: Cappielow Park (16,400).
Club address: Morton, Cappielow Park, Greenock PA15, 2TY.
League: – .
S.F.A. Cup: 1922.
League Cup: – .

PARTICK THISTLE
Founded: 1876.
Colours: Red and yellow stripes/red.
Stadium: Firhill Park (22,000).
Club address: Partick Thistle, Firhill Park, Glasgow G20 5AL.
League: – .
S.F.A. Cup: 1921.
League Cup: 1972.

RANGERS
Founded: 1873.
Colours: Royal blue/white.
Stadium: Ibrox Park (44,000).
Club address: Glasgow Rangers FC, Ibrox Stadium, Glasgow G51 2XD.
League: 1891 (shared), 1899, 1900, 1901, 1902, 1911, 1912, 1913, 1918, 1920, 1921, 1923, 1924, 1925, 1927, 1928, 1929, 1930, 1931, 1933, 1934, 1935, 1937, 1939, 1947, 1949, 1950, 1953, 1956, 1957, 1959, 1961, 1963, 1964, 1975, 1976, 1978 (37 – record).
S.F.A. Cup: 1894, 1897, 1898, 1903, 1928, 1930, 1932, 1934, 1935, 1936, 1948, 1949, 1950, 1953, 1960, 1962, 1963, 1964, 1966, 1973, 1976, 1978, 1979, 1981 (24).
League Cup: 1947, 1949, 1961, 1962, 1964, 1965, 1971, 1976, 1978, 1979, 1982, 1984, 1985 (13 – record).
Cup-winners' Cup: 1972. Runners-up in 1961 and 1967.
Super Cup: Runners-up in 1972.

ST JOHNSTONE
Founded: 1884.
Colours: Blue/white.
Stadium: Muirton Park (24,950).
Club address: St Johnstone FC, Muirton Park, Perth PH1 5AP.
League: – .
S.F.A. Cup: – .
League Cup: – .

ST MIRREN
Founded: 1876.
Colours: Black and white stripes/black.
Stadium: Love Street (25,800).
Club address: St Mirren, St Mirren Park, Love Street, Paisley PA3 2EJ.
League: – .
S.F.A. Cup: 1926, 1959.
League Cup: – .

SOUTH AFRICA

There was only one team in the 1984 South African season, Soweto giants Kaizer Chiefs. They walked away with four of the five trophies on offer, though, to be fair, they had to sneak in towards the end of the campaign to do so. Starting with the championship, 1983 title-holders Durban City held an eight-point lead at one stage but then collapsed to allow Moroka Swallows to get their noses ahead. Chiefs were still some way back because of a backlog of fixtures which built up because of their heavy cup commitments.

Swallows and Durban met in a controversial match in the penultimate league round. It ended in a 1–1 draw which denied Durban a third title in succession, and left Swallows waiting to see if Chiefs, with games in hand, could overtake their forty-three points total. As it turned out, the Chiefs reached forty-three points with two games to spare, and even though they lost both – by 5–1 and 2–0 – they scraped home on goal average. The Amakhosi, as the Chiefs are popularly known, took the Mainstay Cup by beating Orlando Pirates 1–0 thanks to a late penalty converted by Nelson Dladla.

The most exciting tournament of the year was the new John Player Special Knock-out Cup – very heavily promoted and slickly run with huge attendances. Chiefs were again the victors, but had their hands full in the two-leg final against unrated Bush Bucks from Durban. Bucks lost the first leg 1–0 at home despite dominating play from start to finish, but held Chiefs 1–1 at Ellis Park in Johannesburg to lose only 2–1 on aggregate.

The Chiefs' other triumph was the Sales House Champion of Champions, a sort of Charity Shield-type tournament in which they beat Durban City over two legs. Their only 'failure' in the bid for a clean sweep came in the BP Top Eight Cup, a pre-season direct elimination competition featuring the previous season's top eight finishers in the league. In the final, Wits University beat Moroka Swallows.

The league was to have been cut to sixteen clubs for the 1985 season, with four sides being relegated and only two promoted. However, that decision was later reversed so AmaZulu and Benoni were readmiited to the top flight along with second division play-off winners African Wanderers and Pretoria Callies.

1984–85 League Table

	P	W	D	L	F	A	Pts
Iwisa Kaizer Chiefs	34	19	9	8	58	33	43
Moroka Swallows	34	15	13	6	51	32	43
Durban City	34	15	13	6	56	38	43
Arcadia	34	19	4	11	54	35	42
Hellenic	34	18	6	10	46	41	42
Wits University	34	15	10	9	56	33	40
Ukhamba Black Aces	34	14	12	8	48	32	40
Frasers Celtic	34	16	6	12	51	46	38
Jomo Cosmos	34	15	8	11	52	47	38
Bush Bucks	34	14	6	14	65	60	34
Rangers	34	11	11	12	49	48	33
Cape Town Spurs	34	12	8	14	38	56	32
Orlando Pirates	34	13	5	16	44	43	31
Mamelodi Sundowns	34	10	8	16	31	39	28
AmaZulu	34	9	9	16	30	48	27
Kwikot Benoni	34	8	5	21	24	49	21
Western Tigers	34	6	8	20	36	64	20
Stallions	34	5	7	22	37	81	17

Cup final: Iwisa Kaizer Chiefs 1, Orlando Pirates 0.

But the overall future of domestic competition remained in doubt after the professional league then broke away from the South African National Soccer Association in a dispute over funds. The clubs formed a new league, called the National Soccer League, so now South Africa has two professional leagues and two national bodies.

The SANFA-controlled NPSL was left looking distinctly the worse for wear. Since the abolition of apartheid in soccer in 1977, the NPSL had been the only professional league. But after all the top sides split away, its status – and future – was left in serious doubt.

As South Africa has been suspended from FIFA, there have been no full internationals since 1978, when South Africa thumped Zimbabwe (then Rhodesia) by 7–1 in Harare (then Salisbury). A national squad was, however, selected in 1984, and a game organised between then A and B sides. Former Ipswich, Wolves and Newcastle manager Bill McGarry took charge.

ARCADIA
Founded: 1904.
Colours: White/black.
Stadium: Atteridge Super Stadium (50,000).
Club Address: Arcadia, PO Box 1302, Pretoria 0001.
League: – .
Cup: – .

DURBAN CITY
Founded: 1959.
Colours: Blue/white.
Stadium: King's Park (50,000).
Club address: Durban City, 16 Raymar Avenue, La Lucia, 4051.
League: 1982, 1983.
Cup: – .

KAIZER CHIEFS
Founded: 1970.
Colours: Gold/black.
Stadium: Ellis Park (80,000).
Club address: Iwisa Kaizer Chiefs, Suite 723,Royal Arcade, 63 Pritchard Street, Johannesburg, 2000.
League: 1979, 1981, 1984 (3).
Cup: 1979, 1981, 1982, 1984 (4).

ORLANDO PIRATES
Founded: 1952.
Colours: Black/white.
Stadium: Orlando Stadium (Soweto, 70,000).
Club address: Orlando Pirates, PO Box 62124, Johannesburg, 2000.
League: – .
Cup: 1980.

SOVIET UNION

Zenit Leningrad, the club who, in 1944, became the first team to break the Moscow stranglehold on the prizes in Soviet soccer, came within a whisker of the league-and-cup double in 1984. In the end they had to be satisfied with the championship crown after finishing two points ahead of Spartak Moscow and five in front of outgoing champions Dnepr Dnepropetrovsk.

In the cup, played over the first half of the season, Zenit beat Fakel Voronezh of the second division by 1-0 after extra time in their semi-final and then faced Dynamo Moscow in the final. Zenit were deserved favourites. They were the championship contenders, while Dynamo were next to bottom. But in front of 43,500 fans, in the less-than-half-full Lenin Olympic Stadium, steady rain which made the pitch greasy proved a great leveller. Zenit were without international forward Nikolai Larionov, and, although they attacked for most of the initial ninety minutes, they couldn't find a way through.

Soviet teams – with the occasional exceptions of Kiev and Tbilisi in the last decade – have traditionally found goals hard to come by. In this case it needed extra time to separate the sides, and Zenit, for all their pressure, were on the receiving end. First, Valeri Gazzayev headed in an Aleksander Borodyuk cross in the ninety-seventh minute to put Dynamo ahead. Then, in the 115th, Dynamo made sure. This time Gazzayev was the provider and Borodyuk the finisher. Dynamo duly celebrated winning the cup for the sixth time in their history. Ironically, it was in the Dynamo stadium that Zenit had had their only cup success back in 1944, when they beat TSKA Moscow (the army team) 2-1 in a game which also went to extra time.

Zenit had begun the 1984 season with half a dozen new young faces for team manager Pavel Sadyrin to rebuild a team who had finished fourth the previous year but had a reputation for defensive football. Sadyrin wanted more effort put into attack, and achieved this aim so successfully that Zenit ended up as the league's highest scorers with sixty goals.

They signalled their title intentions in late March, early in the season, with a 2-0 victory over defending champions Dnepr. With star striker Yuri Zheludkov in goal-grabbing form – he scored fourteen in the first half of the season, which is phenomenal by Soviet standards – Zenit took over at the top in July. They scored an exciting win over an inconsistent Tbilisi, now coached by former midfield general David Kipiani, when Zenit hit back from 2-0 down to carry the day 3-2. A home defeat a week later, against unfashionable Chernomoretz, couldn't budge them at the top, and although Spartak kept up the chase Zenit made no mistake in their last two home games to take the title. First came a 1-0 win over Shakhtyor Donetsk – who had beaten Dnepr 2-1 in the Soviet Super Cup – and then a 4-1 victory over Metallist Kharkov.

Sadyrin's policies, which this one-time Zenit player had developed since taking over at the end of the 1982 season, had proved justified, even though Zheludkov missed ten matches on the run-in because of injury and added only three more goals to his half-way total of fourteen. Certainly, had he been fit throughout, he must have finished well ahead of the eventual top league scorer, Sergei Andreyev of SKA Rostov, with nineteen.

Second-placed Spartak had a strange season. After being pipped at the post by Dnepr in 1983, they began strongly, and were early league leaders. Then, however, came one of the most astonishing upsets for years when they crashed

6-1 at home against SKA Rostov. What made this result all the more re-markable was that Spartak had conceded only five goals in their previous eleven matches. National team goalkeeper, Renat Dassayev, had never previously had six put past him at senior level, and, indeed, Spartak's heaviest defeats in their league history were 'only' 5-0, at the hands of Torpedo Moscow in 1945 and 1964, and by Dynamo Moscow in that club's greatest year of 1946. Two of the SKA goals fell to Andreyev, while Spartak's Shavlo missed a penalty, and their late consolation goal was eventually collected by Footballer of the Year Cherenkov.

The next week Spartak recovered with a 3-2 win over Minsk, but lost the league leadership to Dnepr when they went down 1-0 against Zhalgiris of Vilnius. But Dassayev did have something worth celebrating late in the season when he kept his one hundredth clean sheet in his 215th first division game for Spartak. This feat leaves Dassayev, at least in terms of statistics, the greatest Soviet goalkeeper behind Lev Yashin. Mention of Yashin brings the need to record one of the saddest events of the year, the news that the man generally considered as the greatest of all goalkeepers had to have a leg amputated in September, 1984. Yashin had been ill on and off for several years after suffering a stroke. This appeared to cast a shadow over the entire Dynamo club, with which Yashin will always be associated. Apart from the cup final success, they gave their fans little else to cheer about.

In 1983 Dynamo had finished fifteenth and only just avoided relegation. It was ironic that they hit the bottom of the table for the first time ever just three days after winning the cup. A 1-0 defeat by Zhalgiris in Vilnius, the goal coming from the promising Sigitas Yakubauskas, condemned them to this ignominy – though not for long. Battling away in a manner most unfitting for one of the world game's most famous names, they eventually scrambled up into sixteenth place, one point above Pakhtakor Tashkent, and seven clear of neighbours TSKA.

Pakhtakor had been granted a three-year amnesty from relegation by the federation back in 1979 when seventeen first-team players were killed in a domestic air crash on their way to play a league match in Minsk. That amnesty had long since expired, however, so Pakhtakor went down, in company with the army team, TSKA Moscow, who gave up the ghost of a hope long before the end of the season. Their last home match in the first division resulted in a 6-1 thrashing by Chernomoretz, and was watched by a mere 600 fans.

A quiet time of it in mid-table was had by the Soviet Union's two former European club trophy winners. Dynamo Tbilisi, slowly rebuilding but still pulling in an average home crowd of 53,000, finished in seventh place under Kipiani. Their claim to international fame was to have won the Cup-winners' Cup in 1981 – six years after the path-finding victory of Dynamo Kiev.

A problem of personalities appeared to be making itself felt at Kiev, where former European Footballer of the Year, Oleg Blokhin, was the centre of controversy after complaints from successive national managers Konstantin Beskov and Eduard Malofeyev that he spent too much time out on the pitch moaning and not enough time playing. Blokhin remains, even so, the Soviet player who has scored more goals at senior level (well over 250) than anyone else.

Torpedo Moscow, out of the limelight for many years while they drifted along in the middle of the table, emerged to gain attention for the wrong reasons. The club had signed a contract with a western sportswear manufacturer. But instead of the name Torpedo being written across the shirts in the Cyrillic alphabet, there it was in Latin characters at their next league match. The game went ahead – but the federation were not amused, and immediately stepped in. The Torpedo football committee, the team manager, the referee and match observers were all reprimanded and fined for allowing Torpedo to be fooled into displaying such anti-Soviet propaganda.

The Soviet first division is to be streamlined at the end of the 1985 season from eighteen to sixteen clubs to help the national team prepare better for prestige competitions such as the World Cup and European championship.

1984 League Table

	P	W	D	L	F	A	Pts*
Zenit Leningrad	34	19	9	6	60	32	47
Spartak Moscow	34	18	9	7	53	29	45
Dnepr	34	17	8	9	54	40	42
Chernomoretz	34	16	9	9	48	38	41
Dynamo Minsk	34	15	13	6	43	28	40
Torpedo Moscow	34	15	10	9	43	36	40
Dynamo Tbilisi	34	14	8	12	36	41	36
Kairat Alma-Ata	34	13	8	13	44	42	34
Zhalgiris	34	12	11	11	30	38	34
Dynamo Kiev	34	12	13	9	46	30	34
Ararat Erevan	34	12	7	15	46	50	31
Metallist	34	12	5	17	42	53	29
Shakhtyor Donetsk	34	10	9	15	47	46	29
SKA Rostov-on-Don	34	10	7	17	48	58	27
Nefchi Baku	34	9	8	17	30	50	26
Dynamo Moscow	34	8	10	16	35	43	26
Pakhtakor Tashkent	34	10	5	19	37	58	25
ZSKA Moscow	34	5	9	20	24	55	19

Cup final (1984): Dynamo Moscow 2, Zenit Leningrad 0 after extra time.
Cup final (1985): Dynamo Kiev 2, Shakhtyor 1.
Top scorer: Sergei Andreyev (SKA Rostov) 19 goals.

* No point awarded for a draw in the case of any team which has already drawn ten league matches.

ARARAT
Founded: 1937.
Colours: All white.
Stadium: Razdan (70,000).
Club address: Ararat Ereven, Pl. Lenina 2, Erevan.
League: 1973.
Cup: 1973, 1975.

CHERNOMORETZ ODESSA
Founded: 1958.
Colours: White and blue/white.
Stadium: Central (43,000).

Club address: Chernomoretz Odessa, Central Stadium, Shevchenko Park, Odessa 270014.
League: – .
Cup: – .

DNEPR
Founded: 1936.
Colours: Red/white.
Stadium: Meteor (34,000).
Club address: Dnepr Dnepropetrovsk, ul. Kirova 12, Dnepropetrovsk.
League: 1983.
Cup: – .

DYNAMO KIEV
Founded: 1927.
Colours: Blue and white/white.
Stadium: Dynamo Stadium (30,000) but important matches in the Central Stadium (100,000).
Club address: ul. Kirova 3, Kiev.
League: 1961, 1966, 1967, 1968, 1971, 1974, 1975, 1977, 1980, 1981 (10).
Cup: 1954, 1964, 1966, 1974, 1978, 1985 (6).
Cup-winners' Cup: 1975.
SuperCup: 1975.

DYNAMO MINSK
Founded: 1935.
Colours: Blue and white/white.
Stadium: Dynamo (50,000).
Club address: Dynamo Minsk, ul. Kirova 8, Minsk.
League: 1982.
Cup: – .

DYNAMO MOSCOW
Founded: 1923.
Colours: Blue and white/white.
Stadium: Dynamo (51,000).
Club address: Dynamo Moscow, Leningradskii pr 36, Moscow.
League: 1936 (spring), 1937, 1940, 1945, 1949, 1954, 1955, 1957, 1959, 1963, 1976 (spring) (11 – record).
Cup: 1937, 1953, 1967, 1970, 1977, 1984 (6).

DYNAMO TBILISI
Founded: 1925.
Colours: Blue and white/white.
Stadium: Dynamo (75,000).
Club address: Dynamo Tbilisi, pr Cereteli 2, Tbilisi.
League: 1964, 1978.
Cup: 1976, 1979.
Cup-winners' Cup: 1981.

PAKHTAKOR
Founded: 1956.
Colours: Yellow/white.
Stadium: Pakhtakor (60,000).
Club address: Pakhtakor Tashkent, ul. Socializma 21, Tashkent.
League: – .
Cup: – .

S K A
Founded: 1951.
Colours: Red/blue.
Stadium: Central (35,000).
Club address: SKA, Central Stadium, Rostov-on-Don.
League: – .
Cup: 1981.

SHAKHTYOR DONETSK
Founded: 1935.
Colours: Orange and black stripes/black.
Stadium: Shakhtyor (43,000). Sometimes switch important matches to the Lokomotiv Stadium (50,000).
Club address: Shakhtyor Donetsk, Avantgard Sports Society, Donetsk 340045.
League: – .
Cup: 1961, 1962, 1980, 1983 (4).

SPARTAK MOSCOW
Founded: 1922.
Colours: Red with a white hoop/white.
Stadium: Lenin/Olympic (103,000).
Club address: Spartak Moscow, ul. Verhniaia Krasnoselskaia 38/19, Moscow.
League: 1936 (autumn), 1938, 1939, 1952, 1953, 1956, 1958, 1962, 1969, 1979 (10).
Cup: 1938, 1939, 1946, 1947, 1950, 1958, 1963, 1965, 1971 (9 – record).

TORPEDO MOSCOW
Founded: 1924.
Colours: White/black.
Stadium: Torpedo (21,000).
Club address: Torpedo Moscow, Avtozavodskaia ul.23, Moscow.
League: 1960, 1965, 1976 (autumn) (3).
Cup: 1949, 1952, 1960, 1968, 1972 (5).

T S K A
Founded: 1923.
Colours: Red/blue.
Stadium: TSKA share use of the Dynamo Stadium (51,000).
Club address: TSKA Moscow, Leningradskii pr 38, Moscow.
League: 1946, 1947, 1948, 1950, 1951, 1970 (6).
Cup: 1945, 1948, 1951, 1955 (4).

ZENIT
Founded: 1931.
Colours: Blue/white.
Stadium: Kirov (74,000).
Club address: Zenit Leningrad, Aptekarskii pr 16, Leningrad 194044.
League: 1984.
Cup: 1944.

ZHALGIRIS
Founded: 1947.
Colours: Green and white stripes/green.
Stadium: Zhalgiris (20,000).
Club address: Zhalgiris/Vilnius, Eidukiavichiaus str 3/11, Vilnus.
League: – .
Cup: – .

SPAIN

Real Madrid won the UEFA Cup, and traditional rivals Barcelona landed the league championship for the first time in eleven years; so, on the surface, there appeared few problems in Spanish football. But appearances are deceptive. Barcelona and Madrid had to share the headlines with a never-ending stream of problems caused in the main by the game's steady collapse into a sea of debt.

The clubs complained that promised funds hadn't been forthcoming to recompense them for the costly stadia improvements undertaken for the 1982 World Cup; and the players at an increasing number of clubs – eventual league runners-up Atletico Madrid among them – protested that they weren't being paid on time. Concern over back-pay became so acute that one week into the season the players went on strike. The clubs soldiered on for one weekend with scratch sides drawn from their youth and amateur teams, but when the strike had been resolved many of the fans who had stayed away never came back. Barcelona's average gate for league games dropped from the 100,000-plus count of three years ago to around 85,000, even though there was comparatively little live television because of another cash row.

The desperate beligerence of the clubs in this field spread over into a row over the percentage paid by the pools for the use of fixtures. Relations between pools officials and the clubs were so bad that match fixtures were published only a month ahead to make life tough for the betting service. In the end it took government intervention to sort out an increase in the pools fees to 3.5 per cent, which, if properly administered, could put Spanish football into the black for the first time in years.

On a personal level, however, the season was a triumph for Barcelona's new English coach, Terry Venables, and – above all – for Jose Luis Nuñez, controversial president of the Catalan club, which is probably the richest in the world. Just consider their financial set-up, for which the key is the beautiful Camp Nou stadium. When Barcelona secured the right to stage the opening match of the 1982 World Cup finals, Nuñez – by coincidence a millionaire builder – had the stadium's capacity increased from 100,000 to 115,000 (85,000 seated and 30,000 standing).

At the same time the club increased their membership roll from 70,000 to 108,000 (and still had a waiting list!). With the annual membership fee set at twenty-five pounds and season ticket prices on top ranging from forty pounds to £115 for league games alone, that adds up to a guaranteed minimum annual income of more than £10 million. No wonder the club have opened their own bank; no wonder the club have built a 25,000-capacity stadium just across the road for their second division nursery team; no wonder the club are constantly expanding their interests in basketball, handball, ice hockey, field hockey, athletics, volleyball, rugby and ice dancing.

Barcelona is much, much more than a football club. It's a flagship for Catalan independence, and that's why the entire region rose up in joy to swamp Venables and his team after they had secured the league crown for the first time since the days of Johan Cruyff in the mid-1970s. The decision to entrust the most exposed position in European club management to Venables had been that of Nuñez. There is a long tradition of English coaches in Spanish football, from William Garbutt and Arthur Pentland in the 1920s to Ronnie Allen and Vic Buckingham in more recent times. The strength of the influence remains in the language of Spanish football, where the coach is known to all and sundry as the *Mister*.

Nuñez has long been an admirer of the British game. At one time he wanted to buy Liam Brady; at another he tried to contract Bobby Robson. He never gave up on the idea. And that's why Barcelona considered Venables, along with the Swiss-German Helmut Benthaus, when Cesar Menotti decided to quit the club in the summer of 1984. Both men met Nuñez and his senior vice-presidents. When it came to a vote at boardroom level Benthaus had many supporters because of sharing a common language with Bernd Schuster, and West German midfielder, who was now the key player with the imminent departure of Argentina's Diego Maradona. But Nuñez didn't agree. And what Nuñez wants, he gets – so Venables it would be. He arrived as an unknown. But it took just one game to win over players and fans – the first match of the season, in which Barsa won away to Real Madrid. They never looked back, and finished ten points clear of Atletico Madrid, losing only two of their thirty-four games.

But just as that first-day match was a good omen for Barcelona, so it proved a bad one for Real Madrid. Amancio, a former club captain and 1960s star, had been promoted as club coach after two highly successful years with affiliated second division side, Castilla. But his attempts to replace some of Madrid's veterans with his young proteges proved disastrous. Madrid staggered along in the league with confidence, form and morale at their lowest ebb for years. They lost an unprecedented five home matches during the season and anger on the terraces grew to such an intensity that president Luis De Carlos announced his early retirement.

Amancio was dismissed as coach – though kept on the payroll – after the 2-0 defeat away to Internazionale in the first leg of the UEFA Cup semi-final. The bad result was compounded by the discovery that senior players Juanito and Juan Lozano were entertaining some young ladies in their hotel room. Both players were fined and suspended, and Amancio paid with his job for the now obvious total breakdown in discipline. De Carlos then summoned general manager Luis Molowny from the shadows. Molowny, an ex-international forward, is used to stepping in as caretaker. He had filled in before for the likes of Miguel Muñoz, Miljan Miljanic and Vujadin Boskov. And he always wins something. Now, true to form, his talismanic influence worked again. Madrid duly won the return against Inter by 3-0, and went on to ultimate victory in the UEFA Cup final over Videoton of Hungary. The fact that they lost the return 1-0 in front of their own fans hardly mattered. Madrid had made sure of the cup with their 3-0 success in Hungary, and were duly fêted and acclaimed at the final whistle in their own Estadio Bernabeu.

Molowny had summoned the veterans for one last effort and they had answered the call. But clearly the likes of Carlos Santillana, West German sweeper Uli Stielike, Juanito, goalkeeper Miguel Angel and several others were playing on borrowed time. The presence in the dressing rooms after the game not only of the retiring De Carlos but of the new president-elect, Roman Mendoza, underlined the point.

Change was coming. Even before the league cup final, in which Madrid faced neighbours Atletico, it was announced that Stielike was on his way to join Swiss club Neuchatel Xamax. His departure immediately fuelled speculation about Madrid's interest in Atletico's Mexican star, Hugo Sanchez. A dentist by profession, Sanchez had extracted nineteen goals from the league season to win the Trofeo Pichichi as top scorer. He finished two goals clear of Real's Argentine striker Jorge Valdano, who was in turn two goals up on Barcelona's Steve Archibald. The Scot's fine all-round form meant few regrets in Barcelona about Maradona's departure for Napoli and Italy. Without him, Barcelona had at last regained admission to the European Champions' Cup. And success there is now the priority for the insatiable Nuñez and his Catalan 'army'.

1984–85 League Table

	P	W	D	L	F	A	Pts
Barcelona	34	21	11	2	69	25	53
Atletico Madrid	34	16	11	5	51	28	43
Athletic Bilbao	34	13	15	6	39	26	41
Sporting Gijon	34	13	15	6	34	23	41
Real Madrid	34	13	10	11	46	36	36
Real Sociedad	34	11	12	11	41	33	34
Osasuna	34	13	8	12	38	38	34
Español	34	11	12	11	40	44	34
Valencia	34	9	15	10	40	37	33
Zaragoza	34	11	11	12	39	39	33
Racing Santander	34	10	12	12	27	34	32
Sevilla	34	10	11	13	29	41	31
Valladolid	34	7	16	11	39	45	30
Betis Sevilla	34	11	8	15	37	43	30
Hercules Alicante	34	9	12	13	28	45	30
Malaga	34	7	15	12	23	36	29
Elche	34	6	14	14	18	37	26
Murcia	34	6	10	18	24	52	22

Cup final: Atletico Madrid 2, Bilbao 1.
League Cup final: Real Madrid bt Atletico Madrid 2-3, 2-0.
Top scorer: Hugo Sanchez (Atletico Madrid) 19.

ATHLETIC BILBAO
Founded: 1898.
Colours: Red and white stripes/black.
Stadium: San Mames (50,000).

Club address: Athletic Club de Bilbao, Estadio San Mames, Felipe Serrate s/n, Bilbao.
League: 1930, 1931, 1934, 1936, 1943, 1956, 1983, 1984 (8).
Cup: 1903, 1904, 1910, 1911, 1914, 1915, 1916, 1921, 1923, 1930, 1931, 1932, 1933, 1943, 1944, 1945, 1950, 1955, 1956, 1958, 1969, 1973, 1984 (23 – record).
UEFA Cup: Runners-up in 1977.

ATLETICO MADRID
Founded: 1901.
Colours: Red and white stripes/blue.
Stadium: Vicente Calderon (70,000).
Club address: Club Atletico de Madrid, Estadio Vicente Calderon, Avenida Manzanares, Madrid.
League: 1940, 1941, 1950, 1951, 1966, 1970, 1973, 1977 (8).
Cup: 1960, 1961, 1964, 1972, 1976, 1985 (6).
World Club Cup: 1974.
Champions' Cup: Runners-up in 1974.
Cup-winners' Cup: 1962. Runners-up in 1963.

BARCELONA
Founded: 1899.
Colours: Red and blue stripes/blue.
Stadium: Nou Camp (108,000).
Club address: Futbol Club Barcelona, Estadio Camp Nou, Aristides Maillol s/n, Barcelona.
League: 1929, 1945, 1948, 1949, 1952, 1953, 1959, 1960, 1974, 1985 (10).
Cup: 1910, 1912, 1913, 1920, 1922, 1925, 1926, 1928, 1942, 1951, 1952, 1953, 1957, 1959, 1963, 1968, 1971, 1978, 1981, 1983 (20).
League Cup: 1983.
Champions' Cup: Runners-up in 1961.
Cup-winners' Cup: 1979, 1982. Runners-up in 1969.
Fairs' Cup: 1958, 1960, 1966 (3). Runners-up in 1962.
SuperCup: Runners-up in 1979 and 1982.

BETIS
Founded: 1907.
Colours: Green and white stripes/white.
Stadium: Benito Villamarin (50,000).
Club address: Real Betis Balompié, Conde de Barajas 23, Seville.
League: 1935.
Cup: 1977.

ESPAÑOL
Founded: 1900.
Colours: Blue and white stripes/blue.
Stadium: Sarria (40,000).
Club address: Real Club Deportivo Español, C. Maestro Villa s/n, Barcelona 17.
League: – .
Cup: 1929, 1940.

GIJÓN
Founded: 1906.
Colours: Red and white stripes/blue.
Stadium: El Molinon (40,000).
Club address: Real Sporting de Gijón, Plaza Monte de Piedad 2-2°, Gijón.
League: – .
Cup: – .

REAL MADRID
Founded: 1902.
Colours: All white.
Stadium: Santiago Bernabeu (90,200).
Club address: Real Madrid Club de Futbol, Calle Concha Espina 1, Madrid.
League: 1932, 1933, 1954, 1955, 1957, 1958, 1961, 1962, 1963, 1964, 1965, 1967, 1968, 1969, 1972, 1975, 1976, 1978, 1979, 1980 (20 – record).
Cup: 1905, 1906, 1907, 1908, 1917, 1934, 1936, 1946, 1947, 1962, 1970, 1974, 1975, 1980, 1982 (15).
League Cup: 1985.
World Club Cup: 1960. Runners-up in 1966.
Champions' Cup: 1956, 1957, 1958, 1959, 1960, 1966 (6). Runners-up in 1962, 1964 and 1981.
Cup-Winners' Cup: Runners-up in 1971 and 1983.
UEFA Cup: 1985.

REAL SOCIEDAD
Founded: 1909.
Colours: Blue and white stripes/white.
Stadium: Atocha (30,000).
Club address: Real Sociedad de Futbol, Paseo del Arbol de Guernica 24, San Sebastian.
League: 1981, 1982.
Cup: 1909.

SEVILLA
Founded: 1905.
Colours: All white.
Stadium: Sanchez Pizjuan (70,410).
Club address: Sevilla Futbol Club, C. Harinas 18, Seville 1.
League: 1946.
Cup: 1935, 1939, 1948.

VALENCIA
Founded: 1919.
Colours: All white.
Stadium: Luis Casanova (55,000).
Club address: Valencia Club de Futbol, Estadio Luis Casanova, Avenida Sueca s/n, Valencia.
League: 1942, 1944, 1947, 1971 (4).
Cup: 1941, 1949, 1954, 1967, 1979 (5).
Cup-winners' Cup: 1980.

Fairs' Cup: 196.', 1963. Runners-up in 1964.
SuperCup: 1980.

ZARAGOZA
Founded: 1932.
Colours: White/blue.
Stadium: La Romareda (45,000).
Club address: Real Zaragoza Club Deportivo, Ponzano 10-1°, Zaragoza.
League: – .
Cup: 1964, 1966.
Fairs' Cup: 1964. Runners-up in 1966.

SWEDEN

The Angels of Gothenburg, IFK, turned on what passes for heavenly football in Sweden to hang onto the Allsvenskan title for the third successive year. They also went on to reach the quarter-finals of the European Champions' Cup before losing narrowly in two bruising matches against the Greeks of Panathinaikos. The matches had to be played on the international dates in March before the 1985 Swedish season had got into full swing. So there remains strong belief in Gothenburg that had their men been at competitive match fitness they, and not Panathinaikos, would have been facing Liverpool in the semi-finals.

IFK have dominated Swedish football in the 1980s, thanks largely to the work of Sven-Goran Eriksson, the man who masterminded their triumph in the 1982 UEFA Cup – the first major European club prize ever won for Scandinavia. Eriksson left for Benfica in Portugal and later Italy's Roma after the UEFA Cup success. But even though several of IFK's best players followed him into the fully-professional world of continental western Europe, IFK quickly replaced them all and kept on winning – the domestic cup and then the championship in the autumn of 1982, and then the 'double' again in 1983.

They didn't win the cup in 1984, however. That particular honour went to Malmö, who beat Landskrona 1-0 in the final, and then promptly said goodbye to their two best players: Thomas Sunesson, who flew off to join Swiss club Lausanne, and Lars Larsson, who flew even further south to join Italian first division side Atalanta. In the circumstances it was remarkable that Malmö kept going so tenaciously in the league section of the Swedish championship and finished in third place, five points behind IFK.

For much of the season, however, the team who took the headlines in Sweden were AIK, bringing football attention swinging back to Stockholm after years in which the capital appeared to have become a forgotten city, while the title dramas were played out in Malmö and Gothenburg. The turnaround at AIK had been remarkable. In 1982 they finished the league campaign only one point away from relegation. Yet in 1983, with very few changes in personnel, they won the league round after conceding a Swedish record of only twelve goals in twenty-two matches. A vastly improved defence, plus the fine form of goalkeeper Bernt Ljung, made all the difference, and coach Rolf Zetterlund worked hard to ensure that AIK were deadly on the counter-attack. Similar tactics paid off in 1984 – although AIK were caught right at the end of the league stage by IFK.

AIK came to the last match with a one-point lead over IFK. They also had the benefit of being at home to Malmö, while IFK were away to Öster Växjö. AIK lost only their third game of the season, and in front of their own fans, by 1-0. But they could still have finished on top of the league and been the best-placed for the play-offs, if IFK had lost to Öster.

That appeared a distinct possibility as the Växjö club, champions three times in the previous seven years and now desperate to avoid relegation, took the lead through Svensson in the thirty-fourth minute. On the verge of half-time, however, Glenn Schiller equalised, and then shot IFK ahead in the sixty-third minute. Öster couldn't sit back. They were on the same points total as Gefle and Elfsborg, who filled the two relegation spots below them, and they needed to battle for the points. In the seventy-third minute Berggren equalised. But the effort of recovery had taken a lot of steam out of the Öster charge. With five minutes remaining, IFK sneaked away for Torbjörn Nilsson to shoot the winner. IFK had not only won the match 3-2, but had overtaken AIK at the top of the table. Öster had the consolation of knowing that both Gefle and Elfsborg had lost, and that they were thus safe for another year.

Nilsson has had a chequered career. He has had two spells in professional football with PSV Eindhoven in Holland – where he became homesick after little more than a year – and then with Kaiserslautern in West Germany, whom he joined after the UEFA Cup win. Benfica – at the behest of Eriksson – tried to sign Nilsson at the end of the 1982–83 season. But West Germany was quite far enough from Sweden for Nilsson. He was more interested in going home to IFK, which he did in the summer of 1984. Nilsson made his 'debut' in an important 1-0 away win over Hammarby, and ended the campaign as the league's third-equal top scorer with nine goals. He also scored five goals against Avenir Beggen of Luxembourg in the first round of the Champions' Cup, and then further underlined his talent by scoring a beautiful solo for Sweden in a 3-1 World Cup win in Portugal.

1984 Championship

	P	W	D	L	F	A	Pts
IFK Gothenburg	22	14	4	4	43	19	32
AIK	22	12	7	3	28	12	31
Malmö	22	11	5	8	47	24	27
Hammarby	22	11	4	7	42	30	26
Norrköping	22	8	8	6	33	30	24
Brage	22	7	6	9	21	25	20
Kaimar FF	22	5	10	7	17	25	20
Halmstad	22	7	5	10	18	26	19
Örgryte	22	5	7	10	24	38	17
Öster	22	5	6	11	28	36	16
Elfsborg	22	5	6	11	24	39	16
Gefle	22	4	8	10	21	44	16

Play-offs. Quarter-finals: Brage bt Malmö 1-0, 2-2 – IFK Gothenburg bt Halmstad 0-0, 2-1 – Hammarby bt Kalmar 2-3, 3-0 – Norrköping bt AIK Stockholm 1-0, 1-2. Semi-finals: IFK bt Brage 5-1, 2-2 – Norrköping bt Hammarby 0-0, 0-0 (5-4 pens). Final: IFK Gothenburg bt Norrköping 5-1, 2-0.
Cup Final (1985): AIK bt Öster 4-3 on pens after 1-1 draw.
Top scorer: Billy Ohlsson (Hammarby) 14 goals.

And so to the championship play-offs, a direct elimination series with the top eight clubs in the league face-to-face. Immediately there were shocks. Malmö (third) lost to Brage and poor AIK – morale beyond repair – lost on the away goals rule to the revived Norrköping, once the club who boasted Nils Liedholm and the Nordahl brothers.

In the semi-finals IFK thrashed Brage, and Norrköping beat Hammarby thanks to the agility of reserve goalkeeper Mats Johansson. The twenty-two-year-old kept a clean sheet in the match, and then saved a Holmberg spot-kick to give Norrköping a 5-4 penalty shoot-out victory. Drained by all this drama, Norrköping were easy victims for IFK in the final – crashing 5-1 at home and losing the formality of a return by 2-0.

A I K
Founded: 1891.
Colours: Black/white.
Stadium: Fotbollstadion (52,000).
Club address: Allmänna Idrottsklubben, Fotbollstadion, 171 38 Solna.
Championship: 1900, 1901, 1911, 1914, 1916, 1923, 1932, 1937 (8).
Cup: 1949, 1950, 1976, 1985 (4).

BRAGE
Founded: 1925.
Colours: Green/white.
Stadium: Domnarsvallen (18,000).
Club address: I K Brage, Box 69, 781 21 Borlänge.
Championship: – .
Cup: – .

DJURGÅRDENS
Founded: 1891.
Colours: All blue and white halves.
Stadium: Stockholm Stadion (25,000).
Club address: Djurgårdens IF, Klocktornet, Stadion, 114 33 Stockholm.
Championship: 1912, 1915, 1917, 1920, 1955, 1959, 1964, 1966 (8).
Cup: – .

ELFSBORG
Founded: 1904.
Colours: Yellow/black.
Stadium: Ryavallen (15,000).
Club address: IF Elfsborg, Box 550, 501 08 Borås.
Championship: 1936, 1939, 1940, 1961 (4).
Cup: – .

HALMSTAD
Founded: 1914.
Colours: Blue/white.
Stadium: Örjans vall (18,000).
Club address: Halmstads BK, Box 223, 301 04 Halmstad.
League: 1976, 1979.

Cup: – .
Championship: 1976, 1979.
Cup: – .

HAMMARBY
Founded: 1897.
Colours: White/green.
Stadium: Söderstadion (18,000).
Club address: Hammarby Idrottsförening, Box 20056 Södermannagatan 61, 104 60 Stockholm.
Championship: – .
Cup: – .

I F K
Founded: 1904.
Colours: Blue and white stripes/blue.
Stadium: Ullevi (52,000).
Club address: IF Kamraterna Göteborg, Folkungagatan 16, 411 02 Gothenburg.
Championship: 1903, 1908, 1910, 1918, 1935, 1942, 1969, 1982, 1983, 1984 (10).
Cup: 1979, 1982, 1983 (3).
UEFA Cup: 1982.

KALMAR
Founded: 1910.
Colours: All red.
Stadium: Fredriksskans (15,000).
Club address: Kalmar FF, Box 169, 391 22 Kalmar.
Championship: – .
Cup: 1981.

MALMÖ
Founded: 1910.
Colours: Sky blue/white.
Stadium: Malmö (35,000).
Club address: Malmö Fotbollförening, Södra Förstadsgatan 2, 211 43 Malmö.
Championship: 1944, 1949, 1950, 1951, 1953, 1965, 1967, 1970, 1971, 1974, 1975, 1977 (12).
Cup: 1944, 1946, 1947, 1951, 1953, 1967, 1973, 1974, 1975, 1977, 1980, 1984 (12 – record).
World Club Cup: Runners-up in 1979.
Champions' Cup: Runners-up in 1979.

NORRKÖPING
Founded: 1897.
Colours: White/blue.
Stadium: Idrottsparken (35,000).
Club address: IFK Norrköping, Box 88, 601 03 Norrköping.
Championship: 1943, 1945, 1946, 1947, 1948, 1952, 1956, 1957, 1960, 1962, 1963 (11).
Cup: 1943, 1945, 1969 (3).

ÖRGRYTE
Founded: 1887.
Colours: Red and blue stripes/blue.
Stadium: Ullevi (52,000).
Club address: Örgryte IS, Ullevi, 411 40 Gothenburg.
Championship: 1896, 1897, 1898, 1899, 1902, 1904, 1905, 1906, 1907, 1909, 1913, 1926, 1928 (13).
Cup: – .

ÖSTER
Founded: 1930.
Colours: All red.
Stadium: Värendsvallen (20,000).
Club address: Östers IF, Storgatan 12, 352 31 Växjö.
Championship: 1968, 1978, 1980, 1981 (4).
Cup: 1977.

SWITZERLAND

Servette of Geneva finally regained the championship after six years in which bad luck or silly mistakes had persistently upset their ambitions, while on the brink of success. Their last league title had been gained in 1979. In 1980 Servette won the main league programme, but slipped up in the play-offs to finish third; in 1982 they were runners-up, three points behind Grasshoppers; in 1983 they finished one point behind the Hoppers; and in 1984 they lost to Grasshoppers in a play-off after finishing level on points.

But even the eventual regaining of the league title this past season was no straightforward affair. All had been going well until Servette suffered their first defeat of the season early in April, by 3-1 away to closest pursuers, Aarau. In the next few weeks they lost 3-1 at home to Wettingen, and crashed, unbelievably, 8-2 to Sion! This all came on top of outspoken comments by players and officials about the rivalry between midfielders Umberto Barberis and Lucien Favre, and their joint disagreements with coach Guy Mathesz. As usual in football everywhere, ultimately it is the team boss who carries the can and so, several weeks before the season ended in triumph, Servette announced a parting of the ways with Mathesz.

'I don't understand it,' said Mathesz, who appeared to have a point. In his first season Servette had won the cup and lost the league title only after a play-off; now they had won the championship at long last and gone out in the cup only in the semi-finals against eventual winners and league runners-up Aarau. Mathesz had believed all along that Servette would – not could – win the league. But he admitted he had not expected to have so many man management headaches in trying to keep control of a squad of sixteen professionals, all of whom believed they should be in the starting line-up.

It was also puzzling for many of the players that even in a year when average crowds dipped below 5,000, Servette could not manage much more than that for their home games. Mathesz explained it thus: 'St Gallen, Luzen, Basel or Young Boys would pull in 15,000 every week if they had been getting the results we did. The trouble is, fans in Geneva expect Servette always to be top.

If we are not leading the table, they stay away out of disappointment but if we are top and winning games, then the fans say they know the result in advance so there's no point going to the game. We just can't win. Also, I believe the fans are put off by the bad publicity – the media making up rumours and stories which just weren't true.

'I suppose Geneva is such a cosmopolitan city now that many people who live here have no identification with the local institutions – such as Servette.'

Mathesz built his team around a 4-4-2 style, with Schnyder, Barberis, Favre and Decastel in midfield working hard to support strikers Kok and Brigger – the latter finishing as the club's top scorer with nineteen goals. But their success also owed a great deal to veteran national team goalkeeper Erich Burgener and sweeper Alain Geiger, as well as the Belgian international stopper, Michel Renquin.

Below Servette it was very much the year of the underdog, with Aarau finishing second and winning the cup in what was their first final appearance for fifty-five years, third place went to Xamax Neuchâtel under former French international Gilbert Gress, and St Gallen were fourth thanks to the experience of the veteran Czechoslovak defender, Ladislav Jurkemik. Outgoing champions Grasshoppers slid down to sixth place. The players could not get on with Yugoslav coach Miroslav Blazevic, who was dismissed half-way through the season and replaced by the West German, Timo Konietzka. On top of that, star striker Claudio Sulser played only eight games because of the knee injury problems which threaten his carreer, and his goals were badly missed. Basel, Luzern, and relegated Zug and Winterthur were other clubs who parted company with their coaches during the campaign.

This 1985–86 season has seen an interesting change of rules to permit first division clubs to line up two foreign players in addition to the so-called 'Football Swiss' (players who have been operating in the country for at least five years), and Grenzgänger (players who live within a radius of twelve miles beyond the Swiss border). One of the first clubs to take advantage of this

1984–85 League Table

	P	W	D	L	F	A	Pts
Servette	30	19	8	3	71	28	46
Aarau	30	16	10	4	62	43	42
Xamax Neuchâtel	30	14	11	5	59	34	39
St Gallen	30	13	11	6	66	32	37
Sion	30	14	8	8	56	49	36
Grasshoppers	30	11	10	9	53	47	32
FC Zürich	30	11	9	10	59	52	31
Basel	30	11	9	10	46	49	31
Young Boys	30	10	10	10	42	45	30
Lausanne	30	10	9	11	50	57	29
Wettingen	30	7	12	11	31	35	26
Luzern	30	9	8	13	33	53	26
Vevey	30	9	6	15	40	47	24
La Chaux-de-Fonds	30	6	12	12	41	54	24
SC Zug	30	4	6	20	27	71	14
Winterthur	30	4	5	21	32	72	13

Cup final: Aarau 1, Xamax Neuchâtel 0.
Top scorer: Dominique Cina (Sion) 24 goals.

opportunity were Xamax Neuchâtel, who hired the West German sweeper Uli Stielike from Real Madrid. Another West German to sign up was Ronnie Borchers, the former Eintracht Frankfurt and Arminia Bielefeld forward, who joined Grasshoppers.

AARAU
Founded: 1902.
Colours: White/black.
Stadium: Brügglifeld (14,000).
Club address: FC Aarau, Postfach 383, 5001 Aarau.
League: 1912, 1914.
Cup: 1985.
League Cup: 1982.

BASEL
Founded: 1893.
Colours: Blue/red.
Stadium: St Jakob (60,000).
Club address: FC Basel, Postfach 419, 4021 Basel.
League: 1953, 1967, 1969, 1970, 1972, 1973, 1977, 1980 (8).
Cup: 1933, 1947, 1963, 1967, 1975 (5).
League Cup: 1972.

CHAUX-DE-FONDS
Founded: 1894.
Colours: Yellow/blue.
Stadium: Parc des Sports de la Charrière (14,450).
Club address: FC La Chaux-de-Fonds, Case Postale 607, 2301 La Chaux-de-Fonds.
League: 1954, 1955, 1964 (3).
Cup: 1948, 1951, 1954, 1955, 1957, 1961 (6).

GRASSHOPPERS
Founded: 1886.
Colours: Blue and white halves/white.
Stadium: Hardturm (35,000).
Club address: Grasshopper Club, Hardturmstrasse 321, 8005 Zürich.
League: 1898, 1900, 1901, 1905, 1921, 1927, 1928, 1931, 1937, 1939, 1942, 1943, 1945, 1952, 1956, 1971, 1978, 1982, 1983 (19 – record).
Cup: 1926, 1927, 1932, 1934, 1937, 1938, 1940, 1941, 1942, 1943, 1946, 1952, 1956, 1983, 1984 (15 – record).
League Cup: 1973, 1975.

LAUSANNE
Founded: 1896.
Colours: Blue/white.
Stadium: Stade Olympique de la Pontaise (38,000).
Club address: Lausanne Sports, Case Ville 3186, 1002 Lausanne.
League: 1913, 1932, 1935, 1936, 1944, 1951, 1965 (7).
Cup: 1935, 1939, 1944, 1950, 1962, 1964, 1981 (7).

LUZERN
Founded: 1901.
Colours: Blue/white.
Stadium: Allmend (21,200).
Club address: FC Luzern, Postfach 772, 6002 Luzern.
League: – .
Cup: 1960.

NEUCHÂTEL XAMAX
Founded: 1970.
Colours: Red/black.
Stadium: Stade de la Maladière (14,900).
Club address: FC Neuchâtel Xamax, Case Postale 78, 2000 Neuchâtel 8.
League: – .
Cup: – .

ST GALLEN
Founded: 1879.
Colours: Green/white.
Stadium: Espenmoos (15,200).
Club address: FC St Gallen, Postfach 374, 9001 St Gallen.
League: 1904.
Cup: 1969.
League Cup: 1978.

SERVETTE
Founded: 1890.
Colours: All claret.
Stadium: Charmilles (30,000).
Club address: FC Servette, Case Postale 12, 1211 Châtelaine, Geneva.
League: 1907, 1918, 1922, 1925, 1926, 1930, 1933, 1934, 1940, 1946, 1950, 1961, 1962, 1979, 1985 (15).
Cup: 1928, 1949, 1971, 1978, 1979, 1984 (6).
League Cup: 1977, 1978, 1979 (3).

SION
Founded: 1909.
Colours: White/red.
Stadium: Stade de Tourbillon (13,000).
Club address: FC Sion, Case Postake 157, 1951 Sion.
League: – .
Cup: 1965, 1974, 1980, 1982 (4).

YOUNG BOYS
Founded: 1898.
Colours: All yellow.
Stadium: Wankdorf (58,500).
Club address: BSC Young Boys, Thunstrasse 22, 3000 Bern 6.
League: 1903, 1909, 1910, 1911, 1920, 1929, 1957, 1958, 1959, 1960 (10).
Cup: 1930, 1945, 1953, 1958, 1977 (5).
League Cup: 1976.

ZÜRICH
Founded: 1896.
Colours: Blue/white.
Stadium: Letzigrund (21,500).
Club address: FC Zürich, Postfach 364, 8040 Zürich.
League: 1902, 1924, 1963, 1966, 1968, 1974, 1975, 1976, 1981 (9).
Cup: 1966, 1970, 1972, 1973, 1976 (5).
League Cup: 1981.

TURKEY

The old cliche that 'nothing suceeds like failure' appeared strangely appropriate at the end of the Turkish season. Both league and cup had been won by
clubs under the management of coaches forced out of their previous jobs
because of defeats in the final stages of the 1984 European championship. Jupp
Derwall, manager of West Germany until the summer of 1984, had been
snapped up by Galatasaray, while the newly-resigned boss of Yugoslavia,
Todor Veselinovic, also landed up in Istanbul, with Fenerbahçe.

Galatasaray won the cup, Fenerbahçe the league. Galatasaray did not start
the season well. In fact, they lost their first league game 1-0 at home to
Denizlispor to the huge disappointment of fans, who had expected the arrival
of Derwall, Turkish emigrant Erdal Keser from Borussia Dortmund and
Rüdiger Abramczik from Nürnberg, to inspire a goal-rush. But the goals
didn't come. Derwall's assistant and interpreter, Yasar Aslan, was sacked for
allegedly 'plotting against the manager', according to the board, and then
Erdal missed a penalty in a depressing goal-less draw at home to Sakaryaspor.
As if this were not enough, Derwall was also an adviser to the national team
thrashed 8-0 at home by England in the World Cup qualifiers.

Sakarya, having embarrassed Derwall, now turned their attentions on
Fenerbahçe. Their 2-0 victory over the Istanbul club at the start of December
toppled them from the league leadership, and inflicted Fenerbahçe's first
defeat of the season in a game which also saw the expulsion of their national
team goalkeeper, Yasar. As if Fenerbahçe didn't have enough problems, top
striker Selçuk recovered from a broken ankle only to catch pneumonia; they
were eliminated in the cup quarter-finals by Galatasaray.

Beşiktaş, under their own Yugoslav coach, Branko Stankovic, had now
taken over at the top of the table. It was a lead they would hold until they were
held 1-1 away by Genclerbirligi just three matches from the end of the season.
That same day Fenerbahçe beat bottom club Boluspor 3-0 to pull level on
points and ahead on goal difference.

The stage was now set for the most dramatic climax to the Turkish league
since the national championship was inaugurated in 1959. The following
weekend Beşiktaş and Fenerbahçe came face to face. Beşiktaş wasted three
early chances and then went a goal down to Fenerbahçe's international
midfielder, Mujdat. Just before half-time a blunder by Yasar presented
Kovacevic with an equaliser, and Necdet put Beşiktaş ahead ten minutes into
the second half. It was a lead they couldn't hold. Ilyas Tufekci pulled
Fenerbahçe on terms, and when both clubs won their remaining two
games, Fenerbahçe were champions for the thirteenth time.

As for Galatasaray and Derwall, their reward for persistence in the face of adversity was a 2-1, 0-0 victory over Trabzonspor in the cup final. But if the volatile fans expect this to lead to the first league title in twelve years in 1986, they should think again. Derwall was quick to warn: 'It will take at least two years' more work before we're ready to think about that.'

1984–85 League Table

	P	W	D	L	F	A	Pts
Fenerbahçe	34	18	14	2	65	25	50
Beşiktaş	34	19	12	3	49	19	50
Trabzonspor	34	14	14	6	38	26	42
Ankaraguçu	34	12	14	8	33	27	38
Galatasaray	34	11	14	9	34	28	36
Sakaryaspor	34	14	8	12	44	39	36
Kocaelispor	34	11	12	11	30	31	34
Sariyer	34	8	17	9	47	45	33
Ordurspor	34	11	11	12	35	36	33
Eskisehirspor	34	10	12	12	39	48	32
Genclerbirligi	34	9	13	12	41	45	31
Zonguldak	34	9	13	12	31	35	31
Bursaspor	34	9	13	12	39	47	31
Malatyaspor	34	10	11	13	35	46	31
Altay Izmir	34	8	14	12	34	39	30
Denizlspor	34	9	11	14	39	48	29
Antalyaspor	34	11	6	17	33	49	28
Boluspor	34	3	11	20	20	53	17

Cup final: Galatasaray bt Trabzonspor 2-1, 0-0.
Top scorer: Aykut (Sakaryaspor) 20 goals.

ADANASPOR
Founded: 1954.
Colours: Orange and white/white.
Stadium: Adana (25,000).
Club address: Adanaspor K., Valiyolu 284 – Sokak 2–4, Adana.
Championship: – .
Cup: – .

ANKARAGUÇU
Founded: 1910.
Colours: Yellow/blue.
Stadium: Important matches in the 19 May Stadium (35,000).
Club address: MKE Ankaragüçü K., MKE Kurumu, Tandoğan-Ankara.
Championship: 1949.
Cup: 1972, 1981 (2).

BEŞIKTAŞ
Founded: 1903.
Colours: Black and white/white.
Stadium: Inönü (40,000).
Club address: Beşiktaş SK, Siraselviler Cad. No 67/3, Istanbul.

Championship: 1934, 1952, 1960, 1966, 1967, 1982 (6).
Cup: 1975.

BOLUSPOR
Founded: 1965.
Colours: Red/white.
Stadium: Bolu (18,000).
Club address: Boluspor K., Bolu.
Championship: – .
Cup: – .

BURSASPOR
Founded: 1963.
Colours: Green/white.
Stadium: Atatürk (30,000).
Club address: Bursaspor K., Bursa.
Championship: – .
Cup: – .

FENERBAHÇE
Founded: 1907.
Colours: Blue and yellow/white.
Stadium: Fenerbahçe (35,000).
Club address: Fenerbahçe Spor Kulübü, Kiziltoprak, Istanbul.
Championship: 1933, 1935, 1953, 1959, 1962, 1964, 1965, 1968, 1970, 1974, 1975, 1978, 1983, 1985 (14 – record).
Cup: 1968, 1974, 1979, 1983 (4).

GALATASARAY
Founded: 1905.
Colours: Red/yellow.
Stadium: Ali Sami Yen (40,000).
Club address: Galatasaray Spor Kulübü, Hasnun Galip Sokak, Istanbul.
Championship: 1962, 1963, 1969, 1971, 1972, 1973 (6).
Cup: 1963, 1964, 1965, 1966, 1973, 1976, 1982, 1985 (8).

ORDUSPOR
Founded: 1967.
Colours: Purple/white.
Stadium: Ordu (20,000).
Club address: Orduspor K., Ordu.
Championship: – .
Cup: – .

TRABZONSPOR
Founded: 1923.
Colours: Maroon/blue.
Stadium: Trabzon (25,000).
Club address: Trabzonspor K., Trabzon.
Championship: 1976, 1977, 1979, 1980, 1981, 1984 (6).
Cup: 1977, 1978, 1984 (3).

UNITED STATES

Chicago Sting became the last winners of the North American Soccer League Superbowl when they defeated Toronto Blizzard in both legs of their championship play-off. But they were matches played beneath dark clouds. Already Chicago had announced their intention to abandon the NASL to concentrate on the indoor football phenomenon, and almost every day other clubs were collapsing under the weight of debt or disinterest.

In the spring of 1985, NASL commissioner Clive Toye announced that it would be suspending operations for a year 'to re-group'. But whether a revival is possible must appear doubtful after the sad failure of the grandiose attempt to force-feed Americans with the game. While the NASL and its money-burning operations attracted vastly more publicity overseas than in its own back yard, it is worth nothing that soccer has made enormous strides in the United States in schools and colleges. Many parents prefer their youngsters to play soccer than risk life and limb – both their own and other children's – in the fledgling gridiron clubs.

The NASL was launched in 1968 as a unified North American professional football championship after a merger of the rival United Soccer Association and National Professional Soccer League, which had both run the previous year. There were seventeen teams divided into four leagues – two on the East Coast, two on the West. Professional soccer was about to take off at last, or so it seemed to pioneers such as former Wales international Phil Woosnam.

Big names had yet to start flooding in. But by the mid-1970s, when there were twenty-one clubs, the squads had started to feature some famous faces – Eusebio and Simoes from Portugal, Rodney Marsh, George Best and then, to top them all, Pele. His capture by New York Cosmos was a masterpiece of promotion by Toye, the former Fleet Street sports writer who had become so enthralled by the prospects of soccer in the United States that he had got down from the newspaper fence to take a leading role. New York Cosmos were backed by Warner Communications, who needed a big name to justify their continued involvement. In soccer there was no bigger name than Pele, who became so involved in the American (soccer) dream that in the early 1980s he publicly backed the United States against his own country, Brazil, as prospective World Cup hosts.

Cosmos regularly pulled in 70,000-plus to the Giants Stadium in New Jersey. Pele was soon followed by West Germany's Franz Beckenbauer, Yugoslavia's Vladislav Bogicevic, Belgium's François Van der Elst, Italy's Giorgio Chinaglia – now the man in charge – and the West German master coach, Hennes Weisweiler. The club went on long world tours to show off their superstars. But this was a flagship for the NASL, which was shipping water fast. The years when Cosmos didn't make it to the Superbowl final, attendances for the championship decider plummeted. For a brief few years to go and watch Cosmos was fashionable; but to go along and watch soccer for its own sake remained unfashionable.

Pele played three seasons for Cosmos between 1975 and 1977, scoring thirty-one goals in fifty-six games, and performing an immense public relations job for the sport. In those years the NASL hit a peak. In 1979 and 1980 no fewer than twenty-four teams competed, but the bubble was about to burst.

The dreams of huge profits entertained by many of the owners – who knew little about the game, and understood the reasons for its worldwide appeal even less – faded. Television, the newspapers and magazines were too far into gridiron and baseball ever to consider soccer as a serious rival for professional popularity; the international community looked askance at these newcomers who wanted to enlarge the goals, abandon offside, discard drawn matches and generally mess around with laws which had stood the test of a century elsewhere; and, finally, many owners were lured away by the promise of making a much quicker buck in the mushrooming six-a-side indoor soccer leagues.

In 1981 the league cut back to twenty teams; the next year it was down to fourteen; by 1983 that was twelve; by 1984 the slide couldn't be halted, and only nine teams were enrolled. By February 1985 those nine had dwindled further to four: New York Cosmos, Tulsa Roughnecks, Minnesota Strikers and the Canadian team, Toronto Blizzard. A few days later Cosmos announced that they would not deposit the 150,000-dollar bond required if they intended to compete in 1985. Instead, they were planning a series of international club friendlies to await the NASL's reorganisation. So the NASL had been reduced to three clubs, one of those Canadian.

The decision to suspend competition for 1985 followed a few weeks later. The collapse had been well signposted. Chicago's decision to pull out, taken even before their 1984 Superbowl success, was but a straw in a wind which had been blowing for several years.

Significantly, there were only 8,352 fans present to see the Superbowl first leg in which Chicago beat Toronto 2-1 in a game which also saw twelve players shown the yellow caution card. The goals for Chicago came in the second half from Argentine-born Pato Margetic and former Chilean international Manuel Rojas. And it was Margetic, with two more to add to a goal from Chicago defender Mark Simanton, who decided the Toronto return in Chicago's favour before the shutters came down – at least for the time being – on a shattered dream.

1984 NASL League Table

Eastern Conference	P	W	D*	L	F	A	Bns	Pts
Chicago Sting	24	13		11	50	49	44	120
Toronto Blizzard	24	14		10	46	33	35	117
New York Cosmos	24	13		11	43	41	39	115
Tampa Bay	24	9		15	43	61	35	87
Western Conference	P	W	D*	L	F	A	Bns	Pts
San Diego Sockers	24	14		10	51	42	40	118
Vancouver Whitecaps	24	13		11	51	48	43	117
Minnesota Strikers	24	14		10	41	44	35	115
Tulsa Roughnecks	24	10		14	42	46	38	98
Golden Bay	24	8		16	60	62	49	95

Note: Six points for a victory (including overtime wins), four points for a shoot-out victory and one bonus point for every goal scored per game to maximum of three.
* No draws in the NASL.

Championship semi-finals: *Chicago Sting* bt Vancouver Whitecaps 0-1, 3-1, 4-3 – Toronto Blizzard bt *San Diego Sockers* 2-1, 1-0.
Superbowl: *Chicago Sting* bt Toronto Blizzard 2-1, 3-2.
Top scorer: Steve Zungul (Golden Bay Earthquakes) 20 goals.
(N.B.: United States teams are italicized.)

CHICAGO STING
Founded: 1975. Ceased operations November 1984.
Colours: Black/yellow.
Stadium: Comiskey Park (45,500).
Club address: Chicago Sting, 333 North Michigan Avenue, Suite 1525, Chicago.
NASL championship: 1981, 1984.

MINNESOTA STRIKERS
Founded: 1984. Previously Fort Lauderdale Strikers. Abandoned competition 1985.
Colours: Red and yellow/black.
Stadium: Metrodome (62,000).
Club address: Minnesota Strikers, 8100 Cedar Avenue South, Suite 115, Bloomington, Minnesota.
NASL championship: – .

NEW YORK COSMOS
Founded: 1971. Abandoned competition 1985.
Colours: Royal blue and yellow/white.
Stadium: Giants Stadium, East Rutherford, New Jersey (76,891).
Club address: Cosmos, 44 East 50th Street, New York, New York 10022.
NASL championship: 1972, 1977, 1978, 1980, 1982 (5 – record).

TULSA ROUGHNECKS
Founded: 1978. Abandoned competition 1985.
Colours: Red and white/blue.
Stadium: Skelly (41,000).
Club address: Tulsa Roughnecks, PO Box 35190, 6243 East 61st Street, Tulsa, Oklahoma.
NASL championship: 1983.

URUGUAY

Unrated outsiders Central Español came from nowhere to snatch the 1984 Uruguayan league title and become only the fourth club to break the stranglehold held by the big two, Peñarol and Nacional, over the past seventy years – not that Central's celebrations were allowed to last long in the confusing world of Uruguayan football.

A word first about organisation: the league title is decided by a simple European-style home-and-away competition involving all thirteen first division clubs. Then those clubs which had claimed championship success in the past decade *plus* the two other highest-placed clubs in the league went forward to the so-called Colombes Cup. The six clubs who totalled most points in both events progressed again, to the 'liguilla' to sort out the two Uruguayan representatives in the 1985 South American Cup. Winners and runners-up would qualify, as long as one of those two clubs were the league champions. However, if the league champions finished outside the top two they would have to play-off against the 'liguilla' runners-up for the right to join the mini-group winners in the continental competition.

As bad luck would have it, as far as Central Español were concerned, Peñarol won the 'liguilla' ahead of Bella Vista, with Central down in fourth place. But because Peñarol and Bella Vista had finished with the same number of points, it was decided – by a federation ever-ingenious at 'creating' important matches – that they should play off to decide first place and runners-up.

The play-off was dramatic for more than this reason: it was also the last game to be played by Fernando Morena, the veteran Peñarol centre-forward who was retiring after a 700–goal career in Uruguay, Spain and Argentina. Peñarol and Bella Vista finished all-square at 2-2 at the end of extra time so the matter went to penalties. And, in *Roy of the Rovers* style, it was Morena who struck the decisive spot-kick which won the shoot-out 7-5 in Peñarol's favour.

Peñarol's fans carried him shoulder-high from the pitch, and the media cornered him for more than an hour and a half at a press conference in the depths of the famous old Centenario Stadium. The fans had chanted: 'Morena don't go, Morena don't go.' But he made it clear that the problems of returning to action after a serious leg injury meant that he could never regain his attacking power, and he felt it best to quit at the top.

Bella Vista, meanwhile, had a second bite at the South American Club Cup cherry and duly beat Central Español 1-0 – which left the Uruguayan champions beaten to a place in the cup before it had even begun! It's hardly surprising that there has since been lengthy negotiation aimed at preventing such a repeat.

These controversial events took a lot of the gloss from Central's achievement, which was a pity, because apart from becoming one of the few clubs ever to last the pace better than Peñarol and Nacional, they were also the first club ever to land the league title immediately after winning promotion to the top flight.

The club had been founded simply as 'Central' in 1904, but it was only in 1972, after adoption by the large Spanish community in the Palermo suburb of Montevideo, that the 'Español' was added to the title. At that time they were just a local team. But with this new-found support they applied for admission to the Uruguayan second division. It was the second time Central had displayed any ambition. The first occasion had been back in 1944, when they won a pre-season tournament with a team which included three of the most famous names in Uruguayan football history: Juan Lopez, who would become manager of the 1950 World Cup-winners, right-half Rodriguez Andrade who was one of that team's most accomplished footballers, and Walter Gomez who would go on to star in Argentina with River Plate. In those days Central couldn't hang on to their best players. They had to be sold. And that was again the policy of necessity with which Central spent eleven years in the second division on their revival in 1972.

Then, in 1983, they surprised even themselves by winning promotion to the first division. There was no rich supporter to back them. The club committee and coach Liber Arispe had to dig into their own pockets sometimes to pay training expenses and for footballs when membership subscriptions and tiny attendances proved insufficient. The players didn't even expect any special bonuses – merely formed themselves into a co-operative to share out whatever profits might be available at the season's end.

Almost no one expected them to play any sort of role in the first division except battle against relegation. But Arispe had other ideas. He said: 'I had confidence in my players, and knew they could do a reasonable job. Then, as the championship advanced and we managed to stay among the leaders I realised that we might just be able to have to go at the title, especially as Peñarol and Nacional were having problems.'

Central had no internationals. But their players worked themselves into the ground closing down their opponents. The result was that they lost only two league games and had by far the best defensive record, with goalkeeper Hector Tuja conceding seventeen goals in twenty-four matches. In attack Jose Villareal was the league's top scorer with a personal tally of seventeen of Central's total of thirty-nine goals. Ironically, Villareal had begun his career with Peñarol, but moved on because, with Morena around, he was never given a chance, even when Morena was out injured.

So much for Central. What of Peñarol's crisis? First, it must be said that with Peñarol a 'crisis' bears little relation to those suffered by most other clubs throughout the world. The problem of the former world club champions in 1984 was that in the league, while they lost just one of their twenty-four games, they drew more than they won – twelve draws compared with eleven victories. Also, the club reached the end of the year around £2 million in debt, despite a £35,000 sponsorship from a local bank, and a further £60,000 for the six-month loan to Argentine club Boca Juniors of Morena. That was far from being a popular move with the fans and Peñarol ran into further controversy when it was revealed that the financial backing for a newspaper which sponsored their basketball team came from the controversial Unification Church, the so-called Moonies.

Star forward Venancio Ramos was sold to French club Lens to further stave off creditors and Uruguay's right-back Victor Diogo was sold to Brazilian club Palmeiras for £140,000 to raise the cash to pacify the rest of the squad, who were threatening to strike because their monthly pay cheques hadn't come through. The club hoped that qualification for the 1985 South American Club Cup would help alleviate the financial distress. If they had missed out the club's headquarters might well have had to be sold off to make good a £100,000 bill from the state airline. With all those headaches it was a wonder the players managed to finish second in the league and top the 'liguilla'. Their consolation was that at least they finished ahead of deadly rivals Nacional in all competitions.

Nacional began the season in a blaze of optimism by recalling as coach Juan Martin Mujica – a playing member of their 1971 World Club Cup-winners side, and coach when they regained the World Club Championship a decade later. With winger Juan Ramon Carrasco back from an unhappy spell with River Plate in Argentina to partner the new starlet, Carlos Aguilera, the fans were happy.

But that didn't last for long. Nacional were beaten in the South American Cup semi-finals by eventual winners Independiente of Argentina, and when this was quickly followed by a 1-0 defeat at the hands of Bella Vista in the league, Mujica was sacked. Internal squabbling led to the suspensions of two of their best young players, Jorge Villazan and Ernesto Berrueta, and then their joint sale to River Plate of Buenos Aires. Nacional duly finished third in both league and 'liguilla', and that wasn't good enough.

1984 League Table

	P	W	D	L	F	A	Pts
Central Español	24	13	9	2	39	17	35
Peñarol	24	11	12	1	47	23	34
Nacional	24	11	10	3	44	25	32
Danubio	24	12	7	5	35	23	31
Bella Vista	24	10	7	7	25	29	27
Wanderers	24	10	6	8	37	30	26
Rampla Juniors	24	6	12	6	28	28	24
Defensor	24	9	6	9	27	26	24
Huracan Buceo	24	4	10	10	15	28	18
Progreso	24	4	10	10	15	28	18
Sud America	24	5	7	12	27	42	17
Cerro	24	2	11	11	15	38	15
Miramar	24	3	5	16	16	34	11

Top scorer: Jose Villareal (Central Español) 17 goals.

Colombes Cup
Final placings: 1 Peñarol 7 pts. 2 Bella Vista, Defensor and Danubio 5 pts each. 5 Nacional and Central Español 4 pts each.

S. American Club Cup 'Liguilla'

	P	W	D	L	F	A	Pts
Peñarol	5	3	2	0	8	3	8
Bella Vista	5	3	2	0	7	2	8
Nacional	5	3	1	1	10	3	7
Central Español	5	1	2	2	5	6	4
Danubio	5	1	0	4	2	7	2
Defensor	5	0	1	4	2	13	1

Play-offs: Peñarol bt Bella Vista 2-2 after extra time, 7-5 on penalties – Bella Vista bt Central Español 1-0.

BELLA VISTA
Founded: 1900.
Colours: Yellow and white/black.
Stadium: Lucas Obes (20,000).
Club address: Club Atlético Bella Vista, Agraciada 3100, Montevideo.
League: —.

CENTRAL ESPAÑOL
Founded: 1904.
Colours: All red.
Stadium: Palermo (12,000).
Club address: Central Español, c/o Asociacion Uruguaya de Futbol, Guayabo 1531, Montevideo.
League: 1984.

DANUBIO
Founded: 1900.
Colours: All white with black sash.
Stadium: Jardines del Hipódromo (18,000).
Club address: Danubio FC, 8 de Octubre 4584, Montevideo.
League: —.

DEFENSOR
Founded: 1900.
Colours: Violet/white.
Stadium: Luis Franzini (15,000).
Club address: Club Atlético Defensor, Jaime Zudañes 2537, Montevideo.
League: 1976.

NACIONAL
Founded: 1899.
Colours: White/blue.
Stadium: Parque Central (20,000) but important matches in the Centenario (73,609).
Club address: Club Nacional de Fútbol, Avenida 8 de Octubre 2487, Montevideo.
League: 1902, 1903, 1912, 1915, 1916, 1917, 1919, 1920, 1922, 1923, 1924, 1933, 1934, 1939, 1940, 1941, 1942, 1943, 1946, 1947, 1950, 1952, 1955, 1956, 1957, 1963, 1966, 1969, 1970, 1971, 1972, 1977, 1980, 1983 (34).
World Club Cup: 1971, 1980.
S. American Club Cup: 1971, 1980. Runners-up in 1964, 1967 and 1969.
Interamerican Cup: 1972. Runners-up in 1981.

PEÑAROL
Founded: 1891.
Colours: Black and yellow stripes/black.
Stadium: Centenario (73,609).
Club address: Club Atletico Peñarol, Magallanes esquina de Galicia, Montevideo.
League: 1900, 1901, 1905, 1907, 1911, 1918, 1921, 1926, 1928, 1929, 1930 (unfinished), 1932, 1935, 1936, 1937, 1938, 1944, 1945, 1949, 1951, 1953, 1954, 1958, 1959, 1960, 1961, 1962, 1964, 1965, 1967, 1968, 1973, 1974, 1975, 1978, 1979, 1981, 1982 (38 – record).
World Club Cup: 1961, 1966, 1982 (3). Runners-up in 1960.
S. American Club Cup: 1960, 1961, 1966, 1982 (4). Runners-up in 1962, 1965, 1970, and 1983.

WANDERERS
Founded: 1900.
Colours: Black and white stripes/white.
Stadium: Wanderers (10,000).
Club address: Club Montevideo Wanderers, San Fructuoso 1070, Montevideo.
League: 1906, 1909, 1931 (3).

VENEZUELA

Venezuela, an exceptional country in South America because football takes second place in the public's sporting affection behind baseball, produced a chaotic climax to the 1984 season. Deportivo Italia, from the capital, Caracas, won the first stage of the two-part championship and collected the two bonus points on offer – which also made them favourites to win the overall title for the fifth time in sixteen years.

However, at the end of the second stage of matches between the top eight teams in the first round, nothing was resolved – all because a match between Deportivo Tachira and Atletico Zamora had ended prematurely in a pitched battle between players and substitutes, coaches and police. It needed the federation to rule that Tachira had won the game, and the championship.

There was more trouble during a game between Estudiantes and Portuguesa, but trouble in terms of form for Deportivo Italia. Having taken a three-point lead in the second round they were ultimately overhauled as Tachira claimed their third championship in five years. Tachira had underlined their ambition in 1982, when they paid what remains a Venezuelan transfer record of £140,000 for the Colombian championship star Arnoldo Iguaran.

The problem with Venezuelan football is illustrated by the failure as yet to produce an outstanding player of their own. All the big names have to be imported. Often, however, they are veterans – such as Portuguesa's capture in the late 1970s of Brazil's one-time World Cup hero Jairzinho. He didn't find it easy in Venezuela, and thus added another dimension to the problems, in that unsuccessful foreign imports further detract from the sport's image.

It was with the hope of finally putting Venezuelan football straight that the federation produced a report in 1977 suggesting ways the government might invest cash to put the game on a sound footing. The recommendations sat around for two years, although there was nothing revolutionary suggested. The main idea was the creation of a central committee made up of delegates from the amateur game, the professional league, the referees, coaches and student and military sports organisations.

1983 Championship
First Round

	P	W	D	L	F	A	Pts
Deportivo Italia	20	10	7	3	26	14	27
San Cristobal	20	8	9	3	17	10	25
Tachira	20	9	4	7	25	21	22
Portuguesa	20	8	5	7	33	18	21
Universidad de los Andes	20	7	7	6	17	12	21
Zamora	20	7	6	7	23	19	20
Estudiantes	20	7	6	7	17	13	20
Portugues	20	7	6	7	24	24	20
Carabobo	20	5	8	7	12	19	18
Petroleros de Zulia	20	11	11	12	10	31	12
Mineros de Guayana	20	3	5	12	8	34	11

Second round
Final placings: 1 Deportivo Tachira. 2 Deportivo Italia. 3 Atletico Zamora. 4 Universidad de los Andes. 5 San Cristobal. 6 Portuguesa. 7 Portugues. 8 Estudiantes (Merida).

Further proposals would involve creating a unified youth scheme among the professional clubs, cutting the number of imported players from four to two per team, bringing down to twenty-five from twenty-eight the minimum age for signing a professional contract, and replacing all the amateurs still playing at first division level by youth team players or apprentices.

The report sat around gathering dust until interest in reviving and activating these ideas followed hard upon the success of the Merida club, Universidad de los Andes, in reaching the semi-finals of the South American Club Cup in 1984 – albeit after a play-off against the vastly more experienced Peruvian club, Sporting Cristal. ULA became involved in the play-off because the other Peruvian club in their first-round group, Melgar, had fielded an ineligible player.

Coached by a Uruguayan, Alfredo Lopez, ULA relied typically on three imports to mastermind their successes: Colombian defender Rodrigo Cosme, Uruguayan midfielder Richard Nada and Brazilian centre-forward Itamar Acevedo.

DEPORTIVO GALICIA
Founded: 1926.
Colours: Red and white.
Stadium: Main matches in the Estadio Olímpico (25,000).
Club address: Deportivo Galicia, c/o Federacion Venezolana de Futbol, Estadio Nacional, El Paraiso, Apartado 14160, Caracas.
Pro. championship: 1964, 1969, 1970, 1974 (4).

DEPORTIVO ITALIA
Founded: 1952.
Colours: Blue and white.
Stadium: Main matches in the Estadio Olímpico (25,000).
Club address: Deportivo Italia, Centro Profesional, Flor – Los Chirs, Caracas.
Pro. championship: 1958, 1961, 1966, 1972 (4).

ESTUDIANTES DE MERIDA
Founded: 1952.
Colours: All white.
Stadium: Guillermo Soto Rosa (10,000).
Club address: Estudiantes, c/o Federacion Venezolana de Futbol, Estudio Nacional, El Paraiso, Apartado 14160, Caracas.
Pro. championship: 1980.

PORTUGUESA
Founded: 1926.
Colours: Green and white.
Stadium: General José Antonio Páez, Acarigua (11,000).
Club address: Portuguesa, c/o Federacion Venezolana de Futbol, Estadio Nacional, El Paraiso, Apartado 14160, Caracas.
Pro. championship: 1973, 1975, 1976, 1977, 1978 (5 – record).

SAN CRISTOBAL
Founded: 1981.
Colours: Green and white stripes/white.

Stadium: Estadio San Cristobal (20,000).
Club address: Atletico San Cristobal, c/o Federacion Venezolana de Futbol, Estadio Nacional, El Paraiso, Apartado 14160, Caracas.
Pro. championship: 1982.

TACHIRA
Founded: 1978.
Colours: Red and white.
Stadium: Tachira, San Cristobal (12,000).
Club address: Deportivo Tachira, c/o Federacion Venezolana de Futbol, Estadio Nacional, El Paraiso, Apartado 14160, Caracas.
Pro. championship: 1979, 1981, 1984 (3).

UNIVERSIDAD DE LOS ANDES
Founded: 1977.
Colours: Blue and white.
Stadium: Guillermo Soto Rosa, Merida (10,000).
Club address: Universidad de los Andes, c/o Federacion Venezolana de Futbol, Estadio Nacional, El Paraiso, Apartado 14160, Caracas.
Pro. championship: 1983.

VALENCIA
Founded: 1926.
Colours: All white.
Stadium: Misael Delgado (8,000).
Club address: Valencia, c/o Federacion Venezolana de Futbol, Estadio Nacional, El Paraiso, Apartado 14160, Caracas.
Pro. championship: 1971.

WALES

Wales' national team discovered a top-ranking strike partnership in Liverpool's Ian Rush and Manchester United's Mark Hughes. But as the national team fought valiantly against Scotland and Spain to keep their World Cup qualifying hopes alive, so the domestic game lost more ground at professional level. While Wrexham struggled to stay out of the fourth division re-election zone, Newport slipped dangerously down the third, where Swansea manager John Bond appeared to be up to his neck in a permanent financial crisis, and Cardiff were relegated from the second division.

As if the Football League clubs had not been embarrassed enough, it was Bangor City of the Northern Premier League who pipped them all to qualify for the 1985–86 European Cup-winners' Cup. Newport were the last league obstacle in their way in the semi-finals of the Welsh Cup because the other finalists, Shrewsbury, were not eligible for Europe, being English.

Bangor won the first leg of their semi-final against Newport and were a little lucky to emerge from the return, at Somerton Park, with a goal-less draw. Newport dominated most of the match but could not take their chances. Chamberlain came closest with a shot which struck the outside of an upright. In the final Bangor lost 3-1 away and 2-0 at home against Shrewsbury, but it did not matter. They had qualified for Europe for the second time in their history. The first occasion was in 1962–63, when Bangor had been drawn against the Italians of Napoli in the first round of the Cup-winners' Cup. Goals from Matthews and Birch (penalty) brought Bangor a 2-0 win at home, and they would have won through had today's away goal rules been in force after losing the return 3-1. Instead they had to play off at Highbury, Arsenal's ground, where at 22,000 crowd saw Bangor go down 2-1.

Considering their standings in the Football League – or out of it! – Welsh clubs have put up some brave fights over the years in the Cup-winners' Cup. But few achievements could match that of Wrexham in the first round of competition in 1984–85 when they were drawn against Portugal's FC Porto, who had been runners-up to Juventus in the 1983–84 final a few months earlier. Wrexham won their home leg 1-0 at the Racecourse Ground, but, struggling at the foot of the fourth division and with the future of manager Bobby Roberts the subject of increasing speculation, were expected to collect a beating out in Portugal.

In monsoon conditions those forecasts appeared well-founded, when it took Fernando Gomes just five minutes to bring Porto level, and Jaime Magalhaes another quarter of an hour to give them the overall lead. Gomes then made it 3-0 – 3-1 on aggregate – from a penalty and it appeared all over – to everyone except the Wrexham players.

In a remarkable six-minute spell before half-time, skipper Jake King scored his first goals of the season to pull the score back to 2-3 and put the Welshmen ahead on the away goals rule. Porto regained the overall lead through Paolo Futre on the hour. Yet with two minutes remaining, Barry Horne – playing non-league football the previous season for Rhyl – shot Wrexham's third goal past former Chelsea goalkeeper Petar Borota. This time it was too late for Porto to react and Wrexham went through on the away goals rule to meet eventual elimination at the hands of Italy's Roma. Even so, they had done Welsh football proud.

Welsh clubs in the Football League 1984–85

First division:	None							
Second division:	21, Cardiff	42	9	8	25	47	79	35
	* Cardiff relegated							
Third division	18, Newport	47	13	13	20	55	67	52
	20, Swansea	46	12	11	23	53	80	47
Fourth division:	15, Wrexham	46	15	9	22	67	70	54

Welsh cup final: Shrewsbury bt Bangor 3-1, 2-0 (5-1 on agg).

CARDIFF CITY
Founded: 1899.
Colours: All blue.
Stadium: Ninian Park (42,000).
Club address: Cardiff City AFC, Ninian Park, Cardiff CF1 8SX.
Football League: – .
FA Cup: 1927.
Welsh Cup: 1912, 1920, 1922, 1923, 1927, 1928, 1930, 1956, 1959, 1964, 1965 1967, 1968, 1969, 1970, 1971, 1973, 1974, 1976 (19).

NEWPORT COUNTY
Founded: 1912.
Colours: Amber/black.
Stadium: Somerton Park (18,000).
Club address: Newport County FC, Somerton Park, Newport, Gwent.
Football League: – .
FA Cup: – .
Welsh Cup: 1980.

SWANSEA CITY
Founded: 1900.
Colours: All white.
Stadium: Vetch Field (26,237).
Club address: Swansea City FC, Vetch Field, Swansea.
Football League: – .
FA Cup: – .
Welsh Cup: 1913, 1932, 1950, 1961, 1966, 1981, 1982, 1983 (8).

WREXHAM
Founded: 1873.
Colours: Red/blue.
Stadium: Racecourse Ground (30,000).
Club address: Wrexham AFC, Racecourse Ground, Mold Road, Wrexham.
Football League: – .
FA Cup: – .
Welsh Cup: 1878, 1883, 1893, 1897, 1903, 1905, 1909, 1910, 1911, 1914, 1915, 1921, 1924, 1925, 1931, 1957, 1958, 1960, 1972, 1975, 1978 (21 – record).

WEST GERMANY

Bayern Munich, the dominant force in West German football in the 1970s thanks to the inspiration of Franz Beckenbauer, the goals of Gerd Müller and the all-round professionalism of Sepp Maier, Georg Schwarzenbeck, Paul Breitner and Uli Hoeness, are back in charge. They may have disappointed in their Cup-winners' Cup semi-final defeat at the hands of Everton, but in domestic competition Udo Lattek's men gave little away.

Over the last few weeks of the season they perhaps allowed Werder Bremen to come a little too close for comfort at the top of the table; and surprisingly they lost to Bayer Ürdingen in the cup final. But on the last weekend of the league programme a second-half goal from Dieter Hoeness brought a 1-0 away win over relegated Eintracht Braunschweig to seal the title. Since Bremen lost 2-0 to Borussia Dortmund, Bayern finished with a commanding four-point lead.

Dieter Hoeness had also opened the scoring against Ürdingen in the cup final, after only eight minutes in the famous old Olympic stadium in West Berlin which will host the final until the end of the decade as consolation for the city's exclusion from the 1988 European championship schedule. But it took Ürdingen, the rank outsiders, only a minute to draw level through midfielder Horst Feilzer. Bayern realised the match was slipping from them when international defender Wolfgang Dremmler was sent off shortly after half-time, and Ürdingen duly won the cup thanks to a sixty-seventh minute effort from Wolfgang Schäfer, who had played second division football only a year before with Union Solingen. It was the first time Ürdingen had won a national trophy in the club's eighty years, and provided their first-ever entry into the European arena.

Ürdingen's home is in the industrial centre of Krefeld, and this season was only their fifth in the Bundesliga. They first gained entry to the top division in 1975, but were instantly relegated, came back up in 1979, and went down yet again in 1981. It now appears that promotion in 1983 was third time lucky, and they have moved steadily up the table over the succeeding seasons. They are one of the work teams of the Bayer pharmaceutical corporation, but have been generally granted less support than Bayer Leverkusen, who also rank among the best athletics clubs in western Europe. Ürdingen's success owes a great deal to the shrewd judgment of coach Karl-Heinz Feldkamp, who brought to the club in 1984 the full value of experience gained in the Bundesliga with Arminia Bielefeld, Kaiserslautern and Borussia Dortmund.

It was Feldkamp who turned defender Mathias Herget into such a fine sweeper that he became first-choice for the World Cup squad, and Feldkamp who gave the talented Icelandic forward, Larus Gudmundsson, the confidence to match his ability. Another foreign import who proved a useful squad member over the season was Wayne Thomas, a former Peterborough apprentice who moved to the West German regional league from non-League Nuneaton Borough and joined Ürdingen in 1983. He collected a cup-winner's medal after appearing as substitute eight minutes from time.

Out of the title frame in both league and cup were 1983 European champions, Hamburg. Austrian coach Ernst Happel and general manager Günter Netzer announced in mid-season their intention to rebuild. Even before the disappointing season had ended they had set up the signings of Peter Lux, a versatile forward, from Braunschweig, and midfielder Thomas Kroth from Eintracht Frankfurt. Former internationals Jürgen Milewski (in attack) and Jürgen Groh (in midfield) were released when their contracts ended, and the season closed on a note of controversy with Happel suspending both Groh and the 1982 World Cup defender Manni Kaltz. It was the second suspension Kaltz had collected after a season in which he looked very much a shadow of the goal-scoring, fast-raiding right-back of a few years ago.

Hamburg's main problem lay up front, where they have yet successfully to replace Horst Hrubesch. The former Hannover and Fortuna Köln spearhead, Dieter Schatzschneider, had spent one unsuccessful season at the Volksparkstadion, and little more success was achieved by the Scotland striker, Mark McGhee, from Aberdeen. At least in defence Hamburg did appear to have picked up a bargain in the Belgian full-back or sweeper Gerard Plessers. He joined up in mid-season having completed an eighteen-month suspension, imposed for his involvement in the Standard Liège bribes scandal in Belgium. Plessers had trained hard in the meantime, quickly fitted in to the scheme of things, and was soon bossing the defence. Hamburg deserved some good fortune after international stopper or sweeper Holger Hieronymus was forced by injury into premature retirement.

Hamburg remain the last West German side to have won a European trophy. The 1984–85 season wasn't particularly kind to Bundesliga clubs abroad. Stuttgart lost in the first round of the Champions' Cup to unrated Levsky Spartak of Bulgaria, and both Werder Bremen and Borussia Mönchengladbach failed to make it beyond the second round of the UEFA Cup. Hamburg fell in the third round against Internazionale, and exiled West German national skipper Karl-Heinz Rummenigge, who also then disposed of Köln in the quarter-finals.

On the international front, the West German federation, which usually manages to steer a successful diplomatic course, stepped on a minefield with their application to host the finals of the 1988 European championship. West Germany's main rivals for the finals were England, who had European concern over the hooligan element working against them. The only worry for the West German delegation was whether Eastern European votes might be antagonised by the inclusion of West Berlin in the provisional fixtures schedule. Once Berlin had been removed, however, it was all plain sailing, until the West German government and media found out. Then all hell broke loose. Government ministers threatened to withdraw their support for the German staging if West Berlin were not reinstated. But there were also expressions of outrage from the cities of Hamburg, Dortmund and Bochum that they had not been included either, despite boasting stadia with 50,000-plus capacities. As a sop to domestic opinion, the DFB did go back to UEFA and ask if the opening match could be staged in West Berlin. The answer, predictably, was no. But at least this seemed to satisfy political opinion at home.

DFB president Hermann Neuberger, who is also FIFA's senior vice-president and head of the world federation's World Cup organising committee, said: 'Sport and politics should not mix, and certainly sport should not be used by politicians as an instrument of power. I am satisfied we have the support of the vast majority of football fans and that is what really matters.'

1984–85 League Table

	P	W	D	L	F	A	Pts
Bayern Munich	34	21	8	5	79	38	50
Werder Bremen	34	18	10	6	87	51	46
1. FC Köln	34	18	4	12	69	66	40
Borussia Mg	34	15	9	10	77	53	39
Hamburg	34	14	9	11	58	49	37
Waldhof-Mannheim	34	13	11	10	47	50	37
Bayer Ürdingen	34	14	8	12	57	52	36
Schalke 04	34	13	8	13	63	62	34
VfL Bochum	34	12	10	12	52	54	34
VfB Stuttgart	34	14	5	15	79	59	33
Kaiserslautern	34	11	11	12	56	60	33
Eintracht Frankfurt	34	10	12	12	62	67	32
Bayer Leverkusen	34	9	13	12	52	54	31
Borussia Dortmund	34	13	4	17	51	65	30
Fortuna D'dorf	34	10	9	15	53	66	29
Arminia Bielefeld	34	8	13	13	46	61	29
Karlsruhe	34	5	12	17	47	88	22
Eintracht Bwg	34	9	2	23	39	79	20

Cup final: Bayern Ürdingen 2, Bayern Munich 1.
Top scorer: Klaus Allofs (Köln) 26 goals.

The West Germans will now play the opening match in the 1988 finals in the Rheinstadion in Düsseldorf, and then travel to Hannover and Munich for further first round matches. The other group games will be organised in Gelsenkirchen, Cologne, Frankfurt and Stuttgart. The semi-finals have been provisionally set for Düsseldorf and Stuttgart, with the final in Munich's Olympiastadion on 25 June, 1988.

In the meantime, Franz Beckenbauer's national team are on their way to the World Cup finals in Mexico. Beckenbauer took over, with considerable success, from Jupp Derwall after West Germany's European crown was seized by France in 1984. Beckenbauer's rebuilt team won all their first five qualifying matches but he warned: 'If the World Cup were a year later I think we could do quite well. But my team will not be experienced enough in 1986.' With Beckenbauer in charge, that seems hard to believe.

BAYER ÜRDINGEN
Founded: 1905.
Colours: Sky blue/white.
Stadium: Grotenburg-Kampfbahn (26,000).
Club address: Bayer Ürdingen 05, 4150 Krefeld 11, Postfach 110.
League: – .
Cup: 1985.

BAYERN
Founded: 1900.
Colours: All red.
Stadium: Olympiastadion (77,573).
Club address: FC Bayern München, Säbener Strasse 51, 8000 Munich 90.
Championship: 1932, 1969, 1972, 1973, 1974, 1980, 1981, 1985 (8).
Cup: 1957, 1966, 1969, 1971, 1982, 1984 (6).
World Club Cup: 1976.
Champions' Cup: 1974, 1975, 1976 (3). Runners-up in 1982.
Cup-winners' Cup: 1967.
SuperCup: Runners-up in 1975 and 1976.

BORUSSIA DORTMUND
Founded: 1909.
Colours: Yellow/black.
Stadium: Westfalenstadion (53,790).
Club address: BV Borussia, Westfalenstadion, Strobelalle, Postfach 509,4600 Dortmund 1.
Championship: 1956, 1957, 1963 (3).
Cup: 1965.
Cup-winners' Cup: 1966.

BORUSSIA MÖNCHENGLADBACH
Founded: 1900.
Colours: All white.
Stadium: Bökelberg (38,500).
Club address: Börussia Mönchengladbach, Bökelstrasse 165 (Stadion), 4050 Mönchengladbach 1.

Championship: 1970, 1971, 1975, 1976, 1977 (5).
Cup: 1960, 1973.
World Club Cup: Runners-up in 1977.
Champions' Cup: Runners-up in 1977.
UEFA Cup: 1975, 1979. Runners-up in 1973 and 1980.

COLOGNE
* See: Köln.

EINTRACHT BRAUNSCHWEIG
Founded: 1895.
Colours: Yellow/blue.
Stadium: Städtisches Stadion (35,000).
Club address: Eintracht Braunschweig TuS, Hamburger Strasse 210, 3300 Braunschweig (Brunswick).
Championship: 1967.
Cup: – .

EINTRACHT FRANKFURT
Founded: 1899.
Colours: Black and red stripes/black.
Stadium: Waldstadion (61,146).
Club address: Eintracht Frankfurt, Sportplatz am Riederwald, Am Erlenbruch 25, 6000 Frankfurt/Main 60.
Championship: 1959.
Cup: 1974, 1975, 1981 (3).
Champions' Cup: Runners-up in 1960.
UEFA Cup: 1980.

FORTUNA DÜSSELDORF
Founded: 1895.
Colours: All white with red trimming.
Stadium: Rheinstadion (67,861).
Club address: Fortuna Düsseldorf, Flinger Broich 97, 4000 Düsseldorf.
Championship: 1933.
Cup: 1979, 1980.
Cup-winners' Cup: Runners-up in 1979.

HAMBURG
Founded: 1887.
Colours: White/red.
Stadium: Volksparkstadion (61,418).
Club address: Hamburger Sportverein, Hartungstrasse 14–16, 2000 Hamburg 13.
Championship: 1922 (withdrawn), 1923, 1928, 1960, 1979, 1982, 1983 (7).
Cup: 1963, 1976.
League Cup: 1973.
World Club Cup: Runners-up in 1983.
Champions' Cup: 1983. Runners-up in 1980.
Cup-winners' Cup: 1977. Runners-up in 1968.
SuperCup: Runners-up in 1977 and 1983.

KAISERSLAUTERN
Founded: 1900.
Colours: White/red.
Stadium: Betzenberg (33,000).
Club address: 1. FC Kaiserslautern, Stadion Betzenberg, 6750 Kaiserslautern.
Championship: 1951, 1953.
Cup: – .

KICKERS OFFENBACH
Founded: 1901.
Colours: Red/white.
Stadium: Bieberer Berg (31,500).
Club address: Kickers OFC, Bieberer Strasse 282, 6050 Offenbach.
Championship: – .
Cup: 1970.

KÖLN
Founded: 1948.
Colours: All white.
Stadium: Müngersdorf (61,188).
Club address: 1.FC Köln, Postfach 100 768, 5000 Cologne 41.
Championship: 1962, 1964, 1978 (3).
Cup: 1968, 1977, 1978, 1983 (4).

MÜNCHEN 1860
Founded: 1860 (but football section in 1899).
Colours: Sky blue/white.
Stadium: Grünwald (31,509).
Club address: TSV 1860 München, Grünwalder Strasse 114, 8000 Munich 90
Championship: 1966.
Cup: 1942 and 1964.
Cup-winners' Cup: Runners-up in 1965.

NÜRNBERG
Founded: 1900.
Colours: Red/white.
Stadium: Städtisches Stadion (60,000).
Club address: 1. FC Nürnberg, Valznerweiherstrasse 200, 8500 Nuremberg
Championship: 1920, 1921, 1924, 1925, 1927, 1936, 1948, 1961, 1968 (9 - record).
Cup: 1935, 1939, 1962 (3).

SCHALKE
Founded: 1904.
Colours: White/blue.
Stadium: Parkstadion (70,600).
Club address: FC Schalke 04, Postfach 680, 4650 Gelsenkirchen.
Championship: 1934, 1935, 1937, 1939, 1940, 1942, 1958 (7).
Cup: 1937, 1972.

STUTTGART
Founded: 1893.
Colours: All white.
Stadium: Neckarstadion (70,705).
Club address: VfB Stuttgart, Mercedesstrasse 109, Postfach 501 142, 7000 Stuttgart 50.
Championship: 1950, 1952, 1984 (3).
Cup: 1954, 1958.

WERDER BREMEN
Founded: 1899.
Colours: White/green.
Stadium: Weser (40,000).
Club address: Werder Bremen, Weserstadion, 2800 Bremen 1.
Championship: 1965.
Cup: 1961.

YUGOSLAVIA

Sarajevo won the championship for the second time in their history, but they were not sure of the crown until their players left the pitch at the end of their last game of the season. It could have been their toughest match, at home to the reviving Red Star Belgrade, whose morale had improved no end in the few weeks since they had beaten Dinamo Zagreb over two legs to win the Yugoslav Cup. At the same time as Sarajevo were home to Red Star, so Hajduk Split – just two points adrift – were at home to Dinamo Zagreb. Hajduk needed to win to stand any chance of the league title, while Dinamo needed to win to stand any chance of overtaking Vardar Skopje, just above them, for the remaining UEFA Cup qualifying place. As it turned out, Sarajevo beat Red Star 2–1 while Hajduk's ambition – surprisingly – did not match that of Dinamo Zagreb, who produced their best display of the season to win 4–2. Such a result deserved reward but unfortunately for Dinamo, Vardar collected a 2–2 draw away to Velež Mostar and stayed one point ahead.

At the other end of the table Iskra of Bugojno made a minor piece of European football history when they became the first club ever to win the Mitropa Cup and suffer the ignominy of relegation in the same season. The Mitropa Cup – the pre-war forerunner of the current European club tournaments – is now virtually forgotten and played between unfashionable clubs. But Iskra had collected the one and only major title in their history when they topped the table ahead of Banik Ostrava, Atalanta of Italy and Bekescsaba of Hungary.

The Yugoslav season began under a minor depression left by the national team's string of defeats in the European championship finals in France but tempered by third place in the Los Angeles Olympics. There were plenty more upsets for the fans, particularly those of Red Star and Dinamo Zagreb, who both struggled in the early months and had unprecedented spells at the bottom of the table. Dinamo reacted by demoting coach Branko Zebec. One-time Anderlecht boss Tomislav Ivic moved in, and Dinamo immediately responded by winning and moving up the table.

As for Red Star, they hit rock bottom after successive defeats by Hajduk Split (3–1 at home) and 2–1 away in the Belgrade derby against Partizan. Partizan were on the crest of a wave, having a few days earlier put together the 4–0 win against Queen's Park Rangers, which turned their UEFA Cup match against the English club upside down. Against both QPR and Red Star it was lively striker Dragan Mance who scored the first goal. As if Red Star had now decided that enough was enough, they bounced back from defeat by Partizan to thrash Buducnost Titograd 6–2. Halilovic grabbed a hat-trick, Sestic two more and the score would have been even more expressive of Red Star's domination had not Buducnost goalkeeper Zalad been in superb form!

An away draw with Pristina and 2–1 home win over Osijek – Sestic and Halilovic again the scorers – and Red Star were moving upwards towards safety. It was too late now for them to catch leaders Sarajevo but at least they achieved the next best thing, defeating Sarajevo 4–1 in Belgrade with goals from Milovanovic, Sestic, Milko Durovski and fit-again teenage winger, Mitar Mrkela.

Sarajevo remained half-way leaders, however, largely thanks to the excellent form in midfield of international Farukh Hadzibegic. His hard work in both defence and attack appeared to provide Sarajevo with an extra man in many matches. He maintained his remarkable record for never having missed a penalty, until the league restarted after the winter break and he let one go in a 1–0 win over Rijeka.

For virtually all the second half of the season Sarajevo and Hajduk remained locked in the lead, with Sarajevo mostly two points clear. Hajduk knew what it felt like to lead the table. Mostly they played their league matches in the afternoons, while Sarajevo played in the evenings. So Hajduk would go top for a few hours and then hear that their rivals had overhauled them again. Sarajevo had appeared once previously in the Champion's Cup. That was in

Final Table

	P	W	D	L	F	A	Pts
Sarajevo	34	19	10	5	51	30	48
Hajduk Split	34	16	12	6	65	42	44
Partizan	34	14	11	9	46	34	39
Red Star	34	16	6	12	63	38	38
Vardar Skopje	34	16	5	13	67	58	37
Dinamo Zagreb	34	14	8	12	47	38	36
Željezničar	34	11	12	11	53	46	34
Rijeka	34	12	10	12	49	48	34
Sutjeska	34	11	11	12	41	42	33
Pristina	34	13	6	15	44	49	32
Velež Mostar	34	10	12	12	39	44	32
Osijek	34	12	7	15	37	36	31
Sloboda Tuzla	34	10	11	13	28	38	31
Dinamo Vinkovici	34	11	8	15	40	51	30
Buducnost	34	11	8	15	31	49	30
Vojvodina	34	9	11	14	36	47	29
Iskra	34	8	11	15	32	50	27
Radnički	34	8	11	15	25	46	27

Cup final: Red Star Belgrade bt Dinamo Zagreb 2–1, 1–1 (3–2 agg).
Top scorer: Zlatko Vujovic (Hajduk) 25 goals.

1967–68 when three of their goals in the 2–2, 3–1 first round victories over Olympiakos of Cyprus were scored by the man who guided them to their 1985 league success, Bosko Antic. In the second round they came up against ultimate winners Manchester United, and lost 0–0, 2–1.

Despite a string of indifferent results at international level over several years now, Yugoslavia remains one of the game's premier nations when it comes to exporting not only playing but coaching and managerial talent.

CRVENA ZVEZDA
*see: Red Star

DINAMO ZAGREB
Founded: 1945.
Colours: All blue.
Stadium: Dinamo (55,000).
Club address: Nogometni Klub Dinamo, Maksimirska 128, 41000 Zagreb.
League: 1948, 1954, 1958, 1982 (4).
Cup: 1951, 1960, 1963, 1965, 1969, 1980, 1983 (7).
Fairs' Cup: 1967. Runners-up in 1963.

HAJDUK SPLIT
Founded: 1911.
Colours: White/blue.
Stadium: Poljud (55,000).
Club address: NK Hajduk, Stadion Poljud, 58000 Split.
League: 1927, 1929, 1950, 1952, 1955, 1971, 1974, 1975, 1979 (9).
Cup: 1967, 1972, 1973, 1974, 1975, 1976, 1977, 1984 (8).

OLIMPIJA
Founded: 1945.
Colours: All green.
Stadium: Bežigrad (20,000).
Club address: NK Olimpija, Cankarjeva 1, 61000 Ljubljana.
League: – .
Cup: – .

PARTIZAN
Founded: 1945.
Colours: Black and white stripes/black.
Stadium: J N A (Yugoslav National Army: 55,000).
Club address: F C Partizan, Humska 1 (stadion JNA), 11000 Belgrade.
League: 1947, 1949, 1961, 1962, 1963, 1965, 1976, 1978, 1983 (9).
Cup: 1947, 1952, 1954, 1957 (4).
Champions' Cup: Runners-up in 1966.

RADNIČKI
Founded: 1923.
Colours: Blue/white.
Stadium: Cair (20,000).
Club address: FC Radnički, Sportska hala Cair, 18000 Niš.

League: – .
Cup: – .

RED STAR
Founded: 1945.
Colours: Red and white stripes/red.
Stadium: Crvena Zvezda (95,000).
Club address: F C Crvena Zvezda (Red Star), Ljutice Bogdana 1/a, 11000 Belgrade.
League: 1951, 1953, 1956, 1957, 1959, 1960, 1964, 1968, 1969, 1970, 1973, 1977, 1980, 1981, 1984 (15 – record).
Cup: 1948, 1949, 1950, 1958, 1959, 1964, 1968, 1970, 1971, 1982, 1985 (11 – record)
UEFA Cup: Runners-up 1979.

RIJEKA
Founded: 1945.
Colours: White/mauve.
Stadium: Kantride (20,000).
Club address: NK Rijeka, Korzo 38, 51000 Rijeka.
League: – .
Cup: 1978, 1979.

SARAJEVO
Founded: 1947.
Colours: Red/white.
Stadium: Grbavice (35,000).
Club address: FC Sarajevo, Maršala Tita 40, 71000 Sarajevo.
League: 1967, 1985.
Cup: – .

SLOBODA TUZLA
Founded: 1919.
Colours: Red/black.
Stadium: Tusnj (20,000).
Club address: FC Sloboda, Ozrenskog odreda 8, 76000 Tuzla.
League: – .
Cup: – .

VARDAR
Founded: 1945.
Colours: Red/black.
Stadium: Gradski (18,000).
Club address: FK Vardar, Kej 13 Novembri, kula 1, 91000 Skopje.
League: – .
Cup: 1961.

VELEŽ MOSTAR
Founded: 1949.
Colours: Red/white.

Stadium: Bijel (25,000).
Club address: FC Velež, Stjepana Radica 41, 79000 Mostar.
League: – .
Cup: 1981.

VOJVODINA
Founded: 1914.
Colours: Red and white halves/white.
Stadium: Vojvodina (20,000).
Club address: FC Vojvodina, Zarka Zrenjanina 8, 21000 Novisad.
League: 1966.
Cup: – .

ŽELJEZNIČAR
Founded: 1921.
Colours: All blue.
Stadium: Grbavice (35,000).
Club address: FK Zeljeznicar, Dinarska 27, 71000 Sarajevo.
League: 1972.
Cup: – .

WORLD CLUB CUP
1960: Real Madrid bt Peñarol 0-0, 5-1.
1961: Peñarol bt Benfica 0-1, 5-0, 2-1 (play-off in Montevideo).
1962: Santos bt Benfica 3-2, 5-2.
1963: Santos bt Milan 2-4, 4-2, 1-0 (play-off in Rio de Janeiro).
1964: Internazionale bt Independiente 0-1, 2-0, 1-0 aet (play-off in Madrid).
1965: Internazionale bt Independiente 3-0, 0-0.
1966: Peñarol bt Real Madrid 2-0, 2-0.
1967: Racing Club bt Celtic 0-1, 2-1, 1-0 (play-off in Montevideo).
1968: Estudiantes de la Plata bt Manchester United 1-0, 1-1.
1969: Milan bt Estudiantes 3-0, 1-2.
1970: Feyenoord bt Estudiantes 2-2, 1-0.
1971: Nacional (Ur) bt Panathinaikos 1-1, 2-1.
1972: Ajax Amsterdam bt Independiente 0-1, 3-0.
1973: Independiente bt Juventus 1-0 (in Rome).
1974: Atletico Madrid bt Independiente 0-1, 2-0.
1975: No competition.
1976: Bayern Munich bt Cruzeiro 2-0, 0-0.
1977: Boca Juniors bt Borussia Mönchengladbach 2-2, 3-0.
1978: No competition.
1979: Olimpia (Asuncion) bt Malmö FF 1-0, 2-1.
1980: Nacional bt Nottingham Forest 1-0 (in Tokyo).
1981: Flamengo bt Liverpool 3-0 (in Tokyo).
1982: Peñarol bt Aston Villa 2-0 (in Tokyo).
1983: Gremio Porto Alegre bt Hamburg 2-1 aet (in Tokyo).
1984: Independiente bt Liverpool 1-0 (in Tokyo).
Winners: 3 – Peñarol. 2 – Independiente, Internazionale, Nacional, Santos.
1 – Ajax Amsterdam, Atletico Madrid, Bayern Munich, Boca Juniors,
Estudiantes de la Plata, Feyenoord, Flamengo, Gremio, Independiente,
Milan, Olimpia Asuncion, Racing Club, Real Madrid.

SOUTH AND CENTRAL AMERICA
S. American Club Cup (Copa Libertadores)
1960: Peñarol bt Olimpia (Par) 1-0, 1-1.
1961: Peñarol bt Palmeiras (Brz) 1-0, 1-1.
1962: Santos bt Peñarol 2-1, 2-3, 3-0 (play-off in Buenos Aires).
1963: Santos bt Boca Juniors 3-2, 2-1.
1964: Independiente (Arg) bt Nacional (Ur) 0-0, 1-0.
1965: Independiente bt Peñarol 1-0, 1-3, 4-1 (play-off in Santiago).
1966: Peñarol bt River Plate 2-0, 2-3, 4-2 aet (play-off in Santiago).
1967: Racing Club (Arg) bt Nacional 0-0, 0-0, 2-1 (play-off in Santiago).
1968: Estudiantes (Arg) bt Palmeiras 2-1, 1-3, 2-0 (play-off in Montevideo).
1969: Estudiantes bt Nacional 1-0, 2-0.
1970: Estudiantes bt Peñarol 1-0, 0-0.
1971: Nacional bt Estudiantes 0-1, 1-0, 2-0 (play-off in Lima).
1972: Independiente bt Universitario (Peru) 0-0, 2-1.
1973: Independiente bt Colo Colo (Ch) 1-1, 0-0, 2-1 (play-off in Montevideo)
1974: Independiente bt Sao Paulo 1-2, 2-0, 1-0 (play-off in Santiago).
1975: Independiente bt Union Española (Ch) 0-1, 3-1, 2-0 (play-off in Asuncion).

1976: Cruzeiro (Brz) bt River Plate 4-1, 1-2, 3-2 (play-off in Santiago).
1977: Boca Juniors and Cruzeiro 1-0, 0-1, 0-0 aet; Boca 5-4 on penalties.
1978: Boca Juniors bt Deportivo Cali (Col) 0-0, 4-0.
1979: Olimpia bt Boca Juniors 2-0, 0-0.
1980: Nacional bt Internacional (Brz) 0-0, 1-0.
1981: Flamengo bt Cobreloa (Ch) 2-1, 0-1, 2-0 (play-off in Montevideo).
1982: Peñarol bt Cobreloa 0-0, 1-0.
1983: Gremio (Brz) bt Peñarol 1-1, 2-1.
1984: Independiente bt Gremio 1-0, 0-0.

Winners: 7 – Independiente. 4 – Peñarol. 3 – Estudiantes de la Plata. 2 – Boca Juniors, Nacional, Santos. 1 – Cruzeiro, Flamengo, Gremio, Olimpia, Racing Club.

Central & N. American Club Cup (Copa CONCACAF)
Winners: 1963 Guadalajara (Mex). 1964 Guadalajara. 1965 Guadalajara. 1966 Racing Club (Haiti). 1967 Alianza (El Salvador). 1968 Toluca (Mex). 1969 Cruz Azul (Mex). 1970 Shared: Cruz Azul, Saprissa (Costa Rica) and Transvaal (Surinam). 1971 Cruz Azul. 1972 Olimpia (Honduras). 1973 Transvaal. 1974 Deportivo Municipal (Guatemala). 1975 Atletico Español (Mex). 1977 America (Mex). 1978 Comunicaciones (Guatemala). 1979 Deportivo FAS (El Salvador). 1980 UNAM (Mex). 1981 Transvaal. 1982 UNAM. 1983 Atlante (Mex).

Interamerican Cup (Copa Interamericana)
1969: Estudiantes (Arg) bt Toluca (Mex) 2-1, 1-2, 3-0 (play-off in Montevideo.)
1972: Nacional (Ur) bt Cruz Azul 1-1, 2-1.
1973: Independiente bt Olimpia (Hond) 2-1, 2-0.
1974: Independiente and Dep. Municipal (Guat) 0-1, 1-0, 0-0 aet; Independiente on penalties.
1976: Independiente and Atletico Español (Mex) 2-2, 0-0, 0-0 aet; Independiente on penalties.
1978: América (Mex) bt Boca Juniors 0-3, 1-0, 2-1 (play-off in Mexico City.)
1980: Olimpia (Par) bt FAS (El Salvador) 3-3, 5-0.
1981: UNAM (Mex) bt Nacional 3-1, 1-3, 2-1 (play-off in Los Angeles).

Winners: 3 – Independiente. 1 – América (Mex), Estudiantes de la Plata, Nacional, Olimpia (Par), UNAM.

EUROPE
Champions' Cup
1956: Real Madrid bt Reims 4-3 (in Paris).
1957: Real Madrid bt Fiorentina 2-0 (in Madrid).
1958: Real Madrid bt Milan 3-2 aet (in Brussels).
1959: Real Madrid bt Reims 2-0 (in Stuttgart).
1960: Real Madrid bt Eintracht Frankfurt 7-3 (in Glasgow).
1961: Benfica bt Barcelona 3-2 (in Bern).
1962: Benfica bt Real Madrid 5-3 (in Amsterdam).

1963: Milan bt Benfica 2-1 (at Wembley).
1964: Internazionale bt Real Madrid 3-1 (in Vienna).
1965: Internazionale bt Benfica 1-0 (in Milan).
1966: Real Madrid bt Partizan Belgrade 2-1 (in Brussels).
1967: Celtic bt Internazionale 2-1 (in Lisbon).
1968: Manchester United bt Benfica 4-1 aet (at Wembley).
1969: Milan bt Ajax Amsterdam 4-1 (in Madrid).
1970: Feyenoord bt Celtic 2-1 aet (in Milan).
1971: Ajax bt Panathinaikos 2-0 (at Wembley).
1972: Ajax bt Internazionale 2-0 (in Rotterdam).
1973: Ajax bt Juventus 1-0 (in Belgrade).
1974: Bayern Munich and Atletico Madrid 1-1 aet. Replay: Bayern 4, Atletico Madrid 0.
1975: Bayern 2, Leeds United 0 (in Paris).
1976: Bayern 1, Saint-Étienne 0 (in Glasgow).
1977: Liverpool 3, Borussia Mönchengladbach 1 (in Rome).
1978: Liverpool 1, Club Brugge 0 (at Wembley).
1979: Nottingham Forest 1, Malmö FF 0 (in Munich).
1980: Nottingham Forest 1, Hamburg 0 (in Madrid).
1981: Liverpool 1, Real Madrid 0 (in Paris).
1982: Aston Villa 1, Bayern 0 (in Rotterdam).
1983: Hamburg 1, Juventus 0 (in Athens).
1984: Liverpool 1, Roma 1 (in Rome). Liverpool 4-2 on penalties.
1985: Juventus 1, Liverpool 0 (in Brussels).

Winners: 6 – Real Madrid. 4 – Liverpool. 3 – Ajax Amsterdam, Bayern Munich. 2 – Benfica, Internazionale, Milan, Nottingham Forest. 1 – Aston Villa, Celtic, Feyenoord, Hamburg, Juventus, Manchester United.

Cup-winners' Cup
1961: Fiorentina bt Rangers 2-0, 2-1.
1962: Atletico Madrid and Fiorentina 1-1 aet (in Glasgow). Replay: Atletico Madrid 3, Fiorentina 0 (in Stuttgart).
1963: Tottenham Hotspur bt Atletico Madrid 5-1 (in Rotterdam).
1964: Sporting (Portugal) and MTK Budapest 3-3 (in Brussels). Replay: Sporting 1, MTK Budapest 0 (in Antwerp).
1965: West Ham United bt TSV 1860 München 2-0 (at Wembley).
1966: Borussia Dortmund bt Liverpool 2-1 aet (in Glasgow).
1967: Bayern Munich bt Rangers 1-0 aet (in Nuremberg).
1968: Milan bt Hamburg 2-0 (in Rotterdam).
1969: Slovan Bratislava bt Barcelona 3-2 (in Basel).
1970: Manchester City bt Gornik Zabrze 2-1 (in Vienna).
1971: Chelsea and Real Madrid 1-1 aet (in Athens). Replay: Chelsea bt Real Madrid 2-1.
1972: Rangers bt Dynamo Moscow 3-2 (in Barcelona).
1973: Milan bt Leeds United 1-0 (in Salonika).
1974: Magdeburg bt Milan 2-0 (in Rotterdam).
1975: Dynamo Kiev bt Ferencváros 3-0 (in Basel).
1976: Anderlecht bt West Ham United 4-2 (in Brussels).
1977: Hamburg bt Anderlecht 2-0 (in Amsterdam).
1978: Anderlecht bt F K Austria 4-0 (in Paris).

1979: Barcelona bt Fortuna Düsseldorf 4-3 aet (in Basel).
1980: Valencia and Arsenal 0-0; Valencia 4-3 on penalties (in Brussels).
1981: Dynamo Tbilisi bt Carl Zeiss Jena 2-1 (in Düsseldorf).
1982: Barcelona bt Standard Liège 2-1 (in Barcelona).
1983: Aberdeen bt Real Madrid 2-1 aet (in Gothenburg).
1984: Juventus 2, Porto 1 (in Basle).
1985: Everton 3, Rapid Vienna 1.

Winners: 2 – Anderlecht, Barcelona, Milan. 1 – Aberdeen, Atletico Madrid, Bayern Munich, Borussia Dortmund, Chelsea, Dynamo Kiev, Dynamo Tbilisi, Everton, Fiorentina, Hamburg, Juventus, Magdeburg, Manchester City, Rangers, Slovan Bratislava, Sporting Club, Tottenham, Valencia, West Ham United.

Fairs'/UEFA Cups
Fairs' Cup:
1958: Barcelona bt London XI 2-2, 6-0.
1960: Barcelona bt Birmingham City 0-0, 4-1.
1961: Roma bt Birmingham City 2-2, 2-0.
1962: Valencia bt Barcelona 6-2, 1-1.
1963: Valencia bt Dinamo Zagreb 2-1, 2-0.
1964: Zaragoza bt Valencia 2-1 (in Barcelona).
1965: Ferencváros bt Juventus 1-0 (in Turin).
1966: Barcelona bt Zaragoza 0-1, 4-2.
1967: Dinamo Zagreb bt Leeds United 2-0, 0-0.
1968: Leeds United bt Ferencváros 1-0, 0-0.
1969: Newcastle United bt Ujpest Dozsa 3-0, 3-2.
1970: Arsenal bt Anderlecht 1-3, 3-0.
1971: Leeds and Juventus 2-2, 1-1; Leeds on away goals rule.
* In a play-off between the first and last winners of the Fairs' Cup, to decide who should keep the original trophy, Barcelona beat Leeds 2-1.

UEFA Cup:
1972: Tottenham Hotspur bt Wolverhampton Wanderers 2-1, 1-1.
1973: Liverpool bt Borussia Mönchengladbach 3-0, 0-2.
1974: Feyenoord bt Tottenham 2-2, 2-0.
1975: Borussia Mg bt Twente Enschede 0-0, 5-1.
1976: Liverpool bt Club Brugge 3-2, 1-1.
1977: Juventus and Athletic Bilbao 1-0, 1-2; Juventus on away goals rule.
1978: PSV Eindhoven bt Bastia 0-0, 3-0.
1979: Borussia Mg bt Red Star Belgrade 1-1, 1-0.
1980: Eintracht Frankfurt and Borussia Mg 2-3, 1-0; Eintracht on away goals rule.
1981: Ipswich bt AZ'67 Alkmaar 3-0, 2-4.
1982: IFK Gothenburg bt Hamburg 1-0, 3-0.
1983: Anderlecht bt Benfica 1-0, 1-1.
1984: Tottenham and Anderlecht 1-1, 1-1; Tottenham 4-3 on penalties.
1985: Real Madrid bt Videoton 3-0, 0-1.

Winners (both Cups): 3 – Barcelona. 2 – Borussia Mönchengladbach, Leeds

United, Liverpool, Valencia. 1 – Anderlecht, Arsenal, Dinamo Zagreb, Eintracht Frankfurt, Ferencváros, Feyenoord, IFK Gothenburg, Ipswich, Juventus, Newcastle, PSV Eindhoven, Real Madrid, Roma, Tottenham Hotspur, Zaragoza.

European SuperCup
1972: Ajax Amsterdam bt Rangers 3-1, 3-2.
1973: Ajax bt Milan 0-1, 6-0.
1975: Dynamo Kiev bt Bayern Munich 1-0, 2-0.
1976: Anderlecht bt Bayern 1-2, 4-1.
1977: Liverpool bt Hamburg 1-1, 6-0.
1978: Anderlecht bt Liverpool 3-1, 1-2.
1979: Nottingham Forest bt Barcelona 1-0, 1-1.
1980: Valencia bt Nottingham Forest 1-2, 1-0.
1982: Aston Villa bt Barcelona 0-1, 3-0.
1983: Aberdeen bt Hamburg 0-0, 2-0.
1984: Juventus bt Liverpool 2-0.

Mitropa Cup
* The Mitropa (Mittel-Europa = Central Europe) Cup was the forerunner of today's European tournaments.
1927: Sparta Prague bt Rapid Vienna 6-2, 1-2.
1928: Ferencváros bt Rapid Vienna 7-1, 3-5.
1929: Ujpest Dozsa bt Slavia Prague 5-1, 2-2.
1930: Rapid Vienna bt Sparta Prague 2-0, 3-2.
1931: FC Vienna bt WAC Vienna 3-2, 2-1.
1932: Bologna (It) walkover.
1933: FK Austria bt Ambrosiana-Inter (It) 1-2, 3-1.
1934: Bologna bt Admira Vienna 2-3, 4-1.
1935: Sparta bt Ferencváros 1-2, 3-0.
1936: FK Austria bt Sparta 0-0, 1-0.
1937: Ferencváros bt Lazio 4-2, 5-4.
1938: Slavia bt Ferencváros 2-2, 2-0.
1939: Ujpest Dozsa bt Ferencváros 4-1, 2-2.
1955: Voros Lobogo (later MTK) bt UDA Prague (later Dukla) 6-0, 2-1.
1956: Vasas Budapest bt Rapid Vienna 3-3, 1-1, 9-2.
1957: Vasas bt Vojvodina (Yug) 4-0, 1-2.
1959: Honved bt MTK Budapest 4-3, 2-2.
1960: New format based on national representation. Winners: Hungary.
1961: Bologna bt Nitra (Cz) 2-2, 3-0.
1962: Vasas bt Bologna 5-1, 1-2.
1963: MTK bt Vasas 2-1, 1-1.
1964: Sparta Prague bt Slovan Bratislava 0-0, 2-0.
1965: Vasas bt Fiorentina 1-0.
1966: Fiorentina bt Trencin (Cz) 1-0.
1967: Spartak Trnava bt Ujpest Dozsa 2-3, 3-1.
1968: Red Star Belgrade bt Spartak Trnava 0-1, 4-1.
1969: Inter Bratislava bt Union Teplice 4-1, 0-0.
1970: Vasas bt Internazionale (It) 1-2, 4-1.

1971: Celik Zenica (Yug) bt Salzburg 3-1.
1972: Celik Zenica bt Fiorentina 0-0, 1-0.
1973: Tatabanya (Hun) bt Celik Zenica 2-1, 2-1.
1974: Tatabanya bt Zilina (Yug) 3-2, 2-0.
1975: Innsbruck bt Honved 3-1, 2-1.
1976: Innsbruck bt Velez Mostar 3-1, 3-1.
1977: Mini-league system. Winners: Vojvidina Novisad.
1978: Partizan Belgrade bt Honved 1-0.
Since then played on a mini-league system. Winners: 1980 Udinese. **1981** Tatran Presov (Cz). **1982** Milan. **1983** Vasas. **1984** Iskra (Yugo).

Overall winners: Pre-war – 2 – Bologna, FK Austria, Ferencváros, Sparta Prague, Ujpest Dozsa. 1 – FV Vienna, Slavia Prague, Rapid Vienna.
Post-war – 6 – Vasas. 2 – Celik Zenica, Innsbruck, MTK Budapest, Tatabanya. 1 – Bologna, Fiorentina, Honved, Inter Bratislava, Iskra, Milan, Partizan Belgrade, Red Star Belgrade, Sparta Prague, Spartak Trnava, Tatran Presov, Udinese, Vojvodina.

Latin Cup
* Immediate post-war predecessor of today's tournaments.
First edition (finals only):
1949: Barcelona bt Sporting Portugal 2-1.
1950: Benfica bt Bordeaux 2-1 (after a 3-3 draw).
1951: Milan bt Lille 5-0.
1952: Barcelona bt Nice 1-0.
    National representation winners: Spain.
Second edition (finals only):
1953: Reims bt Milan 3-0.
1955: Real Madrid bt Reims 2-0.
1956: Milan bt Bilbao 2-1.
1957: Real Madrid bt Benifica 1-0. National representation winners: Spain
Discontinued

Cup of the Alps
Winners: 1960 Italy (club representation). 1961 Italy (club representation). 1962 Genoa. 1963 Juventus. 1964 Genoa. 1966 Napoli. 1967 Eintracht Frankfurt. 1968 Schalke. 1969 Basel. 1970 Basel. 1971 Lazio. 1972 Nîmes. 1973 Servette. 1974 Young Boys Bern. 1975 Servette. 1976 Servette. 1977 Reims. 1978 Servette. 1979 Monaco. 1980 Bordeaux. 1981 Basel. 1982 Nantes. 1983 Monaco. 1984 Monaco.

International Football Cup
* Organised each summer to serve pools betting in central and southern Europe and parts of Scandinavia.
1961 group winners: Slovan Bratislava, Banik Ostrava, Spartak Hradec Kralove, 1st Vienna, Feyenoord, Ajax, Orgryte, Sparta Rotterdam. Final: Ajax bt Feyenoord 4-2.
1962 group winners: Red Star Bratislava (later Inter), Padova, Servette, Ujpest Dozsa, OFK Belgrade, Rijeka, Tatabanya, Pecsi Dozsa. Final; Red Star Bratislava bt Padova 1-0.

1963 group winners: Standard Liège, Sampdoria, Modena, Rouen, Rapid Vienna, Bayern, Orgryte, Norrköping, Slovnaft (formerly Red Star, later Inter) Bratislava, Slovan, Polonia Bytom, Odra Opole. Final: Slovnaft bt Polonia 1-0.

1964 group winners: Hertha W. Berlin, DWS Amsterdam, Kaiserslautern, Liège, Lok Leipzig, Empor Rostock, Szombierki Bymtom, Karl-Marx-Stadt, Malmö, Slovnaft, Polonia Bytom. Final: Polonia bt Lok Leipzig 0-3, 5-1.

1965 group winners: Lugano, Fortuna Geelen, Norrköping, Orgryte, Motor Jena, Empor Rostock, Lok Leipzig, Chemie Leipzig. Final: Lok Leipzig bt Norrköping 0-1, 4-0.

1966 group winners: Eintracht Frankfurt, DWS, Go-Ahead Deventer, Ado Den Haag, Zablebie Sosnowiecz, IFK Gothenburg, Gornik, Inter Bratislava, Vorwärts, Norrköping. Final: Eintracht Frankfurt bt Inter Bratislava 3-2, 1-1 aet.

1967 onwards: No play-offs or finals have been staged. Once the mini-leagues have been completed the tournament ends. Prize money is spread among the group winners.

Major Spanish pre-season tournaments

Trofeo Teresa Herrera (La Coruna). Winners: **1946**Sevilla. **1947** Bilbao. **1948** Barcelona. **1949** Real Madrid. **1950** Lazio. **1951** Barcelona. **1952** Valencia. **1953** Real Madrid. **1954** Sevilla. **1955** Coruna. **1956** Atletico Madrid. **1957 Vasco da Gama (Brz).** **1958** Nacional (Ur). **1959** Santos. **1960** Sevilla. **1961** Sporting Portugal. **1962** Coruna. **1963** Monaco. **1964** Coruna. **1965** Atletico Madrid. **1966** Real Madrid. **1967** Ferrol. **1968** Vitoria Setubal. **1969** Coruna. **1970** Ferencváros. **1971** Red Star Belgrade. **1972**Barceloana. **1973** Atletico Madrid. **1974 Peñarol.** **1975** Peñarol. **1976** Real Madrid. **1977** Fluminense. **1978** Real Madrid. **1979** Real Madrid. **1980** Real Madrid. **1981** Dynamo Kiev. **1982** Dynamo Kiev. **1983** Bilbao. **1984** Roma.

Trofeo Ramon de Carranza (Cadiz). Winners: **1955** Sevilla. **1956** Sevilla. **1957** Sevilla. **1958** Real Madrid. **1959** Real Madrid. **1960** Real Madrid. **1961** Barcelona. **1962** Barcelona. **1963** Benfica. **1964** Betis. **1965** Zaragoza. **1966** Real Madrid. **1967** Valencia. **1968** Atletico Madrid. **1969** Palmeiras. **1970** Real Madrid. **1971** Benfica. **1972** Bilbao. **1973** Español. **1974** Palmeiras. **1975** Palmeiras. **1976** Atletico Madrid. **1977** Atletico Madrid. **1978** Atletico Madrid. **1979** Flamengo. **1980** Flamengo. **1981** Cadiz. **1983** Cadiz. **1984** Gijon.

A F R I C A
Champions' Cup

1964: Oryx Douala (Cam) bt Stade Malien (Mali) 2-1.

1966: Stade Abidjan (Iv.Cst) bt Real Bamako (Mali) 1-3, 4-1.

1967: TP Englebert (Zaire) bt Asante Kotoko (Gh) 1-1, 2-2 w/o.

1968: TP Englebert bt Étoile Filante (Togo) 5-0, 1-4.

1969: Ismaili (Eg) bt TP Englebert 2-2, 3-1.

1970: Asante Kotoko bt TP Englebert 1-1, 2-1.

1971: Canon (Cam) bt Asante Kotoko 0-3, 3-0, 1-0.

1972: Hafia (Guin) bt Simba (Ug) 4-2, 3-2.

1973: Vita Club (Zaire) bt Asante Kotoko 2-4, 3-0.

1974: CARA (Congo) bt Mehalla (Eg) 4-2, 2-1.

1975: Hafia bt Enugu Rangers (Nga) 1-0, 2-1.

1976: Mouloudia Chalia (Alg) bt Hafia 0-3, 3-0 and penalties.
1977: Hafia bt Hearts of Oak (Gh) 1-0, 3-2.
1978: Canon bt Hafia 0-0, 2-0.
1979: Union Douala (Cam) bt Hearts of Oak 0-1, 1-0 and penalties.
1980: Canon bt AS Bilima (Zaire) 2-2, 3-0.
1981: JET (Alg) bt Vita Club 4-0, 1-0.
1982: Al Ahly (Eg) bt Asante Kotoko 3-0, 1-1.
1983: Asante Kotoko bt Al Ahly 0-0, 1-0.
1984: Zamalek (Eg) bt Shooting Stars (Nig) 2-0, 1-0.

Winners: 3 – Canon (Cam), Hafia (Guin). 2 – Asante Kotoko (Gh), TP
Englebert (Zaire). 1 – Al Ahly (Eg), CARA (Congo), Ismaili (Eg), JET
(Alg), Mouloudia Chalia (Alg), Oryx (Cam), Stade Abidjan (Iv.Cst), Union
Douala (Cam), Vita Club (Zaire), Zamalek (Eg).

Cup-winners' Cup
1975: Tonnerre (Cam) bt Stella (Iv.Cst) 1-0, 4-1.
1976: Shooting Stars (Nga) bt Tonnerre 4-1, 1-0.
1977: Enugu Rangers (Nga) bt Canon (Cam) 4-1, 1-1.
1978:. Horoya (Guin) bt Mahd (Alg) 3-1, 2-1.
1979: Canon bt Gor Mahia (Ken) 2-0, 6-0.
1980: TP Mazembe (Zaire) bt Africa Sports (Iv.Cst) 3-1, 1-0.
1981: Union Douala (Cam) bt Stationery Stores (Nga) 0-0, 2-1.
1982: Arab Contractors (Eg) bt Power Dynamos (Zam) 2-0, 2-0.
1983: Arab Contractors bt Ogaza Lomé (Togo) 1-0, 0-0.
1984: Al Ahly (Eg) bt Canon (Cam) 1-0, 0-1 on pens.

Winners: 2 – Arab Contractors (Eg). 1 – Al Ahly (Eg), Canon (Cam), Enugu
Rangers (Nga), Horoya (Guin), Shooting Stars (Nga), Tonnerre (Cam), TP
Mazembe (formerly TP Englebert; Zaire), Union Douala.

A S I A
Champions' Cup
1967: Hapoel Tel-Aviv bt Selangor Select (Malaysia) 2-1 (in Bangkok).
1969: Maccabi Tel-Aviv bt Yangzee (S. Korea) 1-0 (in Bangkok).
1970: Taj Club (Iran) bt Hapoel Tel-Aviv 2-1 (in Tehran).
1971: Maccabi Tel-Aviv bt Police Club (Iraq) walkover.
Discontinued.